# Cotton Kingdom of the New South

# Cotton Kingdom
# of the New South

A History of the Yazoo Mississippi Delta
From Reconstruction to the Twentieth Century

## Robert L. Brandfon

Harvard University Press
Cambridge, Massachusetts
1967

To Frederick Merk

# Preface

Mississippi is a poor state. In the national ranking it is at the bottom of every economic and social indicator. This is so because Mississippi is a casualty of the New South. The economic and social goals of the New South, or the period following reconstruction, embodied the fulfillment of agricultural hopes and ambitions that no longer were relevant to the industrialization characterizing the rest of the United States during the same time. Despite the flood of lofty rhetoric during the 1880's about factories and railroads and capital investment, southern energy was devoted principally to agriculture, just as it had been before the Civil War. There were a few notable exceptions such as cotton textiles and the beginnings of the cigarette industry, but these were offshoots from the South's chief agricultural products. An active iron manufacture during the last part of the nineteenth century developed around the ore fields centering in Birmingham, Alabama. The emphasis of Birmingham's millmen, however, was on the manufacture of iron, just when their northern counterparts were turning to steel, where lay the profits of the future.

Thus basically little had changed since 1860; even the major crops were the old antebellum staples, cotton, tobacco, sugar, and rice. What then was the difference between Old and New Souths? Do historians have any justification for making a distinction? I think they do. The difference between the two Souths was a consciousness in the latter of efficiency. Rhetoricians of the New South were unafraid to argue that

not every area of their section was capable of economic fulfillment. If, they argued, certain parts were developed according to their natural potential (like their predecessors
southern propagandists of the 1880's relied on nature for
justification), the benefits would be shared by all southerners.
Outside capital investment was essential for the development
of these particularly blessed southern areas. But, the philosophers warned, it could not be attracted unless southerners
bent their efforts to efficiency. The philosophers were correct
in assuming that outside capital would invest in places where
the outlook for profits was greatest. But they were wrong
in assuming that the end result would be prosperity for all
the South. On the contrary, the new South was a miserable
landscape dotted only by a few rich enclaves that cast little
or no light upon the poverty surrounding them.

The Yazoo Mississippi Delta was one of these enclaves.
Even in a physical sense the Yazoo River and the high bluffs
that parrallel the river cut it off from the rest of the state of
Mississippi. By the twentieth century the four million acres
of this once impenetrable frontier of alluvial swamp was a
cotton kingdom as rich and vibrant as any area in Texas. It
far surpassed the decayed antebellum cotton kingdom around
Natchez and was richer than the black prairie belts in eastern
Mississippi and south central Alabama. Those who owned
farms in the Delta, no matter what the size of their holdings,
were referred to as planters, an antebellum synonym for the
leaders of southern society. But the title of planter, the
reliance upon cotton as the cash crop, and the heavy use of
Negro labor (the Yazoo Delta had the highest concentration
of Negroes in the nation) were but surface reflections of the
antebellum tradition. Underneath the romantic "moonlight
and magnolia" was the businesslike quest for profits. By the
twentieth century, the largest of the planters of the Yazoo
Delta were some of the wealthiest planters in the world. And
they lived in Mississippi, the poorest state in the Union!

This book attempts to explain this ambiguity by focusing on some of the factors that went into the successful development of the Yazoo Mississippi Delta. These factors—land speculation, railroads, and immigrants—were familiar developmental influences. Contemporaries were aware of the patterns these factors always followed. But when introduced into the Yazoo Mississippi Delta they were compelled to undergo certain changes in order to meet the all pervading theme of the Delta—efficient cotton growing. This book describes these changes and concludes with their political effects. The enclaves of wealth amidst overwhelming poverty produced the setting for new political configurations that jolted the South for decades thereafter. Thus the history of the development of the Yazoo Mississippi Delta transcends local history. It is the starting point for the history of the South in the twentieth century.

\* \* \*

My greatest debt in writing this book is to my wife Sylvia Patino Brandfon who painstakingly read every word of every draft. Wielding a ruthless blue pencil, her criticisms of style and organization were mixed with just the right proportion of encouragement. I have benefited also from the comments of Michael A. Weinberg who read an earlier draft and especially from the many suggestions of Joseph L. Featherstone who read and criticized the final manuscript. I am deeply indebted to the continued and unflagging support of Professor Frank B. Freidel of Harvard University to whom this subject was first submitted as a doctoral dissertation.

Grateful acknowledgment is made to Professor William R. Taylor of the University of Wisconsin, to Professor Paul Wallace Gates of Cornell University who led me to the Illinois Central Railroad collection, to Mr. Stanley Pargellis and Mr. Lawrence W. Towner of the Newberry Library for permission to use the Illinois Central Railroad archives deposited there, to Mr. E. H. Cahill, assistant secretary of the Illinois Central Railroad for permission to use other railroad records, to Charlotte Capers, director of the Mississippi Department of Archives and History, and her staff, to Carleton J. Corliss of Washington, D.C., to Harold Pinkett, former Chief of the Agricultural Section of the National Archives, and finally to a host of people in Jackson, Greenville, and Clarksdale, Mississippi, who in the best traditions of southern hospitality made a lonely Yankee feel at home.

This book is dedicated to Frederick Merk, Gurney Professor, Emeritus, in Harvard University, whose standards of scholarly excellence have been an inspiration for me as they have for a generation of American historians.

Cambridge, Massachusetts                    Robert L. Brandfon
July 1966

# Contents

## MAPS

# Cotton Kingdom of the New South

# CHAPTER 1

# The New South:
# A New Old Land

Reporting on the economic recovery of the United States from the depression of 1873, the secretary of the British embassy in Washington emphasized prosperity's national character. What was new about this latest upturn in the American business cycle, he commented in 1878, was the South's share of the sunshine. "We have seen," he wrote, "the wonderful progress made in the North, East and West, but we have still to be astonished . . . at the progress in the produce of the South, from her soil, from her mines, and from her industries." "The planters," he continued the following year, "show themselves more at ease financially, and are energetic in improving their places with improved machinery and implements . . . there is a better feeling of confidence in their financial condition. Outside capital is being employed in the Southwest, and manufacturing industries are developing." Summing up the general mood in the United States over the South's prospects, he concluded that there is "a new phase of affairs in the South which must be noticed."[1]

[1] Great Britain, *Parliamentary Papers, 1878-9,* LXIX, 335, 337; *1880,* LXXII, 159, 429; *1881,* LXXXIX, 177; a historical survey of New South themes in

For southerners the renewal of prosperity for the first time in almost a generation set loose a heady optimism and an outpouring of fanciful rhetoric from its editorial pages, pulpits, and political stumps. It is true that the contrast of prolonged years of war, defeat, and reconstruction may have magnified out of proportion the degree to which prosperity had actually returned to the South. But Americans are an optimistic people, and pessimism, even under the bleakest of circumstances, as they were for a defeated southern people, is always momentary, something to look back upon and preferably to forget. The future was more important. Southerners were advised everywhere to look to the future where they would behold a New South.

What was this New South? Primarily it was a unanimous desire to achieve for the South an economic position equal to that of the North. (Defeat in war had in no way lessened the old feelings of sectional rivalry.) There were, however, differences in the terms New South spokesmen used. Some interpreted southern calls for such things as factories, diversification, and capital investment as a desire for industrialism. On the other hand, there was little or no history of industrialism in the South and consequently little understanding among southerners of the complexities involved in the industrial process. As far as southerners were concerned, it was only natural that the object of factories, diversification, and capital investment should be not the development of unfamiliar industrial patterns but the strengthening of agriculture in general and cotton agriculture in particular. Spokesmen for the New South had not surrendered the old faith in the power of cotton. They could scarcely conceive of wealth in any other form, and thus stood on common ground with the

Jacob E. Cooke, "The New South," *Essays in American Historiography; Papers Presented in Honor of Allan Nevins*, ed. Donald Sheehan and Harold C. Syrett (New York, 1960), 50-75.

southern electorate, most of whom were farmers who were sometimes vehement in support of anything to make agriculture more prosperous.

Besides representing a hopeful prospect for an agriculturally prosperous future, the term New South also denotes a condition during the later part of the nineteenth and early part of the twentieth centuries. And as a condition, the New South remains a generally unhappy memory. While its leadership never failed to extoll outside exploitation of southern natural resources or the sale of southern railroads to northern syndicates, the results of these developments could not be justified as being relevant to the South's agricultural objectives. On the contrary, they portended not equality but colonial subservience to the rival North. In a few areas, such as the Yazoo Mississippi Delta, where cotton agriculture with the support of northern railroads and outside capital investment achieved new successes, the objectives of the New South were realized. But for most southerners the years of the New South brought only continued depression, distress, and much bitterness. During the period the South's ties to agriculturalism were made stronger than before the war. Moreover, this was an agriculturalism whose sinking poverty was in marked contrast to the buoyant prosperity of northern industrialism. Thus, as a condition as well as a prospect for the future the New South was nothing new but was rather a further compounding of all the old evils of sectionalism— evils characterized by deepening of former intersectional rivalries and a wider gap between the poor South and the rich North.

If disillusion was the end of the New South, optimism was its beginning. By 1880 a number of signs indicated glowing prospects for the future. Cotton production in 1879 reached 5.7 million bales, exceeding by over one million bales the prewar production peak. Thus, the South once again dominated world cotton production. More important were rising prices. Despite the 700,000 bale increase over 1878, average cotton prices continued their steady upward climb, from 10.8 cents to 12 cents a pound. This rise in the face of increased production reflected the steadily increasing exports of American cotton to Great Britain, the world's leading cotton manufacturer. In 1863, at the mid-point of the American Civil War, less than 1 per cent of American cotton was exported to Britain, but each year thereafter saw a steady return of British spinners to their old dependence upon the southern states for raw cotton. In 1878, the percentage of American cotton used by British mills rose sharply—by nine points—and attained once again the prewar average level of 76.5 per cent. American consumption also increased. By 1880, American mills were consuming 31 per cent of the South's cotton growth, or approximately 1.7 million bales.[2] Thus, in production, price, and sales, cotton had more than regained the ground lost during war and reconstruction and appeared to many to be on the threshold of even greater strides.

Southern cotton consumption also seemed to be moving into a new era. In 1880, American consumption of raw cotton was no longer largely confined, as of old, to the northeastern states. During the last two years of the 1870's, southern consumption of raw cotton increased from 186,489 bales to 221,337 bales, reflecting the sharp increase during the decade in the number of southern spindles, from 334,771 to 714,078.[3] The year 1880 marks the beginning of the

[2] U.S. Department of Commerce, Bureau of the Census, *Cotton Production and Distribution, Season of 1915-1916*, Bulletin 134 (Washington, 1916), 51; Robert H. Jones, "Long Live the King?" *Agricultural History*, XXXVII (July 1963), 167, 169; U.S. Bureau of Statistics, Joseph Nimmo, Jr., *Report on the Internal Commerce of the United States*, Treasury Department Document No. 142 (Washington, 1881), 197-198.

[3] *Compendium of the Ninth Census of the United States* (Washington, 1872), 896. This included both mule and frame spindles; Great Britain, *Parliamentary Papers, 1881*, LXXXIX, 190-193; Nimmo, *Report on the Internal Commerce of*

South's cotton spinning industry.[4] Production had begun in the South forty years earlier, but after 1880 the promotion of cotton spinning took on for southerners the character of a religious crusade[5] whose object, among other things, was to realize a prewar argument: If the South was the world's chief supplier of raw cotton, why should not it enjoy all the fruits of that monopoly by spinning cotton as well as by growing it?[6]

A significant category of statistics, which for many supported the view of "a new phase of affairs in the South," was the revival of the South's rail system. It is true that during the decade of the 1870's, track mileage in ten southern states did not increase materially—from 11,163 to 14,908 miles. More important were the widespread improvements and their effects. Iron rails were replaced with steel and relaid to conform to the national gauge. Great sums were expended to modernize rolling stock. All these improvements were made with outside capital and quickly resulted in extraordinary profits for the investors. Dividends from southern railroads during the decade rose from $901,396 to $3,525,977, or the greatest increase in railroad profits during the ten-year period of any section in the nation.[7] These improvements and the

*the U.S.*, 409; Edward Atkinson, "Report on the Cotton Manufactures of the United States," in U.S. Department of the Interior, *Report on the Manufactures of the United States at the Tenth Census, 1880* (Washington, 1883), 16, Table I.

[4] Broadus Mitchell, *The Rise of Cotton Mills in the South*, in Johns Hopkins University Studies in History and Political Science, XXXIX, No. 2 (Baltimore, 1921), 59, 63.

[5] Jack Blicksilver, *Cotton Manufacturing in the Southeast: An Historical Analysis*, Georgia State College of Business Administration, Studies in Business and Economics, Bulletin No. 5 (Atlanta, 1959), 4-5.

[6] James H. Hammond, "Southern Industry," in *The Industrial Resources of the Southern and Western States*, ed. James D. B. DeBow (New Orleans, 1853), III, 31-35; Robert R. Russell, *Economic Aspects of Southern Sectionalism* (Urbana, 1924), 123-150 and passim; Charles T. James, *Practical Hints on the Comparative Cost and Productiveness of the Culture of Cotton and the Cost and Productiveness of Its Manufacture* (Providence, 1849).

[7] Henry V. Poor, *Manual of the Railroads of the United States for 1881* (New York, 1881), lxxviii-lxxix.

introduction of outside capital resulted in the integration
of southern rail lines into the national rail system, and, by
the end of the century, the price paid by southerners for this
development was the placing of both the control and the
profits of southern railroads into the hands of northeastern
capitalists.[8]
Other developments were hailed by New South spokesmen
to hold out great promise for the South's future. The first
of these was the discovery of the South's forests by northern
timbermen, who were concerned about the rapid depletion
of their eastern timber reserves. The full exploitation of
southern timber resources did not come about until later in
the century, but interest in southern yellow pine was awak-
ened during the decade of the 1870's[9] stimulating a rise in
southern land values, which had been seriously shattered as
a result of war and reconstruction. In the mid-1870's, investment in southern railroads was stimulating internal southern
trade. By August 1880, for example, the Illinois Central
Railroad had extended its lines southward from Cairo, Illinois, to New Orleans and was engaged in a short but bitter
rate war for southern trade with the resurrected Louisville
and Nashville Railroad, also expanding in all directions. The
L & N, blessed with its strategic location, had been spared by
the warring armies; it remained intact to exploit the rich
mineral lands in northern Alabama.[10] Commenting on all the

[8] John F. Stover, *The Railroads of the South, 1865-1900* (Chapel Hill, 1955),
xiii-xviii and passim.
[9] Stanley F. Horn, *This Fascinating Lumber Business* (Indianapolis, 1951),
98, 102; Robert V. Reynolds and Albert H. Pierson, *Lumber Cut of the United
States, 1870-1920,* U.S. Department of Agriculture, Bulletin No. 1119 (Washington, 1923), 30; U.S. Bureau of the Census, *Tenth Census* (Washington,
1880), IX, 489; Nollie Hickman, *Mississippi Harvest: Lumbering in the Longleaf Pine Belt, 1840-1915* (Oxford, Miss., 1962), 58-87; James W. Silver, "Paul
Bunyan Comes to Mississippi," *Journal of Mississippi History,* XIX (April
1957), 95-98; U.S. Federal Trade Commission, *Report on War-Time Costs and
Profits of Southern Pine Lumber Companies* (Washington, 1922), 3.
[10] Report of the [Illinois Central R.R.] Directors, January, 1881, Illinois

schemes for railroad expansion and their consequent effects on the development of southern trade and lands, the *Railway Review* hailed the year 1880 as marking "an epoch in the history of the Southern States."[11]

Adding still further to optimistic prospects for a New South was the return of federal largess to southern interests. During the Grant Administration, the South was a Republican rotten borough and therefore politically invisible. It did not share in the "Great Barbecue" from 1865 to 1873, when huge government subsidies and land grants to railroads and protective tariffs to industry were passed to bulge the purses of northern capitalists. To make matters worse, the depression of 1873 and the revelations of government scandals cast a self-righteous cloud upon all government subsidies, effectively closing the doors of the treasury just when the South was regaining its political voice in the Congress. As C. Vann Woodward has pointed out, by the time the South had restored to itself a measure of recognition she arrived at the government table, "only to find the victuals just about cleaned up."[12] But this does not tell the entire story. Since the beginnings of the 1870's the South had received increasingly large appropriations for internal improvements. By 1876, these had reached $1.2 million. Two years later, during the first regular congressional session after the Compromise of 1877, which marks the return of the South into the national councils, appropriations for southern rivers, dams, docks, rivulets, and bayous doubled to $2.4 million, representing, for the first time, a significant southern share of national expenditures

Central Railroad Archives, Newberry Library, Chicago; Jean E. Keith, "The Role of the Louisville and Nashville Railroad in The Early Development of Alabama Coal and Iron," *Business Historical Society Bulletin*, XXVI (Sept. 1962), 165-174; Louisville and Nashville Railroad, *Annual Reports, 1879-1880; Commercial and Financial Chronicle* (New York), Aug. 28, 1880, p. 217; *Railway Review* (Chicago), Aug. 14, 1880, pp. 409-410, Aug. 28, 1880, p. 439.

[11] *Railway Review*, June 19, 1880, p. 300.

[12] C. Vann Woodward, *Reunion and Reaction* (Boston, 1951), 60.

for internal improvements. In Calhoun's day, the South generally turned its back on internal improvements at federal expense.[13] From the time of the Compromise of 1877 to the present, however, nothing but calamity awaited all southern congressmen who failed to derive for their constituencies at least a small bit of the great government pork barrel.

Neither was this the only sign that the South had at last joined the Union. After the Compromise of 1877, congressmen from the lower Mississippi Valley states succeeded, after years of patient arguing, in convincing congressmen from the upper valley that flood protection and navigation were one and the same. Out of this union of mutual interests was passed, in 1879, a bill creating the Mississippi River Commission, committing the resources of the federal government to levee protection for the people of the lower Mississippi Valley.[14] This gave another powerful stimulus to land values there. Even the old skeleton of the Texas and Pacific Railroad Bill, which called for a huge federal subsidy for a southern railroad to the Pacific, was dragged once again from the closet, given a momentary airing, and then laid to rest forever in committee.[15] Despite this setback the South was assuredly on the receiving end of congressional logrolling. For spokesmen of the New South this fact was evidence that economic benefits were bound to follow and that a new era had begun.

[13] The Swamp Land Act of 1850 which caused hundreds of thousands of federal acres to be donated to several southern states for purposes of land reclamation, is one conspicuous exception. But this was explained away as being an "indirect" assistance.

[14] U.S. *Statutes at Large*, XVIII, Ch. 411, XX, Ch. 3; 43d Cong., 1st Sess. (1874), *Congressional Record*, II, 3585-3587, 4988, 5083-5084; U.S. Congress, House, *Alluvial Basin of the Mississippi River*, 43d Cong., 2d Sess. (1875), House Ex. Doc. 127, Serial 1648, p. 19; Arthur DeWitt Frank, *The Development of the Federal Program of Flood Control on the Mississippi River* (New York, 1930), 40-44.

[15] *The Texas Pacific Railroad*, 45th Cong., 2d Sess. (1878), House Report 238, Serial 1822, House Report 619, Serial 1824. See especially minority report of William R. Morrison of Illinois.

Friendly northern sentiment also made its contribution to the spirit of optimism. By the end of the 1870's many northerners, weary of the "bloody shirt," sought conciliation with the South in the name of national progress. The return of prosperity as well as the maturing of a generation that had never known the war, made it easier to forgive and to forget. Fifteen years after Appomatox, northerners pointed out the historical lessons of the South's past and its prospects for the future. It was agreed that the major reason for the South's previous backwardness was the debilitating consequences of slavery. Slavery and the social system it engendered had imprisoned the American spirit for business enterprise. Now that southern life had been liberated from false and immoral ideals, there was no reason why the South with her resources, natural and human, should not join the rest of America in the forward march of industrial progress. The business of the New South, northern business circles advised, should be business, and the first step was to attract the attention of the world by advertising the spirit and integrity of the southern people. "Let them put their shoulders to all the wheels of industry," cried the New York *Commercial and Financial Chronicle*, "and show an example of self-reliance and self help," and these virtues, more than anything else, would encourage a flow of investment capital. The South, it seemed to some, was taking these steps, and the northern business public, which had previously viewed the South as "a sort of buried region," was now seeing it as "a new old land now to be discovered, occupied and inhabited."[16]

The rise of cotton prices, the rejuvenation of southern railroads, the stimulation of land values, the return of the South to the political councils of the nation, and the North's encouragement of its former enemies were developments injecting a degree of confidence among every element of the

[16] *Commercial and Financial Chronicle*, Aug. 28, 1880, p. 218.

southern people. Even those in continually sinking economic conditions were willing for the moment to listen to descriptions of the broad savannahs laid before them by New South rhetoricians. It is too harsh a judgment to attribute cynical motivations to these spokesmen of the New South. To some, no doubt, casting flowery words before the masses might serve as a convenient opiate masking personal aggrandizements. For most of these leaders, however, New South rhetoric was a mixture of political ambition, large pecuniary interests, a firm belief that future prosperity lay in an alliance with the money of the northeast, and genuine southern pride.

General John B. Gordon, hero of Appomatox, lawyer, senator, and governor of the state of Georgia, was an outstanding example of New South leadership. His speculative activities touched every important aspect of New South enterprise—railroads, mines, cotton factories, and cotton lands. In May 1880, convinced that the South really stood, as Henry Grady of the *Atlanta Constitution* said, "on the threshold of a prosperity more brilliant than that of the past,"[17] Gordon resigned his seat in the United States Senate "to consult my inclinations and the imperative interests of my family." These inclinations and interests began with a high salaried position as general counsel for the ever prospering Louisville and Nashville Railroad. From this vantage point Gordon embarked upon a brief but prosperous railroad building career himself.[18] The idea was to bring to life the long-cherished dream of the citizenry of Atlanta, a western railroad to the rich Alabama coal fields and beyond. For over a year, Grady's *Atlanta Constitution* had been booming the advantageous ways in which this "grand highway of com-

[17] Allen P. Tankersley, *John B. Gordon: A Study in Gallantry* (Atlanta, 1955), 322-326. For the establishment of the Gordon Cotton Mills Company in Carroll County, Miss., see *Laws of the State of Mississippi, 1882* (Jackson, 1882), Ch. CCCXLVII; *Atlanta Constitution*, Jan. 11, 1882, June 10, 1879.

[18] Tankersley, *John B. Gordon*, 302, 304; *Atlanta Constitution*, May 20, 1880.

merce" would give employment to the poor, increase the value of Atlanta real estate, and otherwise "make Atlanta the empire city of the South."[19] Armed with an old railroad charter General Gordon reportedly went west through the states of Alabama and Mississippi promising a railroad in return for donations of municipal bonds and mineral lands. Obtaining these for nothing he promptly sold (for three-quarters of a million dollars in cash) the bonds, lands, and charter to the rich northern stockholders of the Richmond and Danville Construction Company, thus making, as the *Railway Review* commented, "something out of nothing in true Yankee style."[20]

Notwithstanding his personal profits, Gordon's machinations succeeded in giving Atlanta a western railroad, and, more important, he had interested northern capital in southern enterprise. As he warned the legislators of Mississippi, northern capital was the key to the South's future prosperity and nothing in southern legislation should bar the way to secure it. In a passage typical of New South rhetoric, Gordon did not doubt that the South was "about to enter upon an era of progress and prosperity never known in her history."

> The North, with its unparalleled material development and its accumulated wealth, stands, for the first time in the history of the country, ready to delve in your mines, build your furnaces, construct your railways, erect your factories, spin your cotton, convert your timber into implements of husbandry, that they and you may unite to make this southern country what nature intended it, the richest and most productive country upon earth. With this disposition on the part of the North, with the barrier of slavery gone, with the passions of the war fast dying out, with a hearty

[19] *Atlanta Constitution*, Feb. 21, 1879; Fairfax Harrison, *History of the Legal Development of the Southern Railway* (Washington, 1901), 423-425; *Railway Review*, Sept. 10, 1881, p. 507; *Atlanta Constitution*, Feb. 23, March 27, April 15, May 24, 1881; *The Georgia Pacific Railway; Prospectus and Reports* (New York, 1882), 3-7; Stover, *Railroads of the South*, 240.
[20] *Railway Review*, Aug. 27, 1881, p. 476.

welcome from our people, with a soil unrivaled in its fertility; with a climate enabling us to produce two crops in one season, with staples demanded by the civilized world, and with the fact now made manifest that cotton can be manufactured here to greater profit than elsewhere, what can prevent the realization of our hopes except a failure to appreciate the situation, or mistakes in the legislation of these states?[21]

Gordon's career and his prospects for the South's future afford a closer look at the aspirations behind the term "New South." In the employment of northern capital spokesmen for the New South sought a more tangible prescription for southern prosperity than sermons on the virtues of union and common heritages. The nation, they argued, could better unite upon a quest for business profits. This was the trend of the nation and the South should not lose its share of the future by clinging to irrelevant memories. Northern and foreign capital were eager to invest in the South. In the two years after 1879, according to Henry Grady's estimates, six huge syndicates had invested $100,000,000 in southern railroads. The South, Grady reasoned, had to have capital stimulation before it could share in the bright new era that had opened up before it. By their heavy investment in southern railroads, northern and foreign capitalists had committed themselves to the South's growth for, obviously, there could be no profits from a barren country. In response to fears that the South was selling itself into colonialism, Grady replied that the sale of southern railroad stock at "advanced prices" to New York capitalists was not surrendering southern economic freedom. On the contrary, he argued, the result of these sales would put money into southern hands and southerners would in turn invest it in factories and real estate. Thus, the sale of southern railroad stock and charters would not only raise desperately needed capital, it would stimulate

21 *Jackson Weekly Clarion* (Jackson, Miss.), Feb. 15, 1882.

an influx of immigrant labor to the South and raise southern land values. And from these elements the South would regain her former prosperity as well as a new sectional pride within a glorious union.[22]

When the war ended southerners concluded that they had been defeated not only by the North's industrial power but also by the hoards of cheap white immigrant labor that prosperous industries attracted. A burgeoning immigrant population had given the North majority political representation in Congress and a large source of manpower for war. Were the South ever to match the North's strength, it must increase its population. Following this reasoning, reconstruction state governments inaugurated immigration programs. Their success in every case was marred from the start by an inherent inability to appeal to immigrant motives. Why would industrial immigrant labor go to a land where industrialism was nonexistent? How could immigrants be attracted to southern lands as yeoman farmers when political and social instability had shattered land values? Under the weight of these initial disadvantages, most of the programs languished into oblivion during the depression of 1873. But the idea that somehow immigration would enrich the South remained dormant and was revived at the end of the decade when home rule and the proclaimed return of prosperity gave calls for immigration a spurt of new life.

This time the need for a factory labor force had a little more foundation. By 1881, at the time of the International Cotton Exposition in Atlanta, the manufacture of cotton

22 *Atlanta Constitution*, April 15, 20, May 18, July 28, 1881; Raymond B. Nixon, *Henry W. Grady; Spokesman of the New South* (New York, 1943), 6 and passim; C. Vann Woodward, *Tom Watson; Agrarian Rebel* (New York, 1938), 113-123; *Journal of the American Agricultural Association*, I (New York, 1881), 247; Henry W. Grady, "Cotton and Its Kingdom," *Harper's New Monthly Magazine*, LXIII (Oct. 1881), 733; *Jackson Weekly Clarion*, Nov. 10, 1881.

textiles had become a significant part of the southern economy. The arguments for southern textile factories were the same ones used in the 1840's; the natural resources of southern water and coal (steam) power, the vast numbers of marginal farmers eager to learn new skills, and the significant savings in transportation costs by eliminating the shipment of southern raw cotton to northern mills. New South spokesmen were as captivated as their fathers had once been by the logic of the South, the world's greatest grower of cotton, becoming the world's leading cotton spinner. Nailed to the masthead of Grady's *Atlanta Constitution* in 1881 was the slogan of the Atlanta exposition: "The foremost branch of American industry is the culture and manufacture of cotton."[23] A delegation of northern spinners representing the New England Cotton Manufacturing Association was frankly impressed with what they saw at Atlanta. Their spokesman, Edward Atkinson of Boston, one of the nation's leading economists, an important figure in the New England textile industry, and one of the promoters of the Atlanta Exposition, was, like the rest of the delegation, quick to praise southern advances in cotton manufacturing. But, fearing future competition, he tried to divert the South away from spinning by impressing upon his southern friends the importance of the South's time-honored position as grower of cotton.[24] He and his northern colleagues had little to fear. It would be another half century before the number of southern spindles would surpass the North's. The slow and piecemeal development of southern cotton manufacture was, in part, caused by the lack of large-scale northern and foreign investment that

[23] *Atlanta Constitution*, Sept. 30, 1881.

[24] New England Cotton Manufacturing Association, *Proceedings*, No. 31 (Boston, 1882), 38; Edward Atkinson, *Address Given in Atlanta, Georgia in October, 1880* (Boston, 1881); Jack Blicksilver, "The International Cotton Exposition and Its Impact upon the Economic Development of Georgia," *The Atlanta Economic Review*, VII (June 1957), 2.

forced the South to fall back upon its own meager capital resources.

To a larger extent, southern cotton manufacture did not grow rapidly because indigenous southern capital was concentrated, as it had been before the war, in increasing the growth of cotton. As in the days before the war southern faith in the efficacy of cotton agriculture remained immovable. The *Memphis Daily Appeal* proclaimed cotton in 1881 as "more a king today—if in a different sense—than ever before. Properly allied, as he may be, to capital, skill, labor, and allied as he already is to opportunity, he must be stupefied indeed if he does not assume a grander scepter than any he has yet wielded."[25] The newly appointed United States Commissioner of Agriculture, George B. Loring of Massachusetts, reinforced this belief. Before an enthusiastic Atlanta audience he echoed the prewar cotton nationalists. "Cotton stands in such a relation to our commerce and manufacture, that it exerts a great influence upon our prosperity and progress . . . While it is not the largest crop in those southern states and does not occupy the largest area of land, it forms the nucleus around which the other production industries gather, and forms the basis of the transportation and trade of the section adapted to its growth."[26] These statements, repeated countless times, reflected widespread thinking about the cotton grower's position in the grand designs of the Souths, old and new. Cotton was the nucleus of the South's future and the South's future was the future of the nation. It was ironic that this anachronistic theme of the cotton power should be repeated in a period of national reconciliation. It was, as many recognized, the discredited theme of prewar southern nationalists, who disastrously had led the South from the Union.

[25] *Memphis Daily Appeal* (Memphis, Tenn.), Jan. 6, 1881.
[26] Speech of George B. Loring, Nov. 2, 1881, quoted in *Atlanta Constitution*, Nov. 3, 1881.

Yet, in 1881, the theme was vigorously applauded by all the promoters, North and South, of the Atlanta Exposition.

It is not surprising to find the South's planter community fully in accord with the ideals of Henry Grady, for those ideals were in line with their interests. At the outset of the 1880's this was especially true of the planters and prospective planters of the lower Mississippi Valley, which by virtue of its vast expanses of virgin and extraordinarily rich soils afforded a great opportunity for enlarging the cotton kingdom. The National Cotton Planters Association, first organized at Vicksburg, Mississippi, in 1879 as the Mississippi Valley Planters Association, reflected the objectives of the planters of the New South.[27] Their desires for increased railroad facilities and for heavy federal expenditures on levee construction were obvious. Railroads, they discovered, were more reliable than the old-fashioned river boat. Moreover, competition between the two modes of transportation would reduce freight rates. As for levees, the advantages were just as obvious. Not only would the enlargement of the levee system prevent flooding and allow an enlargement of cotton cultivation, but federal appropriations and control would lessen the cotton grower's heavy burden of levee taxation. Likewise, the planters favored southern textile manufacture, or, as Grady popularized it for them, the marriage of the mill to the cotton field. Planter attitudes on this subject were based not on the prosperity that textile manufacturing might bring to the South as a section, but rather on the belief that southern manufacture of cotton would give the planters greater control over their staple, and thus bring about higher prices. As the *Memphis Daily Appeal* explained it, by manufacturing cotton

---

[27] National Cotton Planters Association of America, *Charter of Incorporation* (Vicksburg, 1881); Theodore Saloutos, *Farmer Movements in the South, 1865-1933*, University of California Publications in History, vol. 64 (Berkeley, 1960), 57-58.

cloth at home "we could thus keep the inferior grades of cotton from being made a lever in the distant markets to run down the price of the whole crop, by working it up ourselves and sending away only what was in demand in the markets."[28]

The planters had other reasons for agreeing with the ideals of the New South. They involved the whole concept of the planter and his leadership in the Southern way of life. Lands and slaves had been the twin pillars of the prewar plantation system. With the sharp devaluation of lands and the emancipation of the slaves, the whole social, political, as well as economic structure of the South was violently disrupted. What the planters and would-be planters of the New South sought was a restoration of plantation organization based this time on the businesslike efficiency of industrialism. For these southerners, the lesson of the North's enviable industrial profits was not what it produced but how it went about doing it. This lesson was reflected in the planters' intense concern with costs rather than priding themselves, as in the old days, upon yields. As Frank C. Morehead, president of the National Cotton Planters Association, expressed it in 1881: "It is not the extent of the cotton crop *per se* that I object to—though it would be better if that were curtailed—and that impoverishes us, but the ruinous cost of its production."[29]

The major cost was labor. Share tenancy in all its varying forms was a miserable makeshift for slavery. Inefficiency was its trademark, and the Negro made it worse. He was, according to the planters, shiftless, lazy, stupid, and wholly unreliable as a tenant, without the same constant supervision he had had under slavery. Increasing numbers of cotton growers were voicing doubts about the old assumption that the successful growth of cotton was dependent upon Negro labor. Some went so far as to envision the Negro's displacement from

[28] *Memphis Daily Appeal*, Aug. 21, 1881.
[29] *Ibid.*, May 26, 1881.

the cotton fields. Hope for this turn of events was afforded by the latest laborsaving agricultural machinery that the Atlanta Exposition put on full display before visiting planters.

Machinery and the displacement of the Negro, both leading to efficiency in cotton growing, were dependent upon an influx of capital and cheap credit. "There is one thing," wrote Henry Grady, "that has stood between the southern farmer and unexampled prosperity and that is the lack of capital with which to operate." Credit, Grady claimed, was ruinously expensive, amounting in his own state of Georgia to a full 54 per cent on everything the farmer purchased. But by 1880 Grady claimed that northern and foreign capitalists were finding it profitable to lend money on southern and western mortgages at a mere 7 per cent.[30] Moreover, a new wave of land speculation sweeping the lower Mississippi Valley also gave hope of increased land values upon which further capital could be raised. For the planters of the New South land values still had great meaning, especially in prosperous times (or even in the expectation of prosperous times), when prices would soar. Tenancy might serve temporarily as a replacement for slavery, the second pillar of the prewar plantation system, but in the teeth of the new factory-like cost-conscious ideal of cotton agriculture it would have to give way to efficiency.

According to Frank Morehead, the goal of agricultural efficiency could be brought about through a wages system of labor in the cotton fields. At present, he argued, the planter was forced to continue with the tenant system, which was as inefficient for the plantation owner as it was repressive to tenants who harbored ambitions to yeomanry. A wages system of plantation labor, supported by a free flow of credit and capital, would liberate the planter-owner to diversify and

[30] *Atlanta Constitution*, July 28, 1881; Grady, "Cotton and Its Kingdom," 722-723.

plan his crops according to the needs and prices of the market. Morehead proposed to have capitalists consolidate ten to fifty plantations under one management with a cash system. Under economical centralized management the planter-owner would then be free to invest in the latest agricultural laborsaving machinery, erect his own gins, compresses, and oil mill, "and in fine adopt the same business system throughout that brings success to a railroad or factory." It was in the best interest of the South to dismiss sentiment about the virtues of the small farm. The small cotton farmer and the tenant system were inefficient shackles because they diminished cotton prices, which formed, of course, the foundation of the South's economic structure. "Must we," Morehead asked, "from sentiment, continue to make partners and landlords of pauper labor? Is there any demand on the land owners of the South to treat labor differently from the manner in which it is treated in all other parts of the world?"[31]

No other single expression could have better reflected the goals of the New South, as southerners understood them. These goals were agricultural and not industrial. It is true that a number of factories were erected, but to a large extent these were limited to cotton manufacture. And in the context of the twentieth century this development could hardly be called industrialism. On the contrary, southern cotton manufacture received the support of southerners only because they were convinced that the vertical integration of the cotton industry worked to the better interests of cotton growers. Likewise, the mind of the New South was willing to concede, as the Old South was reluctant to do, that such things as railroads, immigration, and capital were good because they would lead to efficiency in cotton growing, and thus greater profits for the cotton grower, which would in turn enrich southerners

[31] Address of Frank C. Morehead quoted in *Atlanta Constitution*, Dec. 9, 1881.

of all classes and occupations. The place of cotton agriculture in southern thinking was not displaced by fanciful visions of humming factories but remained as dominant for the New South as it had been for the Old.

What was somewhat new was the relocation of the cotton kingdom from the uplands of the Carolinas, Georgia, and the black prairies of Alabama and Mississippi, to the alluvial swamplands of the lower Mississippi Valley and to Texas. Particularly enticing were the alluvial swamplands, scarcely settled before the war, less than one-tenth of which was cultivated by 1880. Their remarkable fecundity, which gave yields of almost one bale of cotton to the acre, was widely recognized, especially by northern capitalists, who naturally concentrated their investments where they would reap the greatest profits. Morehead and Grady agreed that if the twenty counties bordering the Mississippi River between Memphis and Baton Rouge were fully exploited they could outproduce the entire southern cotton crop of 1880, itself a record production of 6.6 million bales. For spokesmen of the New South these alluvial lands represented something more than record production figures. In addition to cotton these lands could grow their own grains, feed, cattle, and, with the large quantities of labor that would naturally be attracted to them, provide a thriving cotton textile industry as well. Thus the automatic self-sufficiency of these lands would provide the kind of agricultural efficiency necessary for the best interests of the southern economy. Through the improvement of river transportation, the building of levees to protect these lands, the stimulation of land values by speculation, and the introduction of capital, immigrant labor, and railroads, the cotton kingdom would become as efficient as any northern factory system, make profits as never before, and thus provide general prosperity for a New South.

By the twentieth century the major part of these alluvial

swamplands—the Yazoo Mississippi Delta—had undergone every one of these developmental influences whose processes and effects are described in the remainder of this book. Profits were made as never before, but the prosperity of these lands did not generate prosperity throughout the South. Indeed, the concentration of railroads, capital, and labor into the alluvial lands to the neglect of the South's poorer cotton lands, which were unable to compete, led to the latter's too rapid deterioration. The realization of New South goals in the Yazoo Mississippi Delta served to accelerate the long-standing divisions between rich and poor in Mississippi, the rich planters of the alluvial lands became richer while the one-time yeoman of the uplands sank deeper and deeper into tenancy and peonage. The sharpness of the divisions between the Delta and the hills made more turbulent the political reactions of the 1890's, and these in turn imprinted upon the South for generations the curious mixture of progressivism and clownishness that was the redneck political order.

# CHAPTER 2

# The Alluvial Empire

THE PEOPLE of the lower Mississippi Valley have lived
by the fate of their great river. The Mississippi River made
their lands, and the remarkable fecundity of the Mississippi's
alluvial lands was the source of a prosperous cotton agriculture, out of which was born, in the years after reconstruction,
a new "Delta" planter society. The wealth of this new society
dramatically separated its members from the surrounding
areas of scrub pine hills, whose poverty-stricken residents
made up the "redneck" country. But if the Mississippi was
the source of the Delta's prosperity, its residents continued
to view the river as a power to contend with, an arbitrary
power capable of destroying in a moment the bountiful gifts
which it previously had given. This danger, peculiar only
to the Mississippi's alluvial lands, served to reinforce the
Delta's separation from the surrounding countryside, at the
same time instilling in the Delta people attitudes of short
term self-interest and an overriding belief that what was
good for the Delta was good for the surrounding countryside.

For the present generation of Delta folk the outstanding
memory of the Mississippi River's awesome power remains
the great flood in the spring and summer of 1927. It was
then that the unchecked tide of the Mississippi River took

with it hundreds of lives and destroyed 450 million dollars
worth of property. It flowed over twelve and one-half million
acres "equal in size to the States of Massachusetts, Connec-
ticut, Delaware, Rhode Island and Maryland combined, and
flooded [the land] to a depth of from 3 to 12 feet, for a
period varying from three to ten weeks."[1] It was, according
to the testimony of former Senator Leroy Percy, one of the
Delta's most prominent citizens, "a yellow sea, stretching a
thousand miles from Missouri to the Gulf of Mexico, from
50 to 120 miles in width, rendering more than 700,000
people homeless, putting 600,000 of them on the charity of
the American people."[2]

But the magnitude of the flood, Percy declared, was not
the cause for the deep feelings of despair and hopelessness
that followed in its wake. The people of the valley had known
disastrous floods before. Aware of the dangers of the river,
they had set to work building levees to protect themselves.
By the 1920's after almost fifty years of mixed successes,
they had built their levees to a point beyond which, their
engineers assured them, flood waters could not possibly go.
The valley folk rejoiced in the confident belief that Mississippi flood disasters were things of the past. Then in the
spring of 1927, "the mighty river mocked, devastated, and
desolated them," bringing the greatest flood in the valley's
history. This flood, declared Percy, who for long years had
been an important leader in the drive for the Delta's levee
protection, "shook the people of the valley to their very souls.
It stripped them of courage and hope. It made them realize
for the first time how puny and futile their efforts to secure
protection had been . . . They realized then that they had

[1] U.S. Congress, House, Committee on Flood Control, *Hearings . . . on the
Control of the Destructive Flood Waters of the United States,* 70th Cong., 1st
Sess. (1927), 2575, 745.
[2] *Ibid.,* 44.

made the fight and lost and that they were powerless to continue the struggle."[3]

The greatest extent of flood damage was confined to the 500 mile area south of Cairo, Illinois, which lies at the confluence of the Ohio and Mississippi rivers. South of Cairo, the Mississippi River follows a serpentine course, constantly twisting and turning for more than 1,200 miles before emptying into the Gulf of Mexico. For years it was held that the exaggerated bends in the river which retarded its tremendous flow were beneficial in the prevention of floods. Great efforts were therefore made to preserve the twisting course of the river by re-enforcing its bends and preventing the force of the river from making natural cut-offs.[4] The "great flood" of 1927 revealed the weakness of this policy.

Charles Ellet, author of the classic engineering report on the Mississippi River in 1852, asks us to imagine the lower Mississippi Valley as "a great plane sloping uniformly from the mouth of the Ohio . . . to the Gulf of Mexico . . . Its northern extremity is elevated two hundred and seventy-five feet above the surface of the sea . . . Its total descent, following the highest surface of the soil, is about three hundred and twenty feet, or at the rate of 8 inches per mile."[5] This plane is the Mississippi River bed, which has a breadth of about 30 to 40 miles at its northern end and widens as it proceeds southward until it reaches a breadth of 150 miles at

[3] *Ibid.*, 44-45.

[4] A cut-off occurs when the force of the flowing river pinches off a bend leaving behind it a curved lake, or "moon lake." Quite a number of these can be seen to the east and west of the main course of the Mississippi, some of which, especially since 1927, are man-made. At times these cut-offs can be disastrous. In 1876, for example, the city of Vicksburg, one of the great river ports of antebellum days, found itself no longer on the Mississippi River. Eventually a diversion canal had to be built, which once again put the city in contact with the Mississippi.

[5] U.S. Congress, Senate, Charles Ellet, Jr., *Report on the Overflows of the Delta of the Mississippi*, 32d Cong., 1st Sess. (1852), Sen. Ex. Doc. 20, Serial 614, p. 15.

the Gulf of Mexico. Containing about 40,000 square miles, the Mississippi's bed, wrote Ellet, "has been formed in the course of ages from the material brought down from the uplands by the Mississippi and its tributaries. The river has therefore raised from the sea the soil which constitutes its own bed."[6]

The Yazoo Mississippi Delta lies in the center of this vast alluvial bed. Diamond-shaped, its western boundary is formed by the channel of the Mississippi River which bends westward from Memphis as far south as Greenville and then turns slightly eastward until reaching Vicksburg. The Delta's eastern boundary is formed first by a formidable line of bluffs, which rise to a height of about 200 feet. Beginning just below Memphis these continue as far south as the city of Greenwood, then bend southwesterly following the line of the Yazoo River, which meets the Mississippi at Vicksburg. The Yazoo Delta, therefore, is an enclosed basin whose protective boundaries give its 7,065 square miles or 4,520,600 acres[7] a geographical distinctiveness of its own.

To the naked eye the Yazoo Delta is flat; but closer observation reveals an uneven surface resulting from the peculiar manner by which the Mississippi River built up the land. Always suspended in its waters are vast amounts of sediment. These represent rich soils washed into the river from all the tributaries of the vast Mississippi watershed embracing thirty-one states, one and one-quarter million square miles, or approximately 41 per cent of the total area of the

6 *Ibid.*

7 U.S. Congress, House, *Reclamation and Rural Development in the South: Part 2, Swamp and Overflow Lands in the Yazoo Basin,* 69th Cong., 2d Sess. (1927), House Doc. 765, p 39. For purposes of statistics I have included the following counties as making up the Yazoo Mississippi Delta: Bolivar, Coahoma, De Soto, Issaquena, Leflore, Quitman, Sharkey, Sunflower, Tallahatchie, Tunica, and Washington. Geographically, however, the Yazoo Delta includes only parts of De Soto and Tallahatchie counties in addition to parts of Holmes, Warren, and Yazoo counties.

contiguous states. While the water is carried along in the channel of the great river, these silt deposits are eventually deposited at its mouth. But when the river overflows its channel banks and the velocity of its flow is thus decreased, these deposits are spread out along the river's natural bed.

The heavier deposits nearest the river bank naturally fall first, and the lighter deposits are spread farther away. Consequently, the borders of the Mississippi River's channel are raised higher than areas farther inland. The rivers within the enclosed Delta Basin react in similar ways. The land nearest the banks of Steele Bayou, Deer Creek, the Big Sunflower River, and the Yazoo River are raised and fall away at right angles to their banks. If we were to take a cross section view of the Yazoo Delta Basin from west to east, we would see the basin sloping eastward from the higher elevations at the foot of the bluffs. But intermittently there would be a series of rises and depressions between the two boundaries.

The Yazoo Delta also slopes gently southward. At its northern end the mean Gulf level is 210 feet. At its southern end it is 90 feet above the Gulf level. Because Delta lands thus slope from north to south and from west to east, the lowest lands, and consequently the wettest lands from the point of view of natural drainage, are those in the southernmost counties of Issaquena and Sharkey, and the part of Warren County lying north of the Yazoo River. In addition to the natural drainage flow from the Delta's streams, these lands receive large doses of flood water from the Mississippi.

In the later winter and spring, when the Mississippi is rising to its full crest and flowing with increasing velocity, the river seeks an outlet. Before levees were built, the river's natural outlets were its tributaries, or its bayous. Flood waters of the Mississippi would back up into the Yazoo River. This, in turn, would overflow its banks, and flood the lowlands of

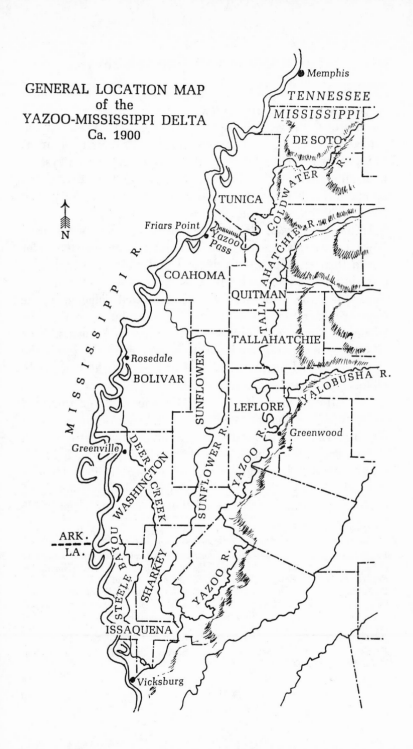

GENERAL LOCATION MAP
of the
YAZOO-MISSISSIPPI DELTA
Ca. 1900

N

Memphis

TENNESSEE
MISSISSIPPI
DE SOTO

COLDWATER R.

TUNICA

Friars Point

Yazoo Pass

TALLAHATCHIE R.

COAHOMA

QUITMAN

TALLAHATCHIE

MISSISSIPPI R.

Rosedale

BOLIVAR

SUNFLOWER

YALOBUSHA R.

LEFLORE

SUNFLOWER R.

YAZOO R.

Greenwood

Greenville

DEER CREEK

WASHINGTON

STEELE BAYOU

SHARKEY

YAZOO R.

ARK.
LA.

ISSAQUENA

Vicksburg

Sharkey, Warren, and Issaquena counties. Likewise the Yazoo would seek outlets. Its backwater would fill up the lower reaches of the Big Sunflower, Deer Creek, and Steele Bayou. And these streams would in turn flood into their tributaries. Thus, in its original state the Mississippi River was a system, with all its tributaries, large and small, playing their parts in maintaining the natural balance and flow of the parent river—The Father of the Waters.

If the velocity of the Mississippi River were not slowed down by merely backing up into its tributaries, the river would then rise out of its channel and spill over its banks, covering the adjacent lands with a brackish yellow-brown film. When the velocity of the river slowed sufficiently, the river would return to its channel having built up the surrounding lands with highly fertile alluvial deposits. This was the process repeated for countless centuries until the farmers arrived on the scene and altered (but did not completely change) the picture.[8]

The alluvial deposits of the Mississippi River provided the planters of the Yazoo Basin with soils of unsurpassed fertility. They are generally divided into four classifications: a dark gray sandy loam, a light gray sandy loam, a bluish gray tenacious "buckshot" clay, and a stiff dark gray (black) "buckshot" clay. "Buckshot" clays cover about two-thirds of the entire basin. Every one of these types has remarkable

[8] The foregoing description is derived from: Ellet, *Report on the Overflows of the Delta of the Mississippi*, passim; *Swamp and Overflow Lands in the Yazoo Basin*, 39-41; *Hearings on the Control of the Destructive Flood Waters of the U.S.*, 319, 429, 2572; U.S. Congress, House, *Mississippi River Commission Report, 1880*, 46th Cong., 2d Sess. (1881), House Executive Doc. 58, Serial 1925, pp. 6-8; U.S. Congress, House, *Report by a Special Board of Engineers on Survey of Mississippi River*, 61st Cong., 1st Sess. (1909), House Doc. 50, Serial 5574, pp. 40-46; a brief popular discussion of the levee system and peculiarities of the Mississippi River in John L. Mathews, *Remaking the Mississippi* (New York, 1909), 34-59; E. N. Lowe, *A Preliminary Study of Soils of Mississippi*, Mississippi State Geological Survey, Bulletin No. 8 (Brandon, Miss., 1911), 182-186.

growing potential.[9] This is especially so of the dark gray "buckshot," found predominantly along Deer Creek. "Taken as a whole," one geologist reported in 1906, "the plant-food percentages in this soil are probably unexcelled by any soil in the world thus far examined."[10] It is called "buckshot" because it dries rapidly and breaks up into little angular fragments. A sticky substance when wet, this soil was once a "great hindrance to wagoners," who cursed it for miring the wheels of their vehicles into its pastelike substance.[11] But the planters never stopped blessing its wondrous yields. Not without exaggeration, some of them claimed that cotton grown on buckshot soil grew 10 to 15 feet high and yielded as much as 1,000 pounds of lint per acre.[12] The potential of these soils, especially when compared, as they usually were, with those of Egypt's Nile Delta, was not lost upon those who first described their geological origins. "The alluvial plain," wrote the Mississippi state geologist in 1857, "is, in an agricultural respect, one of the most important formations, not only in the State of Mississippi, but in all the Southern States: nay, more than that, even in the United States . . . It is still a wilderness; the prejudice of its unfitness for cultivation has only lately subsided, and the axe of the woodman scarcely begun its ravages; but after the lapse of another century, whatever the delta of the Nile may once have been, will only be a shadow of what the alluvial plain of the Mississippi will then be. It will be the central point— the garden spot of the North American continent—where wealth and prosperity culminate."[13]

[9] *Report on Cotton Production in the United States*, U.S. Bureau of the Census, *Tenth Census*, V (Washington, 1884), 44.

[10] U.S. Congress, House, A. F. Crider, *Geology and Mineral Resources of Mississippi*, 59th Cong., 1st Sess. (1906), House Doc. 831, Serial 5016, p. 71.

[11] *Report on Cotton Production in the United States*, in *Tenth Census*, V, 44.

[12] L. Harper, *Preliminary Report on the Geology and Agriculture of the State of Mississippi* (Jackson, 1857), 256.

[13] Lowe, *Preliminary Study of Soils of Mississippi*, 66.

In addition to the soil there were the trees. The farmer and the timber merchant thrilled at the sight of a magnificent virgin abundance of hard and soft woods. Cypress, tupelo, and sweet gum, most measuring 4 to 6 feet in diameter, dominated the Delta forest. There was, however, no dearth of other varieties. On the dark gray sandy loams stood the honey locust, holly hackberry, and sweet gum. On the lighter sandy loams grew maple, water and willow oaks, elm, and more hackberry. On the light colored clays of fine sediment were swamp chestnut, oak and sweet gum, ash, maple, sassafras, and willow oak. And on the "buckshot" soils the growth was sweet gum, overcup, willow and water oak, hackberry, and pecan.[14] There for the taking, these forests represented the first lure to the permanent settlement of the basin.

The basin's humid subtropical climate is perfect for cotton growing; the winters are short and mild, the summers long and hot. Mean monthly temperatures vary from 46° F. in January to 81.9° F. in July, and the mean relative humidity varies from 55 per cent to 71 per cent.[15] In the early hours of some January mornings, the Delta's freezing temperatures are a match for those of any northern city. Highest temperatures during the summer days of cotton growing climb to 95° F. and 100° F., sometimes even higher.[16] But without exception the Delta's evenings bring relief; before the dawn, temperatures are down to 70° or an even cooler 65°. This daily relief from oppressing summer heat is as ideal for the Delta's cotton as it is for its wilted citizenry.

Not so ideal, however, is the heavy precipitation which,

[14] C. E. Dunston, *Preliminary Examination of the Forest Conditions of Mississippi*, Mississippi State Geological Survey, Bulletin No. 7 (Brandon, Miss., 1910), 32-37; John L. Campbell and W. H. Ruffner, *A Physical Survey in Georgia, Alabama, and Mississippi Along the Line of the Georgia Pacific Railway* (New York, 1883).

[15] Arthell Kelley, Some Aspects of the Geography of the Yazoo Basin, Mississippi (unpublished Ph.D. dissertation, University of Nebraska, 1954), 34-36.

[16] *Swamp and Overflow Lands in the Yazoo Basin*, 53.

added to the already wet condition of the lands, makes cotton growing precarious. The Delta's heavy rains are thus a significant point of difference between the Yazoo Delta and Egypt's Nile Valley, a factor often overlooked by the Delta's enthusiastic boomers. The Yazoo Mississippi Basin is the focal point for two main storm belts moving in an easterly direction. These are the Colorado type sweeping along the southwestern plains in the late winter and early spring, and the Texas type covering the Gulf States. When these two meet, rain is heavy and prolonged. Arthell Kelley tells us that maximum rainfall recorded at Greenville during one 24-hour period in April was 8.12 inches. The average annual precipitation is about 50 inches, and is heaviest in the winter and spring seasons (15.42 inches in winter and 15.37 inches in the spring). This is also the time of year when the Mississippi is gathering momentum from the flood tide of its great tributaries. These elements gathering in springtime determine the future of the planter's crops.[17]

For the Delta cotton grower, then, spring planting is a time for proper judgment and a little guesswork. He must be able to judge when the heaviest part of the rainy season has passed away. He cannot afford to wait too long; otherwise he will have difficulty controlling the late spring grasses. Moreover, a late crop is more susceptible to the ravages of the boll weevil, at its height during late July and August. And he must face one other hazard from the elements: this is pelting rain. Summer rains, usually thunderstorms, are short but very heavy. The maximum such rainfall for one 1-hour period recorded in Greenville is 3.18 inches. These hard rains knock the cotton from the open bolls and spot the lint, thereby lowering the grade.[18]

Water, both from the Mississippi River and from heavy

[17] Arthell Kelley, Some Aspects of the Geography of the Yazoo Basin, 39-40.
[18] Ibid., 40.

rainfall, has thus been the source of life and growth and de-struction. This sharp ambivalence in the behavior of natural elements shapes the physical structure of the entire Alluvial Empire and presses down upon the consciousness of its citizens. In the mid-nineteenth century Charles Ellet warned of eventual disaster from the increasing heights of the Mississippi's flood waters. The natural causes for these floods were the irregular movements of the river, winds, river velocity at particular times, and the slope of the river channel. But, Ellet continued, "The floods which now carry annual distress and destruction into the lower Mississippi . . . are essentially the result of artificial causes. The water is supplied by nature, but its *height* is increased by man." The cause for these increasing river heights *"is the extension of the levees."*[19]

Because of the way the rivers spilled over their alluvial deposits, the Yazoo Delta's early settlers took the higher lands immediately adjacent to the rivers. The higher lands bordering the Mississippi were taken first because of their immediate availability to the mainstream of Mississippi River commerce. Later comers settled upon the higher grounds along the lesser Yazoo basin streams. Settlement thus ran in parallel lines separated by the lower lying swamp lands. In the Mississippi's flood time, these rivers and bayous filled, as they always had, and threatened to overflow the lands of the settlers. During these early years of settlement, however, the height of the sluggish overflow rarely exceeded a few inches. Consequently, a "frail embankment along the edge of the river in front of his estate, with wings or lateral banks running back into the swamp,"[20] afforded ample protection for the pioneer farmer.

With additional settlers and cultivation, levees were extended in length and in height along the Mississippi's banks.

[19] Ellet, *Report on the Overflows of the Delta of the Mississippi*, 48.
[20] *Ibid.*

Eventually, the levees were extended so as to divert the Mississippi's natural overflow away from its tributaries. Having nowhere to push its excess water, the great river flowed with increasing velocity and height down its own inadequate channel. In the same way, the bayous and stream outlets of the Mississippi tributary rivers were also leveed, thereby increasing the velocity of flow and the height of those streams. Each year the hand of man changed the natural force of nature without regard for the violent flooding that would most certainly follow. As Ellet succinctly described the situation:

> The water which formerly escaped through these lateral vents, filling up the swamps slowly, or as the flood increased, flowed over the borders of the great river and its tributaries, filling the reservoirs there . . . is now confined by artificial breastworks within the too contracted channel of the river. Consequently, as the levees are extended higher up, more water is excluded from the swamps, and the flood is therefore increased, and forced more rapidly, and in a deeper column, on the country below; thus compelling the lower planters to raise higher and make stronger the frail levees which originally sufficed for the protection of their isolated estates.[21]

During the late 1840's when cotton prices made a comeback from the price disaster of 1844 the great clamor to grow more cotton led to the policy of clearing the swamps by extending the levees. This disastrous policy was further encouraged by the Federal Swamp Land Act of 1850. Under this act vast areas haphazardly labeled "swamp and overflow lands" were granted to the lower Mississippi states for the purpose of putting the proceeds of the sale of these lands into building levees.

With reckless abandon, the lower Mississippi River states, urged on by the land speculators, hastened to enact legisla-

---

[21] *Ibid.*, 49.

tion to project levees and to take advantage of the federal government's largess.[22] "As things are now," warned Ellet soon after the act was passed, "extensive works are in progress to exclude the water from the swamps and swell the floods of the river; while no step has yet been commenced to reduce those floods, or to guard the lower coasts from their consequences."[23]

The history of levee building in the Yazoo Mississippi Delta—constant breaks in the levee line, excessive costs, disgust, distrust, and abandonment—reveal on a small scale the detrimental effects of excessive localism. Mississippi's first levee legislation was passed in 1819. This elementary enactment reveals how flimsy levee protection needed to be. Only $8,000 was considered sufficient to give adequate protection. In the 1830's, with further settlement along the Mississippi River, more complex legislation and larger appropriations were passed. But in each case the finances, control, and responsibility were placed into the hands of local landowners. The result was a patchwork of levee districts each vying for self-protection without regard to possible effects on other districts.

The climax of prewar Yazoo Basin levee building was the establishment in 1858 of the General Levee Board. Its purpose was to direct and coordinate the building of 262 miles of levee along the Yazoo Delta's side of the Mississippi. The work of the Board was conceived as an over-all basin project with integrated levee control, engineering, and administration. It had, however, the usual fatal weakness. Board members were unable to overcome the strong financial control by

[22] Benjamin H. Hibbard, *A History of the Public Land Policies* (New York, 1924), 269-288; Margaret B. Bogue, "The Swamp Land Act and Wet Land Utilization in Illinois, 1850-1890," *Agricultural History*, XXV (October, 1951), 170.

[23] Ellet, *Report on the Overflows of the Delta of the Mississippi*, 50.

parochial planting interests firmly entrenched in the state legislature. Planters were unwilling to go beyond the minimal protection afforded by their own local levee districts, which for them was adequate enough. Had the war not interceded and put an end to the Board, it is all too likely that the multiplicity of local interests would have similarly doomed the Board's designs, particularly if the planters had had an opportunity to contemplate paying for the six and a quarter million dollar estimated cost of the General Levee Board's finished project.[24]

On the other hand, had the project been completed, it would have proved disastrous to the isolated settlements across the river in Arkansas and Louisiana. Higher and firmer levees for the Yazoo Delta would cause the rising flood waters of the Mississippi to seek other outlets downstream or on the western banks. But for this consequence Yazoo Delta planters were unconcerned.

> If both sides of the river cannot be leveed [wrote an enthusiastic supporter] then must we protect ourselves, and let our neighbours in Arkansas suffer . . . They have a much longer line of bank than we; their bank is much lower than ours, and they have numbers of angry rivers pouring their floods to the Mississippi. Nature has done almost everything for our side, and *shame* on the man who doubts our ability to do the rest . . . These lands [of the Yazoo Delta] and the personal property on them is worth not less than seventy millions of dollars, and yield a State revenue of not less than one hundred thousand dollars. If they can be protected from an overflow within the next ten years, the real and personal estate in the valley will not be less than one hundred and fifty millions . . . Shall we abandon and lose this present property, and that which the future promises?[25]

24 Robert W. Harrison, "Levee Building in Mississippi Before the Civil War," *Journal of Mississippi History*, XII (April 1950), 80-92.

25 *De Bow's Commercial Review of the South and West*, New Series (Oct. 1858), 439-440.

The Civil War effectively put an end to the problems (as well as to the finished products) of the General Levee Board. In February 1863 General Grant's army on the march toward Vicksburg blew up the great 18-foot-high levee at Yazoo Pass, and the flood waters of the Mississippi were allowed to inundate the Yazoo Delta. During the war the entire prewar levee line deteriorated, high explosives ripping those levees that might not have already crumbled away from neglect. The great flood of April 1865, "remarkable for its duration," finished the job. Thus all protection was destroyed.[26] At the close of the Civil War, as at the beginning of white settlement, Delta lands lay open to the Mississippi River. They had with a few exceptions returned to their natural condition of alluvial swampland.

But the destruction of the levees and the flooding of the lands did nothing to hold back the postwar drive to cultivate the rich alluvial lands of the Mississippi Valley. The flooding had furthermore renourished the lands. Once again, levees were thrown up with the same disregard for the problems of finance and coordinated flood control. The inquiries on the subject of Mississippi River flood control made earlier by Charles Ellet were as relevant in the post-Civil War era as when he had first made them.

> It is a curious problem now to determine what is to be the effect of all this. While population is taking possession of the plains of Missouri and the prairies of the Mississippi, there increasing the discharge of the streams, and forcing the floods forward, by opening new drains and removing obstructions from the natural channels; States, counties, and individual proprietors, further south, are projecting and executing schemes for the reclamation of the swamps, of which the direct tendency is to cut off all the natural outlets for the surplus water, and confine the volume now

[26] Edwin C. Bearss, *Decision in Mississippi* (Jackson, 1962), 142-151; Robert W. Harrison, "Levee Building," 95-97.

spread by these outlets over vast areas of territory, within the narrow channel of the Mississippi.[27]

As he predicted, the advancing cultivation of the Missouri Valley Plains and the Mississippi Valley Basin, with the subsequent extension of the levees, increased flood heights. For years after the Civil War it was a race to build levees high enough to keep pace with the increasing height of the floods. Complicating the postwar picture once again was the disunified engineering and administration of the differing levee districts, each looking out for its own interests and safety.[28] No one studying the problem of Mississippi floods can escape the fact that the Mississippi River is not merely a river but a system of rivers, bayous, and swamps. Only unified control and administration of the system could coordinate all its parts and bring about permanent protection. But for more than a century this condition was sadly wanting.

The Mississippi River and the human response to the challenge it presented characterized the history of the New South Yazoo Delta. Just as the river had built up the land, so the floods whose silt deposits brought mineral refurbishment also destroyed all the growing crops lying across their path. And, as the levees were built higher, so the increasing vol-

[27] Ellet, *Report on the Overflows of the Delta of the Mississippi*, 51.

[28] Robert W. Harrison, "The Formative Years of the Yazoo-Mississippi Delta Levee District," *Journal of Mississippi History*, XIII (Oct. 1951), 236-248. That the floods were getting greater in proportion to the increasing settlement of the lower Mississippi Valley and the consequent increase in the heights of the levee is revealed by statistics. At the crest of the great flood of 1882, the gauge reading at Greenville, Mississippi, was 41.68. In the flood of 1912, it read 50.76. And during the great flood of 1927, the gauge reached an all time high of 54.6. U.S. Congress, House, *Control of Floods in the Alluvial Valley of the Lower Mississippi River*, 71st Cong., 3d Sess. (1931), House Doc. 798, Serial 9385, p. 84. In 1882, the height of the levees of the Yazoo Basin averaged about 8 feet; in 1927, they averaged 22 feet. U.S. Congress, House, *Flood Control in the Mississippi Valley*, 70th Cong., 1st Sess. (1928), House Report 1072 to accompany H. R. 8219, Serial 8839, p. 335.

ume of flood waters which occasionally broke them became increasingly more destructive. In like manner, as the prospects of capital investment within the Delta multiplied, bringing with them greater visions of quick riches from the large-scale growth of cotton, so it increased in direct proportion the myopic localism of a people whose success tended to isolate them from the rest of Mississippi.

# CHAPTER 3

# The Process of Progress

THE HISTORY of the Yazoo Mississippi Delta begins with its lands. Four million alluvial acres held out great prospects for agricultural wealth, prospects always described in glowing terms. As early as the 1850's, it was commonplace that the future course of progress for the Yazoo Mississippi Delta was the future course of progress for the whole state of Mississippi. This idea stemmed from the knowledge that some of Mississippi's soils were already beginning to deteriorate from overcropping. Thus the Delta's inexhaustible alluvial lands were viewed not only as the richest but also the most permanent source of state income. All that needed to be done was to clear, drain, and cultivate them; and this, it was thought, was only a matter of time. But the Civil War nearly put an end to these hopes. Indeed, by the end of the war the lands were in fearful physical condition. Lacking money and manpower, the state's General Levee Board had to drop its ambitious plans to protect the entire Yazoo Basin from Mississippi River floods. County and private levee districts likewise were forced to lay aside their protective programs. And added to the prolonged neglect of the levees was their destruction by Grant's invading Union armies.[1]

[1] Edwin C. Bearss, *Decision in Mississippi* (Jackson, 1962), 142-151, 200-207; James W. Garner, *Reconstruction in Mississippi* (New York, 1901), 124-125;

All these circumstances stripped Delta lands of protection from floods, and many reverted to their original state of swamp and bog. Thus Wilbur Cash and Charles Nordhoff's description of the entire postwar South as returning to the frontier condition would literally include the Yazoo Delta.[2] But the word "returned" grants too much to the antebellum condition of Yazoo Delta lands. In 1860 less than one-tenth was cleared for cultivation.[3] Although virtually a wilderness, most of the lands were owned, were on the assessment rolls, and, their steadily increasing values rising in direct proportion to the extension of the levees, were considered reliable indicators of prosperity. But wartime damage to the levees followed by a decade of political dislocation reversed the Delta's economic direction, seriously retarding its eventual position as a postwar cotton kingdom, and causing an economic lag from which the state of Mississippi has yet to recover.

The trouble lay in the vicious circle of rising taxes in the face of decreasing land values. The abolition of slavery not only destroyed the prewar plantation labor system but caused, in addition, a drastic change in the South's tax structure. Up to their abolition, slaves were considered personal property, and in antebellum days personal property bore the brunt of local, county, and state taxation. After 1865, the tax burden was placed upon the only remaining major source of tax revenue—real property. This put many Delta landowners in the uncomfortable position of possessing lands whose tax assessment, no matter how small, was infinitely greater than the wealth most of them produced, since fully nine-tenths of the Delta lands were as yet un-

Robert W. Harrison, "Levee Building in Mississippi Before the Civil War," *Journal of Mississippi History*, XII (April 1950), 95-97.

2 Wilbur J. Cash, *The Mind of the South* (New York, 1941), 103; Charles Nordhoff, *The Cotton States in the Spring and Summer of 1875* (New York, 1876), 74.

3 *The Georgia Pacific Railway: Prospectus and Reports* (New York, 1882).

cleared for cultivation and producing nothing. Like all American frontier farmers, the early Delta settlers bought far more land (at bargain rates) than they could farm, holding out lands either for future cultivation, or in most cases for a speculative rise in land values.[4] While the burden of taxation was still on personal property, land speculation was a cheap luxury. It was made easier by the fact that by Mississippi law landowners were enabled to set the value of their lands according to their "intrinsic value," which, freely interpreted for wild lands, meant no value at all and thus, insignificant taxation. The Mississippi Constitution of 1868 not only made all property taxes ad valorem but declared that assessed value was to equal the actual market value of the land.[5] This reform, though motivated by a moral impulse to promote honesty in property assessments, was wholly out of touch with the reality faced by hard-pressed Delta landowners. It had to be ignored and is so to this day. But it was the beginning of a long series of equally unrealistic laws, administrative actions, and judicial decrees whose effects were usually far removed from the ideals that prompted them.

Repair of widespread wartime damage and the accompanying decay of neglect, as well as the reforms of reconstruction, weighed heaviest upon Mississippi's landholding taxpayers. With a new system of public schools, the construction of new insane asylums, poorhouses, bridges, court-

4 For outstanding studies of the pioneer farmer see, Paul W. Gates, "Frontier Landlords and Pioneer Tenants," *Journal of the Illinois State Historical Society*, XXXVIII (June 1945), 143-206; Introduction to Glen A. Blackburn et al., *The John Tipton Papers With an Introduction by Paul Wallace Gates* (Indianapolis, 1942); Theodore L. Carleson, "The Illinois Military Tract: A Study of Land Occupation, Utilization and Tenure," *Illinois Studies in the Social Sciences*, XXXII (Urbana, Ill., 1951).

5 *Revised Code of the Statute Laws of the State of Mississippi* (Jackson, 1848), Ch. 8, Sec. 13; *Revised Code, 1857*, Ch. 3, Art. 10, 12; *Revised Code, 1871*, Sec. 675; Mississippi Constitution, 1868, Art. XII, Sec. 20; Charles H. Brough, "History of Taxation in Mississippi," *Publications of the Mississippi Historical Society*, II (Oxford, Miss., 1899), 116-117.

houses, jails, and especially county roads, it was estimated that by 1874 a landowner had to pay $26 on the thousand dollar valuation, by far the greatest percentage of which represented county levies.[6] Even by the standards of the twentieth century this was heavy taxation, and in those days it was an unprecedented burden. It was especially hard on lands whose yields (and hence income) were decreasing. The once proud cotton areas around Natchez were in this category, and to a lesser extent, the black prairies of eastern Mississippi were also beginning to feel the pinch of over-cropped soils. The situation caused by heavy taxation and deteriorating soils was aggravated by yet another reform in 1874 requiring all state taxes to be paid in unobtainable specie.[7] Increasingly, it behooved landowners to forfeit lands that were not producing an income beyond the tax rate. The resulting mounting forfeitures withdrew vast amounts of land from state and county tax rolls. In April 1871, the amount of lands forfeited was 3,329,324 acres, exclusive of another 3,518 acres in town lots. By 1874 the state auditor estimated that this figure had doubled to over six million acres, or one-fifth of the state's total land area.[8]

The situation was worse among the Delta's landowners. It is true that unlike other Mississippi lands, those of the Yazoo Mississippi Delta were not decreasing in fertility. With better methods of cultivation, many planters were averaging one bale of lint cotton to the acre, with promise of even greater yields in the future. But along with the county and state taxes, Delta landowners were required to pay additional levee taxes. It was estimated that by the end of 1874, a typical Delta

[6] U.S. Congress, Senate, *Mississippi in 1875*, 44th Cong., 1st Sess. (1876), Senate Report No. 527, Serial 1669, 1670, pp. 53, 526, 645, 661; hereafter cited as Boutwell Report.

[7] *Laws of the State of Mississippi, 1874* (Jackson, 1874), Ch. IV, Secs. 11-13.

[8] Mississippi, *Journal of the House of Representatives, 1871* (Jackson, 1871), 503-1117; U.S Congress, House, *Vicksburgh Troubles*, 43d Cong., 2d Sess. (1875), House Report 265, Serial 1659, 531.

landowner paid, in levee taxes alone, $4.15 for every acre he owned. What pained him most was that a good part of these taxes was going to pay off the bad debts of previous levee projects (such as the General Levee Board of 1858) rather than being used to give him the present and future levee protection his interests demanded.[9]

Every Delta planter who had any hopes for the future of his section knew the importance of sound credit. By repaying the past debts of the General Levee Board of 1858, Delta landowners sacrificed to redeem the tarnished credit rating of the state of Mississippi to which, for better or worse, their interests were irretrievably bound. In 1842 the state of Mississippi had repudiated its own Union & Planter's Bank bonds. This stigma of repudiation made it difficult several years later to get creditors for the bonds of the General Levee Board of 1858. By the war's end these bonds, also, were worthless. But many leading Delta planters, such as James Lusk Alcorn, former president of the Board, as well as Governor Benjamin Grubb Humphreys, were determined to salvage, if not the credit of the state, at least the credit of the Yazoo Mississippi Delta, even if most of the bonds had probably fallen into the hands of speculators. A law was passed in 1867 refunding the General Levee Board's debts. New bonds were exchanged for the old on condition that holders of the new issue would relinquish any claims to interest prior to June 1, 1867. The new bonds were called Liquidating Levee Bonds and were secured by a five cent and three cent an acre tax on all Delta lands (according to their proximity to the Mississippi River) until all the debts and liabilities of the General Levee Board were paid in full.[10]

---

[9] Boutwell Report, 661, 1465-1466, 1528.

[10] Charles H. Brough, "The History of Banking in Mississippi," *Publications of the Mississippi Historical Society*, III (Oxford, Miss., 1900), 319-330; Testimony of James L. Alcorn in Ford & Levy *vs.* Delta and Pine Land Company, Justice and Treasury Department, 15168, Record Group 267, National Archives, Washington; Mississippi, *Laws, 1866-67,* Ch. CLXXIII; *Laws, 1871,*

But too often it happens that long-term gains are defeated by their short-term consequences. The price of the Delta's strengthened credit was the five and three cent an acre Liquidating Levee Tax. Delta landowners in 1867 might have thought twice about so committing themselves had they perceived the mounting tax schedules that social reforms would soon bring about. In 1870 county taxes for these reforms rose sharply. With these increasing burdens added on to inescapable Liquidating Levee Taxes, as well as other levee taxes, many Delta landowners found it impossible to hold on any longer to their speculative lands, a fact illustrated dramatically in 1871 when 1,369,093 forfeited acres were reported in the Delta's seven counties.[11]

As long as the cultivated lands were producing a satisfactory income, Delta landowners appear to have acquiesced in the reforms despite their cost and despite the fact that taxes had eaten away their speculative landholdings. However, the unfavorable cotton crop in 1874 with its low yields and low incomes transformed an uncomfortable tax burden into an unbearable one by threatening the landowners with the loss of their cultivable lands. The result was an organized protest of taxpayers, and in the words of one "a general disinclination to pay taxes all over the state."[12] A bipartisan taxpayers' convention was followed by a formal petition of grievances to the Republican governor, Adelbert Ames. This brought about some amelioration but not enough to prevent the landowners (many of whom had been former Whigs and who had sat on the political fence for the past decade) from going

Ch. II; John W. Wade, "Lands of the Liquidating Levee Board Through Litigation and Legislation," *Publications of the Mississippi Historical Society,* IX (Oxford, Miss., 1906), 281-284; Vasser *vs. George,* 47 Miss. 720.

[11] Garner, *Reconstruction in Mississippi,* 311-314, 354-371; J. S. McNeily, "Climax and Collapse of Reconstruction in Mississippi, 1874-1876," *Publications of the Mississippi Historical Society,* XII (University, Miss., 1912), 290-294, 303-305, 336-345; Mississippi, *House Journal, 1871,* pp. 503-1117.

[12] Boutwell Report, 1529.

over to the Democratic party and thereby precipitating the fall in 1875 of the Republican administration.[13]

A change in parties did nothing to change the problem that faced every administration during these years: how to stop the mounting forfeitures and get the lands on the tax rolls once again. In 1872-73, something tantamount to outright donation was resorted to. Two local railroads were offered hundreds of thousands of acres of forfeited lands at the ridiculously low rate of two cents an acre.[14] These railroads were forced to turn down this offer, not simply because it was hedged with reform-like conditions that restricted the railroads from land speculation, but because the railroads, in order to secure legitimate title to the lands, would have had to pay accumulated taxes on them. A good part of these forfeited lands, especially those in the Yazoo Delta, had been accumulating back taxes for more than a decade, and the skimpy capital resources of these railroads were barely enough to lay track, much less to pay the past debts of others. This rejection by the railroads and the protests of the taxpayers' convention made it clear to the legislature that only by abating the accumulated taxes was there any hope of getting the lands sold. Accordingly, an Abatement Act was passed in 1875[15] by which the state gave up all claims to arrearage taxes prior to January 1, 1874.

For Delta lands, however, the mere abatement of state taxes was not enough. Added provisions were necessary to meet the very confused legal conditions arising out of the diffuse ad-

[13] *Ibid.*, 456-462; McNeily, "Climax and Collapse" 343; Mississippi, *Laws, 1875*, Chs. 1, 4-7, 9, 10, 16, 25, 23; David Donald, "The Scalawag in Mississippi Reconstruction," *Journal of Southern History*, X (Nov. 1944), 447-460; Vernon L. Wharton, *The Negro in Mississippi, 1865-1890* (Chapel Hill, 1947), 177-179, 181-198.

[14] Mississippi, *Laws, 1872*, Ch. LXV; *Laws, 1873*, Ch. CCXCIII; N. H. Harris to S. Gwin, April 12, 1881, Mississippi State Auditor's Archives, Series G. No. 159, Department of Archives and History, Jackson, Miss.

[15] Mississippi, *Laws, 1875*, Ch. II.

ministration of tax forfeited lands. Besides the state and counties, the Delta's three chief tax levying agencies were two levee boards that shared the Delta's leveeing activities, and the Liquidating Levee Board, which levied taxes to pay off the debts of the General Levee Board of 1858. Taxes for every one of these agencies were due on different dates; hence, there was a welter of claims over which lands had been forfeited for nonpayment of taxes. Moreover, the amount of land forfeited for nonpayment of state taxes made up the smallest portion of the total, and the Abatement Act applied only to state tax delinquent lands. Thus, unless all the forfeited lands could be passed to state control the benefits of the Abatement Act would hardly apply at all to Delta lands. The provisions of the Abatement Act marked the beginning of a campaign to consolidate the administration of all forfeited lands— county, levee, and state—into the hands of the state. By its terms, lands of the Liquidating Levee Board were made liable for state taxes, which, of course, the Board was in no position to pay. As a result, 1,788,165 acres held by the Board were in 1875 put up for sale, and when no one attempted to purchase them, were struck off to the state. Additional Liquidating Levee Board lands likewise passed on to the state when the legislature decided in 1876 to abolish the independent status of the Board altogether and place it under state control. Also in 1876 one of the levee districts was done away with, its lands passing to the state. Other forfeited tax lands belonging to certain Delta counties also passed under state sovereignty. In all, by 1878, the state auditor reported that 2,365,214 acres of Yazoo Delta land, or more than half the area of the Delta, were held by his office and therefore withdrawn from taxpaying status.[16]

[16] Prophet vs. Lundy, 63 Miss. 608; Wade, "Lands of the Liquidating Levee Board," 293-294; Mississippi, *Annual Report of the State Auditor, 1876* (Jackson, Miss., 1876); *Annual Report of the State Auditor, 1878* (Jackson, Miss., 1878).

If the legislature had achieved administrative consolidation, it obviously had failed to gain the larger object of the
Abatement Act—to get the lands on the taxpaying rolls again.
As many lands remained on the tax rolls as before the drive
to consolidate them under state control. Moreover, the continuing discontent of the Delta landowners, whose recent
commitment to the Democracy was uncertain, was unnerving
to the newly installed Democratic administration. It is true
that under Democratic rule after 1875 the reforms of reconstruction were cut drastically, with a consequent lowering of
the tax rate, and that Democratic county assessors were willing
to place a far lower assessment on lands despite the constitutional requirement that all lands be assessed according to
their market value. But this relief was not enough. More than
half the Delta's acres were still not paying their share of
taxes, a burden that had to be made up by lands that were on
the tax rolls. Moreover, one year after the return to Democratic rule complaints about the tax drag took on a new aspect.
In 1876, Congress repealed the restrictive southern homestead
law, thus opening up federal lands in the South to large-
scale speculation. Delta lands would not be covered by this
act, for there were no lands open for homesteading. But it
was certain that speculative activities prompted by the repeal
would spill over into the Delta, whose fertile lands held out
greater opportunities than any other lands in Mississippi.
The Delta landowner wanted an end to the tax drag of the
past. He wanted to concentrate his energies on making the
most of the future.

The administration was ready to do what it could to relieve the Delta planters' burden, but it had no plan of action.
Early in 1877, Governor John M. Stone dropped the problem
into the lap of the legislature, which proceeded to take the
most direct course of relief it knew. This was a tax cut, which
partially repudiated the terms of the 1867 Liquidating Levee

Act. The five and three cent taxes were cut in half, and the
face value of the Liquidating Levee Bonds was reduced by
two-thirds.[17] Even though this reduction was in accord with
the actual market worth of the bonds, the bondholders protested loudly, claiming an impairment of the contract that
allegedly existed between themselves and the state as a result
of the Liquidating Levee Act of 1867. The state supreme
court in the celebrated case of Gibbs *vs.* Green upheld the
bondholders and forced a settlement the outcome of which
had far-reaching effects upon the Delta's history. According
to the court's decree, the five and three cent taxes remained,
but all lands forfeited for failure to pay them were to be sold,
with the proceeds of sale going to retire the bonds at par. In
this way the lands were made additional security for the
bonds. The sale price of these forfeited lands was to equal
only the Liquidating Levee Taxes in arrears beginning with
January 1, 1874, the Abatement Act having discharged all
taxes prior to that date. Actual payment for the lands was
made even easier by the fact that by Mississippi law only 5
per cent of the purchase price was to be in currency, the
remainder could be paid in the bonds, scrip, or other evi-
dences of debt of the Liquidating Levee Board.[18] Here was an
excellent method of retiring this paper whose value was
heavily debased. Likewise, the good credit rating of the Delta
was again maintained. But, more important, by reducing the
price of these lands to a negligible fraction of the taxes due
on them, the promoters of this settlement were inviting large-
scale land speculation as the only hope of getting the lands
sold. Thus the Gibbs case was the starting point for a chapter
in the Yazoo Delta's history, a chapter that would test anew
the theories about land speculation as a factor in the development of frontier societies.

---

17 Mississippi, *Laws, 1877*, Ch. V.
18 Gibbs *vs.* Green, 54 Miss. 606; Green *vs.* Gibbs, No. 326 Chancery Court,
Hinds County (Jackson, Miss.), 1st District *Minutes*, II, 230-231.

Historians of land speculation in the United States usually have concerned themselves with the effects of speculation on frontier land development or with its profits (or lack of them) to the speculator. The speculator has been rightly pictured as the cutting edge of the frontier, the man or syndicate of men who pre-empted the land and then proceeded to skin the settlers who followed. But little has been said of the motives of the settlers and the state and county governments, many of whom encouraged speculation as a positive good to the development of the country. Speculation, it was believed, if given the right direction, would give higher market value to frontier lands, which would in turn attract capital development, railroads, and other improvements. These would cause land values to increase even further; the cycle would be on its way. In short, land speculation was the starting point for progress. On the other hand, it had its pitfalls, mainly its tendency to withdraw lands from sale for longer periods of time and for higher prices than was healthy for development. All too often, unfortunately, this was the case, with the result that land speculation retarded development, was accompanied by a growth of frontier tenancy, and was therefore eventually condemned as immoral by a disappointed and frustrated public.

The Yazoo Delta's landowners never condemned speculation and had little to fear from the possibility of the growth of frontier tenancy. On the contrary, being landlords they sought to increase tenancy. If by encouraging outside land speculators the millions of forfeited acres could be returned to the tax rolls and the restrictive burdens of taxation thus be done away with, the landlords would be enabled to accumulate the necessary capital for the expansion of their plantations. This would put the Delta's economy on the move, and the ensuing confidence generated among the Delta's landlords would infect outside capital investors. These latter would furnish the massive capital needed for improvements in transportation, land clearing and drainage, and the leveeing of rivers, and would bring about an influx of cheap tenant labor. If to these ends speculation could be directed, controlled, and encouraged by the laws, courts, and judgment of the state's political leadership, it would prove the antidote for the economic sluggishness of the Delta's growth and put the Delta, and thus the rest of the state of Mississippi, on the path to economic progress.

So speculation was encouraged as one more attempt to get the lands sold and onto the tax rolls again. Neither partial donation of the lands nor the abatement of taxes on them had been successful in accomplishing this object. Indeed, the end results of both measures had strayed far from the course set by the legislature. Likewise, the compromise resulting from Gibbs *vs*. Green was the furthest thing from the minds of Mississippi's legislators when by the Abatement Act they acted to reduce the burdens of the Liquidating Levee Taxes from the shoulders of the Delta landowners. Were the results of large-scale land speculation also to be different from the benefits expected from it? How could the Delta landowners and the officials of the state of Mississippi be certain that their needs, as well as those of the speculators would be met? These questions were all answered by the leading promotor of the Gibbs settlement, William L. Nugent.

The son of a well-to-do Louisiana sugar planter, Nugent migrated as a young man to the Yazoo Delta. Settling in Greenville, he took up the law and was admitted to the Mississippi Bar. Possessed of a sharp wit, a facile pen, and an ability to convince others of his sincerity, he soon won the notice and respect of his profession. A sign of this was the relocation of his law practice to Jackson, the state capital, where there was a wider field of legal pasturage. Even so, the law was not the sole source of his income. He was part owner of at least two large Delta plantations located in

Bolivar County, then one of the Delta's wealthiest cotton growing areas. As a leading planter, he was thoroughly familiar with the needs of his section and thus was a logical spokesman to whom the administration turned for advice on how to treat the problem of the Delta lands. As attorney for the Jackson Bank of J. & T. Green, it was his handiwork in the Gibbs settlement that made the promotion of large-scale land speculation an administration policy.[19]

The hoped for results from the invitation to land speculation were immediately evident. In the four years after the Gibbs settlement in 1877, only 600,000 acres, or about one-quarter of the Delta's forfeited lands, were sold, and these in piecemeal lots. Slow as these sales were, the administration could at least take heart that the sales reflected a growing confidence in the Delta's future. It was this confidence buttressed by the flush of southern prosperity at the end of the 1870's that was prelude to two dramatic land sales in the summer of 1881.[20] The first of these was a 774,000 acre sale to the Memhpis and Vicksburg Railroad, a local corporation (owning not a mile of track) whose purchase of these lands was motivated by the knowledge that both it and its valuable right-of-way franchise were soon bid to a powerful northern railroad syndicate, headed by one of the greatest of railroad entrepreneurs, Collis P. Huntington. By the beginning of the 1880's he and his partners were building a national coast to coast super trunk line whose connecting link lay in the stretch of alluvial land between Memphis and Vicksburg. The suc-

[19] *Goodspeed's Biographical and Historical Memoirs of Mississippi* (Chicago, 1891), II, 515-517; Nugent *vs.* Levee Commissioners, 58 Miss. 197; Dunbar Rowland, *Courts, Judges and Lawyers of Mississippi, 1798-1935* (Jackson, 1935), 240; Wirt A. Williams, ed. *History of Bolivar County, Mississippi* (Jackson, 1948), 361, 490; "The Proceedings of a Mississippi Convention in 1879," *Journal of Negro History*, IV (January 1919), 51-54.

[20] Mississippi, *House Journal, 1886*, p. 572; Green *vs.* Gibbs, No. 326, Chancery Court, Hinds County (Jackson, Miss.), 1st District *Minutes*, II, 519-520, 522-523, 579.

ceeding effects from this sale to the Huntington group determined the major part of the Yazoo Delta's history and will be taken up in later chapters. Curiously enough, however, it was not this sale that attracted attention at this time. Rather, all the notice was given to the 706,000 acres of Delta lands sold to a peculiar group of land speculators, from whose activities Nugent was convinced the entire Delta would benefit.

Much was made of the fact that the people involved in this sale were British capitalists. This by itself was enough to evoke confidence. For despite suspicions about the conspiratorial intents of British capital to enslave the Americans, it was a fixture in the agrarian mind that the acid test of any really valid large-scale enterprise in America was its degree of English support. Nugent must have done a masterful job of propagandizing the role of British capital because tradition still has it that during the early part of the 1880's British capitalists were swarming all over the lands of the lower Mississippi Valley.[21] In fact, very little British money was involved in this sale of Delta lands, and it certainly did not have the backing of large English banking houses. It is not even certain that the chief player in this land adventure, a certain Colonel Byron Henry Evers, was English to begin with. His background was obscure, and there is reason to believe that he was traveling under an alias and that he was Edward Evers, a man earlier convicted in Missouri of swindling.[22] When he first met Nugent sometime during the late

[21] *Atlanta Constitution,* Jan. 10, 1882; C. Vann Woodward, *Origins of the New South, 1877-1913* (Baton Rouge, 1951), 118-119.

[22] State of Missouri *vs.* Evers and Evers, 49 Missouri 544. Unless otherwise noted, the following discussion is based on court records pertaining to the case of Byron H. Evers *vs.* Thomas Watson, 314 U.S. District Court (Western Division of Northern District, Miss.), Box 9, Container 94092, National Archives and Record Services, East Point (Atlanta), Georgia. The collection also includes records of Byron H. Evers *vs.* S. Gwin, 392 U.S. Circuit Court (Miss.), Dysart *vs.* George F. Phillips et al., 397 U.S. District Court (Miss.), and Jordan and Jordan *vs.* Phillips, Marshall and Co., 71262 Court of Common Pleas, Hamilton Co. (Cincinnati) Ohio. For a complete account of the involved deal-

spring of 1881 and became his client, Evers had the limited
financial backing of two London bond and share brokers,
George Frederick Phillips and William Marshall. This was
the entire extent of the so-called British capital.

Nevertheless, Nugent was clever enough to make the most
out of popular conceptions of British capital. No one knew
better than he that the chief ingredient for successful speculation was to excite anticipation about the land's future value.
More than two-thirds of the lands in his own county of Bolivar
were still in their wild state. For the most part they probably
were forfeited for taxes and hence, as far as the Delta's
landlords were concerned they had little or no value. The
situation was worse in many other parts of the Delta. For
some landowners these forfeited wild lands were a great
temptation to commit illegal depredations of the standing
timber on them. (It was charged that county officials turned
their eyes the other way when these acts occurred.) But there
was no future in this. The real future of these lands was to
get them into cultivation, for only when these lands were
producing cotton did they have value. Delta landowners like
Nugent were eager to do this but lacked the means to purchase them and continue to pay the taxes on them, as well
as to undertake the slow and expensive process of clearing,
draining, and otherwise making them fit for production. If,
however, the value of these wild lands could somehow be
raised, the increase could be used as security for loans. Thus,
the purpose of land speculation was not merely to facilitate
the sale of the lands and get them on the tax rolls, but arti-
ficially to raise their value and thereby increase their chances
to be permanently productive. The rise in value of these forfeited lands would correspondingly create higher values for
Delta lands already in cultivation.

ings in this case see Robert L. Brandfon, Planters of the New South: An
Economic History of the Yazoo Mississippi Delta (unpublished Ph.D. dissertation, Harvard University, 1961).

That the forfeited lands were sold to "British capitalists" might alone have brought this about. But Nugent had greater plans. His use of the reputation attached to British capital was but part of a larger scheme to integrate a number of forces that would ensure even higher values. He was aware that General John B. Gordon was planning to build the Georgia Pacific Railroad west from Birmingham to the Mississippi River. This was a project that would cut through the widest part of the Yazoo Delta and, incidentally, across some of the lands involved in this speculation. Everyone knew that the advent of a major railroad such as Gordon's Georgia Pacific would cause a rise in the value of all Delta lands since Delta products would be given a modern transportation outlet to the cities of the eastern seaboard. Nugent hoped to capitalize on this development by selling the lands temporarily to Gordon and then transferring them to Evers. His was a complex plan, but one that he could easily direct because all the principals in the transaction were his clients. By a court order and with the full consent of the state administration, 706,326 acres were sold to the Georgia Pacific (in the name of the general's brother, Eugene C. Gordon) for the agreed upon sum of $48,454.22 or approximately 6½ cents an acre.[23] Although the deeds were made out in Gordon's name they were bought for him by Evers. The latter purchased them under the terms of the Gibbs settlement, paying 5 per cent in currency and 95 per cent with the bonds of the Liquidating Levee Board. These Evers purchased at a substantial discount from the Bank of J. & T. Green, which had been persuaded to sell them to him by Nugent. By the end of November 1881, all the deeds earlier made out to Gordon were transferred to the name of Bryon H. Evers. And now

[23] Green *vs.* Gibbs, No. 326, Chancery Court, Hinds County (Jackson, Miss.), 1st District *Minutes,* II, 579; Washington County, Mississippi, *Deed Book, 0-2,* pp. 227-238, Courthouse, Greenville, Miss.

both Nugent and the state administration had only to await the expected fruits of this juggling.

Both were to be disappointed, but not entirely for the same reason. Although the Delta landowners and the state administration were agreed about the importance of getting the lands on the tax rolls again, they differed over what was to happen to the lands thereafter. The administration looked to this speculation as a means of settling the lands with white yeoman farmers, for one of the ideals of the New South was to increase the southern white population by encouraging immigration. The reconstruction immigration program for the state of Mississippi was a casualty of the political turmoil in 1875. It was revived a few years later, and reached its peak in 1882 when the legislature appropriated $25,000 to further the work.[24] Meager as it was, this sum was far more than any previous grant, and coincided with Evers' alleged intentions to settle his newly acquired lands with yeoman farmers. In December 1881, he formed the British and Mississippi Land Company and gave word to the press that if the state of Mississippi would aid his syndicate he promised within the next four years (or in time for the gubernatorial election of 1885) to settle up his lands with "100,000 English immigrants, 60,000 of which will be voting as soon as naturalized."[25]

There is no existing evidence for other widespread assurances about the benefits expected from Evers' speculation, but statements by the administration indicate that more were given. The state auditor, for example, reported that during 1881 two million acres of Mississippi lands were restored to the assessment rolls. Echoing current ideas about the po-

[24] Mississippi, *Journal of the Senate, 1882* (Jackson, 1882), 235; Mississippi, *Biennial Report of the Commissioner of Immigration, 1882* (Jackson, 1882), 8, 18-19.

[25] *Magnolia Gazette* (Magnolia, Miss.) quoted in *Memphis Daily Appeal*, Dec. 14, 1881; *New York Tribune*, Dec. 27, 1881.

tency of foreign (British) capital, he said, "the fact that about one-half of these large acreages was bought by foreign capital and that similar investments of foreign money are continually being made, encourages the hope that our population will, ere long, be augmented by the introduction of a useful and valuable class of foreign immigrants."[26] During the gubernatorial canvass of 1881, the Democrats pointed with pride to the fact that it was they who had solved the twenty-year headache of Mississippi's six million forfeited acres. And they assured the voting masses that the encouragement of large-scale land speculation, which had put these lands in a taxpaying category once again, was also the means by which these lands would be developed and improved for the betterment of the entire state of Mississippi.[27]

To be sure, Delta landowners applauded the theory of bringing in new immigrants, especially if they were white. By the beginning of the 1880's, the Delta was fast filling up with thousands of Negroes forced from depleted soils in the older South. So great was this black flood that Nugent, for example, voiced his fears for the "conservation of our institutions."[28] On the other hand, Delta landowners never envisioned their area as a home for prosperous small white cotton farmers. They reasoned that there was no such thing as a prosperous small cotton farmer. Everyone knew that really profitable cotton growing involved, in addition to extraordinary soils as those of the Yazoo Delta, economies of production, chief among which was cheap tenant labor.

It was, therefore, idle to think that 100,000 English im-

[26] Mississippi, *Report of the Auditor of Public Accounts, 1881* (Jackson, 1881), pp. 55-56.

[27] State of Mississippi *vs.* Delta and Pine Land Company, No. 922, Chancery Court, Hinds County (Jackson, Miss.) ; Mississippi, *Governor's Messages, 1882* (John M. Stone), Department of Archives and History, Jackson, Miss.; Robert Lowry to Col. Byron H. Evers, Oct. 25, 1882, in Gastrell *vs.* Wineman, 521 U.S. Circuit Court, Eastern District, Miss.

[28] Mississippi, *House Journal, 1886*, p. 576.

migrant yeomen, even if Evers somehow delivered them, could be fitted into the prospects of the Delta's landowners. What they sought from this speculation was not a significant increase in the numbers of Delta property owners but rather a reservoir of land for future expansion. Held out from piecemeal sale by Evers, they reasoned, these lands would constantly be paying taxes, which in addition to relieving present tax burdens, would allow Delta planters to purchase them later without tax accumulations. Likewise, the speculative process of bidding up prices on anticipated values would give the lands increased worth; higher purchase prices to the planters would offset by the greater advantage of being able to borrow more heavily on the land's future productive capacity. Finally, several years of taxpaying by Evers would strengthen the land's legal status by consolidating Evers' fragile tax titles into fee simple ownership, thereby making the lands safer to purchase in the future.

All these advantages—the economic ones for the landowners and the political ones for the administration—hinged on Evers' ability to pay taxes on these lands and thereby prevent them from becoming forfeit once again. This he was never able to do. Evers did not have the money. His English partners and sources of capital, Phillips and Marshall, were a far cry from the great English banking houses. They were small time entrepreneurs—amateurs whose monetary resources and knowledge of American land speculation were wholly inadequate for the undertaking Evers had engaged them in. Nugent knew of Evers' limited financial resources, although he was never fully aware (until it was too late) of just how limited they really were. Faced with this serious handicap, Nugent planned to raise money by widening the scope of the enterprise. This was in the accepted manner of land speculation. By selling part of Evers' interest but not the lands themselves (that is, their titles) the lands would be valued not at their market price, which was worth very little, but rather at their much greater anticipated value. It was for the purpose of escalating their anticipated values that Nugent had arranged with General Gordon to have the lands bought in Gordon's name, thereby giving the impression that the General's Georgia Pacific was about to extend its lines through the Yazoo Delta.

During the involved arrangement with Gordon, Evers succeeded in selling an undivided half interest in his lands, according to the plan, to a Chicago group of land speculators, Thomas Watson and his sons, Matthew and William. Allowing these adventurers into the affair was a mistake. To be sure, faced with Evers' financial limitations and eager to get the lands sold, Nugent had no other choice but to give his consent, for it was the Watsons who had the money. But the choice of the Watsons was poor judgment. These men, foreseeing the interests of northern lumbermen in the South, had for years been engaged in speculating with southern timber and mineral lands. Their strictly exploitative desires precluded any developmental interests in the lands of the Yazoo Delta such as Nugent or the state administration had in mind. Moreover, a long history of opportunism had involved them in innumerable lawsuits, all of which produced the hopelessly confused legal trail that characterized their every movement.[29] The Delta speculation was no exception. Indeed, the Watsons' share of Evers' interest was an invitation for all who had previous legal claims against the Watsons to clamor for ancillary shares in the Delta lands. There was a long list of such people. Although the records of this speculation are scattered and incomplete, no fewer than twenty-eight different parties eventually became embroiled in it. Heretofore, Nugent masterminded every step. All the original

---

[29] Watson *vs.* Austin et al., 63 Miss. 469.

principals—the Bank of J. & T. Green, General John B. Gordon's Georgia Pacific Railroad, and Evers (who represented Phillips and Marshall) were his clients. Even the state administration could be added to this list, for the auditor, treasurer, governor, and legislature submitted just as willingly to Nugent's leadership. However, the Watsons and all the litigants that followed in their wake were another matter. From the time they entered the speculation, Nugent lost his guiding control with results frustrating to the developmental expectations of both Delta planters and the state of Mississippi.

When the Watsons found out Evers' true condition (the aura of British capitalists notwithstanding), they made haste to take advantage of his financial weakness. In January 1882 they began a series of protracted lawsuits against Evers and his London partners, claiming full ownership and title to Evers' Delta lands because the money they had paid to Evers for a half interest was equal to the sum Evers had paid originally for the land. In other words, they claimed, it was their money that Evers had used to buy the land in the first place. Because of the intricacy of the sale to Gordon their claim was legally a powerful one. The long years of legal wrangling that followed damaged the entire proceedings. Because Evers lacked cash to pay taxes on the lands, his plan was to raise the necessary tax money by selling large segments of them. He reasoned he could get a good price for the lands, if only for the fact that his ownership of them raised their values. But their sale to others was made impossible by the Watsons' suits, which by challenging Evers' ownership jeopardized his legal right to sell them, put a cloud over the titles, and frightened away prospective buyers. In March 1883, as a result of Evers' failure to pay taxes, all 706,000 Delta acres fell back into the hands of the state. The magic of land speculation was not producing the effects expected from it.

But this did not cause the state administration to lose faith in the process. Under Nugent's urging the legislature was persuaded to extend Evers one extra year to redeem his lands and thus relieve the state from the persistent headache of the Delta's forfeited lands.[30]

This measure did not reach to the heart of the problem. What Evers needed was not time to pay the taxes, but exemption from them altogether. But for whatever reasons, the state of Mississippi was unwilling to grant Evers the kind of help his situation demanded. The result was that a shortsighted policy of demanding a few years of back taxes lost for the state the greater long-run gain that might have come about had Evers, under Nugent's guidance, been able to retain his lands. In July 1884, the Bank of J. & T. Green, with whom Evers had deposited his small savings, collapsed wiping out forever any hope that Evers could salvage the speculation in his interest. Immediately thereafter his allies began to desert him, shifting allegiance to the Watsons, who were successful in demanding that Evers' titles to the lands be put into the hands of a federal receiver, with final judgment on the interests of all the parties to be rendered by a federal court. Having lost in this way its jurisdiction, the state of Mississippi was powerless to direct the speculation in such a way that would favor the interests of the Yazoo Delta and the state of Mississippi. That the state government should want to direct it at this stage, however, would have been a new departure, for at no time during the preceding four years had it taken a positive role. Had it done so, the outcome might have been more to its satisfaction.

As a condition of the alliance, the Watsons forced all the other parties into an agreement by which the party who paid the taxes on the lands would be granted them, providing that if the lands were sold the proceeds of the sale would be di-

[30] Mississippi, *Laws, 1884*, Ch. CLXXII.

vided pro rata according to each party's original investment.
It was on this basis that the United States district court de-
creed in October 1885 that if within six months Evers were
to pay the Watsons an agreed upon sum he would receive
the Delta lands free of all the Watsons' liens and encum-
brances; otherwise the lands (in the hands of a federal receiver) would be sold, the proceeds being applied to the
amount owed the Watsons. It was a foregone conclusion that
Evers could never hope to raise the money to pay the Watsons.
He had failed to raise money enough merely to pay the taxes.
It was equally certain that when the lands were sold at auction
in March 1886, the Watsons would be the chief buyers. Based
on the terms of the court degree, they would get the lands at
bargain rates, since the sale price amounted to the taxes for
1885 (all previous taxes having been abated as a result of
the judicial proceedings). In the end, having paid the taxes
for just one of the five years that this proceeding involved, the
Watsons took possession of 450,000 acres of their own choos-
ing, and neither Evers, Nugent, nor the state of Mississippi
could do anything about it.[31]

It was incongruous that the state of Mississippi was unable
to realize a penny from the sale of its own lands. Nor was
this all. It had not received any taxes on these lands since
Evers first purchased them in 1881; most of the lands had
not been yielding taxes since the Civil War. For a quarter
of a century these lands were totally unproductive from the
standpoint of revenue, not to mention agricultural production. Whatever else the administration may have thought of
the fact that the Watsons wound up owning hundreds of
thousands of the very best lands in the state, it was quick to
make certain that at least they would not become forfeit
again. In 1886 the Watsons received a Mississippi charter
to incorporate the Delta and Pine Land Company behind

---

[31] Byron H. Evers et al. *vs.* Thomas Watson et al., 156 U.S. 527.

whose corporate shield their titles immediately were transferred. Two years later the legislature granted a sweeping
confirmation of the Watsons' titles, upholding the validity of
all the proceedings by which the Watsons had acquired their
ownership.[32]

As with Evers the state government was ready to grant the
Watsons this kind of permissive legislation. But just as with
Evers, the legislation for the Watsons was no guarantee that
they would continue to pay taxes and thus keep the lands on
the assessment rolls. Neither was legislation passed nor administrative action taken to encourage the Watsons to use
their vast holdings in the interests of the Delta planters.
Likewise the Watsons' designs contradicted the larger hopes
of the Mississippi government when it embarked upon the
policy of speculation and the lands were first sold to Evers.
Despite the fact that the company's charter gave it wide
powers for future land development (powers which in 1919
under entirely different owners would be used to develop the
world's largest cotton plantation in the Yazoo Delta), it was
an absentee landlord with all the evils attendant upon it. The
only goal of the handful of stockholder-directors sitting in
Chicago was to sell the lands and divide the proceeds of sale
among themselves without regard to any questions of land
settlement and development. The company's undeviating policy was to sell its property as timber lands, the minimum
purchase being 10,000 acres for cash with no provisions for
credit. No steps were taken to encourage immigrant yeoman
farmers to these Delta lands.[33] Moreover, the Delta and Pine

[32] Mississippi, Secretary of State, *Record of Incorporations*, III, 122-123;
Office of Secretary of State, Jackson, Miss.; Mississippi, *Laws, 1888*, Ch.
XXIII.
[33] Wirt Adams *vs.* Delta and Pine Land Company, 89 Miss. 817; Delta and
Pine Land Company *vs.* Edgar S. Wilson, No. 916, Chancery Court, Hinds
County (Jackson, Miss.), 1st District; Augusta Hawks *vs.* Edgar W. Wilson,

Land Company's policy worked against the expansive interests of the Delta planters. By selling its lands to timber firms
the company not only prolonged the day when the planters
could buy them, but by the twentieth century, when the lands
finally became available for purchase, they were classified as
cutover or "improved" lands carrying much higher prices
than they were worth during the 1880's.[34]

In short, the outcome of this speculation contradicted the
theory that prompted the state of Mississippi and the Delta
planters to encourage land speculation. The advantages of
higher land values expected from speculation favored only
the absentee Watsons and their partners and were not shared
by the Delta planters who sought to convert higher land values
into sources of new capital. Thus the rapid opening up, improvement, settlement, and cultivation of some of Mississippi's most prized lands never materialized. Not at least
out of this speculation. What was left, unfortunately, was
a residue of disenchantment with the spokesmen who had
championed land speculation as a means of bringing about
a prosperous southern order. At no time, despite the importance of the Delta's development to the rest of Mississippi's economy, did the state government take the lead in
guiding the actions of the speculators so as to bring about
a more satisfactory end. With faint knowledge of the Evers-
Watson proceedings, Mississippi's public, by the hard times
of the mid-1880's, was quick to condemn all land speculation as a means by which "giant corporations and purse-
proud syndicates," had robbed Mississippi's people of their

No. 931, Chancery Court, Hinds County (Jackson, Miss.), 1st District; Edward
P. Skene to J. C. Welling, Jan. 28, 1897, and Stuyvesant Fish to Chaplin,
Milne, Grenfell & Co., Ltd., March 2, 1903, in Stuyvesant Fish Letters, Illinois
Central Railroad Archives, Newberry Library, Chicago.

[34] U.S., Congress, House, *Swamp and Overflow Lands in the Yazoo Basin*,
69th Cong., 2d Sess. (1927), House Doc. 765, Serial 8735, pp. 77, 81-89.

birthright.[35] To the extent that the Delta's land remained undeveloped thus retarding the entire state's agricultural development, these feelings were not too wide of the mark.

[35] Address by Frank Burkett, July 31, 1895, quoted in William D. McCain, The Populist Party in Mississippi (unpublished M.A. thesis, University of Mississippi, 1931), 46.

Thus, what happened to these Delta lands followed the pattern of federal lands all over the South. As Paul Gates says: "Southerners had good reason to reconsider their attitude on land policy. They realized that the reopening of the southern lands to large-scale purchasing had not brought the economic expansion they had expected; instead it had resulted in the purchase of large tracts of valuable lands by speculators, generally non-residents, who withheld them from development while they waited for their profits." Paul W. Gates, "Federal Land Policy in the South 1866-1888, *Journal of Southern History*, VI (July 1940), 327.

# CHAPTER 4

# A Marriage of Interests

AT THE SAME TIME that large-scale land speculation was failing as a massive spur to the Yazoo Delta's economy, another major development was shaping the area. This was the establishment of a modern railroad system, which, by the end of the nineteenth century, had numerous branch lines reaching into every corner of the Delta. The distinguishing feature about the Delta's rail system was that, when completed, it was an essential part of one of the leading trunk line railroads in the nation—the Illinois Central Railroad. The Yazoo Delta trade became the cream of the Illinois Central profits. Placed within the orbit of an organization counted as one of the blue chip corporations in the United States, the Yazoo Delta's economy acquired characteristics that distinctively set the landowning planters of the Delta apart from their poorer southern neighbors to the east. Attached to the major north and south rail artery of the nation, the Delta's economy was part of one of the great mainstreams of national commerce. Attached also to the Illinois Central's balance sheet the interests of the Yazoo Delta became the interests of the Illinois Central.[1] Thus was woven a marriage

[1] Certain aspects of the Illinois Central Railroad's history have been studied: e.g., Paul W. Gates, *The Illinois Central Railroad and Its Colonization Work*

of interests, the impact of which was as profound upon the thinking and attitudes of the Delta's populace as upon the rest of the state of Mississippi.

It was natural that the Delta's rail system should develop along north and south lines. Her streams ran in that direction, and before the advent of the railroads, the Delta's many streams were the arteries of her commerce. They formed a small-scale replica of the South's great water artery. Between the Mississippi River on the west and the Yazoo River on the east, there are three major rivers, all of which enter into the lower Yazoo before emptying into the Mississippi. These are Steele Bayou, Deer Creek, and the Big Sunflower River. In addition there are scores of smaller waterways many of whose names are delightfully descriptive—Panther Creek, Bear Creek, Dry Bayou, Otter Bayou, Bogue Phalia, Clear Creek, Puzzle Bayou, Bee Bayou, Muddy Bayou, Quiver River, and the Little Sunflower False River. On the map it would seem that there was no need for any other form of communication than the river steamboat, which plying up and down the rivers, bogues, brakes, creeks, and bayous could connect every part of the Delta. In reality, however, the Delta's streams made for very unsatisfactory transportation. Uncontrolled spring flood waters from the northern bluffs combined with heavy rains to overwhelm its narrow channels causing such serious obstructions to river commerce as caving banks, overhanging trees, and partially sunken logs the roots of which had to be

(Cambridge, Mass., 1934) ; Edwin S. S. Sunderland, *Illinois Central Railroad, Main Line of Mid-America; The Simplification of Its Debt Structure, 1938-1952* (New York, 1952) ; John F. Stover, *The Railroads of the South, 1865-1900* (Chapel Hill, 1955), ch. VIII and passim. A general account from 1851 to 1950 is Carlton J. Corliss, *Main Line of Mid-America; The Story of the Illinois Central* (New York, 1950). The most satisfactory account, however, of the Illinois Central Railroad's activities in the South can be derived only from its vast archives (from 1851-1906) deposited in the Newberry Library, Chicago. All statements concerning the Illinois Central's activities have been derived mainly from these sources.

blasted out. Snags presented no problem during the early summer months when river levels were at their highest. But by autumn the waters receded and the snags were left uncovered. As a result, the Delta's many waterways were least accessible at harvest time when river transport was most needed. Thus cotton growers were forced to store their cotton at riverside warehouses, to wait there for the next spring freshets, or else haul their harvests westward over almost impassable swamps to the banks of the Mississippi where river boat transit was more reliable.[2]

In 1873 Congress began to appropriate funds for clearing away the hulks of ships sunk in the Yazoo River during the Civil War. Within a few years, appropriations were increased to dredge other Delta streams for the purpose of improving navigation.[3] As the dredging began stimulating steamboat commerce, railroading entered the Delta and very rapidly replaced the seamboat and the necessity for dredging as well. Nevertheless, dredging appropriations continued down through the end of the century, mainly as a boon to the Delta's short-lived but lively lumber industry, which depended upon the rivers to barge the lumber downstream. Any other kind of river traffic had long since dried up. As the president of the principal steamboat line on the Yalobusha River testily observed in 1902, traffic on the Yalobusha "would not support a catfish."[4]

Before 1880, planters were generally not in favor of giving up the steamboat, especially since congressional appropriations for dredging had become more or less of a habit. Nu-

[2] U.S. Congress, Senate, *Report of Captain W. H. H. Benyuard to Brig. Gen. Humphreys*, 45th Cong., 3d Sess. (1879), Senate Exec. Doc. 42, Serial 1828, pp. 3-4.
[3] U.S. Army, *Annual Reports of the Chief of Engineers, 1873-1919* (Washington, 1873-1919), Vicksburg Division.
[4] U.S. Congress, House, *Examination of the Yalobusha River*, 58th Cong., 2d Sess. (1903), House Doc. 201, Serial 4672, p. 3.

merous steamboat companies provided the competition that kept down freight rates. Railroads were, therefore, regarded as a supplement to the steamboat—as a means of connecting the north and south streams as well as the valuable cultivated high grounds that ran parallel to them. Thus the numerous local railroading schemes of the 1870's projected for the most part in east and west directions. Only the ambitious names of the proposed companies carried hopes that they would ever become more than links between the Delta's riverboat traffic. By the late 1870's two narrow gauge single track lines had been built through the efforts of local planter capital. These were the Greenville, Columbus and Birmingham Railroad, which in 1880 crawled 31 painful miles from Greenville eastward across the paths of swamps, bayous, and rattle-snakes to Johnsonville, and the Mobile and Northwestern Railroad in the Northern Delta, whose 39 miles of track were all that existed of original visions to build something greater. Local interest and local capital were both lacking for any-thing more.[5] If the Delta were to have an enlarged modern railroad system that would replace the steamboat, outside capital and interest would have to bring it about.

The beginnings of the Delta's rail era lie in the interrela-tions between the nineteenth century American railroad and the boundless visions of the rugged entrepreneurs who ran them. Speculation was the common denominator. Eager to cash in on the opportunities of a rapidly expanding economy, railroad promoters rushed to build without the proper kind of capital backing. They floated bonds to begin construction. This is normal in any enterprise. But wholly lacking cash, railroad managers then went on to float additional bonds to cover interest payments on the construction bonds. The rail-

[5] William D. McCain and Charlotte Capers, eds., *Papers of the Washington County Historical Society* (Jackson, Miss., 1954), 311-326; *The Mobile and Northwestern Railroad: Address to the People of Mobile* (Mobile, 1870).

road's sole source of cash income was its earnings, which in a new country were highly unpredictable. This income was used first to meet fixed interest charges on the railroad's bonds, anything left over being passed on in dividends and increased stock value. But because of the need to overcome the chronic shortage of investment capital and the need to attract it by whatever means, railroad managers were always granting higher interest rates and higher dividends than the actual capital assets of the road would allow. Thus, even if its securities were not watered to begin with (the exception and not the rule), a new railroad's fixed obligations were dangerously high, a situation fraught with temptation for speculative dealers who toyed with American railroad securities.

Under these conditions hard times and depression were, of course, automatically fatal. On the other hand, prosperity could prove to be just as bad. Prosperity brought more competition and an intensified scramble for freight and passenger earnings. In the face of competition retrenchment and economy were out of the question, not only because they were foreign to the expansive nature of the nineteenth century entrepreneur, not only because it was believed (especially in good times) that there was still plenty of room for industrial and agricultural expansion, but also because the railroad's fixed obligations made it mandatory to increase its earnings merely to keep pace with its debts. There had to be expansion else a railroad would lose freight and passenger traffic to its competitors, automatically causing decreased earnings and discouraging prospective investors. And without cash reserves and the possibility of investors the railroad would be unable to meet its obligations and would without exception wind up (as so many American railroads did in this period) amid the wreckage of court receivership. The antidote to debt was expansion in the hopes that expansion would mean an increase in earnings sufficient to meet mounting debts. But lacking cash reserves, the only way to expand was to boom another bond issue, glorifying out of all proportion the future profits for prospective investors. Thus, the exaggerated visions of a Beriah Sellers in the *Gilded Age* were those of a man not only possessed with a sublime faith in the golden future (of the new country) but of a man with his back to the wall. Success in raising additional creditors, however, meant another increase in fixed obligations, putting more pressure on the railroad's earning capacities. Yet the debt was raised still higher, if for no better reason than the hope that expansion would stave off the day of final reckoning that some blindly believed might somehow never come at all. Born of speculation the typical nineteenth century American railroad was a vicious circle of its own creation. To understand this setting is to know the background of the Yazoo Delta's railroad history.

Placed firmly within the speculative whirligig was Collis P. Huntington, one of America's greatest railroad entrepreneurs, whose bold plan for a super continental railroad combined with the speculative character of American railroading to produce a new departure for the Yazoo Delta's economy. Having amassed a fortune in the West, Huntington turned, in 1869, to the East, taking over the Chesapeake and Ohio Railroad and extending it 200 miles through the Appalachian Mountains to the point on the Ohio River that bears his name. This was the first step in Huntington's dream to connect the east and west coasts by one main rail line. Part of the process was to buy out bankrupt lines, of which the South had a plentiful supply. Thus, it was through the South that the line between his eastern and western roads could be made most cheaply. In 1882, in conjunction with Richard T. Wilson, whose New York banking firm made a practice of picking up the pieces of impoverished southern railroads,

Huntington purchased the franchises of several Mississippi railroad companies. These were the Memphis and Vicksburg and the Mississippi Valley and Ship Island railroads.[6] Despite a decade of unified management these two roads had done little to build a road, for by 1882 all that existed of a projected rail line from Memphis to New Orleans was a 25-mile strip of narrow gauge track extending south from Vicksburg. Yet the Huntington-Wilson group was willing to pay over $400,000 for the roads and their franchises.[7] In part, this was because the franchise included 774,000 acres of Yazoo Delta lands (part of the millions of acres forfeited for taxes during the 1870's), which the owners of the two Mississippi railroads just one year earlier presciently had picked up from the state at bargain rates.[8] But the larger reason was neither the lands nor the possibility of developing them into lucrative freight earnings, but rather because the franchise included the right-of-way through the Yazoo Delta, whose flat contours provided gradeless terrain and thus cheaper operating costs.

The chief aim of the Huntington-Wilson group was to build a railroad connecting Memphis to New Orleans in the most economical way possible. Its interests were therefore at best inferentially related to the Yazoo Delta. But this did not lessen the impact of this railroad upon the area. No sooner had arrangements been made for the sale of the two Mississippi roads than track laying began. By the fall of 1884 the 454-mile length of track from Memphis to New

[6] Cerinda W. Evans, *Collis Potter Huntington* (Newport News, Va., 1954), II, 573-575; Stover, *Railroads of the South*, 103, 184; Major James M. Edwards, History of the Louisville, New Orleans and Texas Railroad, in Stuyvesant Fish Letters, Illinois Central Railroad Archives, Newberry Library, Chicago.

[7] *The Weekly Clarion* (Jackson, Miss.), April 12, 1882.

[8] E. Martin to State Auditor, Aug. 21, 1881, Series G. No. 159, Mississippi State Auditors Archives, Department of Archives and History, Jackson, Miss.; Mississippi, *Senate Journal, 1882*, p. 5; Green *vs.* Gibbs, Hinds County Chancery Court, *Minute Book*, II, 519-520.

Orleans was formally opened for traffic. Named the Louisville, New Orleans and Texas Railway Company, it was no
fly-by-night operation. Its authorized capital stock was
$10,000,000 and its immediate success justified this huge
outlay. To the surprise of its owners the success of the L.N.O.
& T. was due not only to the fact that the road was a major
northern outlet for the products of New Orleans, and the
entrepôt for an expanding Latin American trade, but also
because of the very profitable earnings from the products
of the Yazoo Delta.[9]

Delta planters previously had been apathetic about railroads. The steamboat had always been good enough. Yet,
once they tasted the advantages of an all-weather, all-season
transportation system, they hastened to make the most of it.
The old river wharfs and warehouses were abandoned, and
urgent demands were made for more railroads, or more
specifically, an expansion of the Louisville, New Orleans and
Texas. "What they want," reported a spy for the Illinois
Central Railroad, "is rail facilities, and [they] are ready to
welcome first comers."[10] Planters in one district, for example, reportedly were willing to put up $300,000 for the
L.N.O. & T. to build in their area. And the city of Greenville
on the Mississippi subscribed $25,000 in L.N.O. & T. stock
for the construction of additional rail facilities including
a river wharf for handling coal. The eagerness of the planters
was matched only by the energy and resourcefulness of the
L.N.O. & T.'s vice president and general manager, James M.
Edwards, who was responsible for capitalizing upon the
popular approval of the planters for railroad expansion.[11]

9 Mississippi, *Laws, 1882*, pp. 874-875, 920-932; *Laws, 1884*, 936; Secretary
of Yazoo and Mississippi Valley Railroad to Mayes and Longstreet, Aug. 22,
1903, Fish Letters; Edwards, History of the Louisville, New Orleans and Texas
Railroad.
10 Henry P. Farrar to John G. Mann, June 1, 1888, Fish Letters.
11 John G. Mann to Edward T. Jeffery, June 13, 1888; Edward T. Jeffery
to Stuyvesant Fish, June 12, 1888; George W. Carlisle to John G. Mann, June
13, 1889; John Dunn to Stuyvesant Fish, May 17, 1890, *ibid.*

During the latter part of the 1880's two frail narrow gauge roads, which existed within the L.N.O. & T.'s orbit were absorbed, their track relaid with steel, widened to conform with the standard gauge, and otherwise fully integrated into the rest of the railroad. By 1892, after fewer than ten years of operation the L.N.O. & T. had doubled its length to 807 miles (exclusive of 132 miles of sidings) of which more than half lay in the Yazoo Delta.[12]

A transportation system connecting the Delta with the nation's largest markets had a great stimulative effect upon the area's economy, bringing to life the potential wealth that a generation of publicists had claimed for it. Expansion was the propelling force. Despite two severe floods in 1882 and 1884, the decade of the 1880's brought about a doubling of the Delta's cultivatable acreage. Cotton production in the Delta's eleven counties rose from 225,907 bales in 1879 to 366,401 ten years later. Corn, the Delta's second largest crop also saw a marked increase, from 2,606,117 to 3,408,317 bushels.[13] So great was the urge to expand that even some low-lying swamp areas, once scorned by the early pioneers, were being cultivated. As one observer described it, "the planters . . . instead of as formerly, confining themselves to the ridges, the ground is now broken on the ridges, and between them cotton and corn are growing down to the water's edge of the bayous."[14] And, above all, expansion and the prosperity that went with it gave greater value to Delta

[12] These roads were the Mobile and Northwestern in the northern Delta and Natchez, Jackson and Columbus Railroad, which went northwest from Natchez as far as Jackson. With the purchase of this latter road the L.N.O. & T. had direct access to the state capital and could draw off trade from the Illinois Central's main line in the South. William E. Rogers, *Report of the L.N.O. & T. to the President of the Illinois Central Railroad May 16, 1892* (Chicago, 1892), 3 and passim.

[13] *Agriculture*, U.S. Bureau of the Census, *Tenth Census*, III (Washington, 1883), 195, 231; *Agriculture*, in *Eleventh Census*, III (Washington, 1895), 372-373, 395.

[14] Henry P. Farrar to John G. Mann, June 1, 1888, Fish Letters.

lands, both cultivated and wild. The railroad succeeded in giving life to the rich Delta lands where the old formulas of large-scale land speculation had failed.

Expansion interacted with other forces to produce a new outlook for the Delta people, black and white. The decade of the 1880's saw the beginnings of federal efforts to bring about flood control, a factor that gave an important degree of confidence to those planning to farm in the Delta's wilderness. The same decade also saw a relative stabilization of cotton prices. The attendant wealth accumulated from the combination of expansion and steady prices attracted hoards of Negroes then drifting out of the worn-out lands to the east. Enticed by planter labor agents who sketched a new paradise, the hapless Negroes flocked into the Yazoo Delta providing the planters with a cheap and readily available labor force for further expansion and a multiplication of profits. Without the kinds of outlets provided by the railroad, there could have been no such expansion and no such profits. And the railroad did something more—less tangible, but just as significant. It provided the Delta planter with a new level of social sophistication. It was possible for planters and their families to travel swiftly to New Orleans and Memphis where the experiences of city life provided them with a degree of cosmopolitanism not held by most Mississippi farmers. In other words, it was during this period of the 1880's, a period of expansion stimulated by the railroad, a period of prosperity and rising land values, that the Delta farmer was separated from his brother in the hills. One became a planter, the other remained a farmer, and with the passing years, as the differences became more marked, so the enmity between them grew in like proportion.

If the Louisville, New Orleans and Texas Railroad had been good for the Delta, the benefits were reciprocal. From 1887 to 1891, the railroad's gross receipts tripled. Its third annual report in 1889 revealed net earnings per mile of

$55.45 as compared with $38.65 during the previous year. Indeed, by the time of this report the volume of business in the Delta was so large that the road's officers complained of their inability to handle it all.[15] Ironically, however, the L.N.O. & T.'s success caused the end of its independent existence, for its aggressive and expansive policies, especially at its major terminal point of New Orleans, ran athwart the more powerful interests of the Illinois Central Railroad. By the end of the 1880's the L.N.O. & T. had become a serious contender of the Illinois Central for New Orleans north and south rail traffic, and this was a situation the Illinois Central could not tolerate for very long.

The reasons for the Illinois Central's presence in New Orleans, as well as the circumstances that led it into the economy of the Yazoo Mississippi Delta, exemplify once again the fortuitous chain of events involved in economic development. Chartered in 1851, the Illinois Central was the creation of a two-and-a-half million acre federal land grant within the state of Illinois. In its early years, at least, because of its efforts to sell its huge landholdings to farmer-settlers and thus build up agricultural freight, the Illinois Central was more of a land company than a railroad.[16] Nevertheless, in a short time a railroad took shape and its tracks extended from Cairo, Illinois, at the confluence of the Ohio and Mississippi rivers, northward forming a Y, one terminal to the northeast at Chicago and the other to the northwest at Dunleith, Illinois. The location of its track and the extent of its landholdings made the Illinois Central a leading factor in the maturing economic and political life of the state of Illinois. And the road was acutely aware of its importance.

[15] Louisville, New Orleans and Texas Railroad, *Annual Report, 1889* (New York, 1890) ; Stover, in his *Railroads of the South*, 184, says that the L.N.O. & T. was sold because "of the lack of traffic in a region as yet largely underdeveloped." But the enthusiastic annual reports of the L.N.O. & T. do not bear out this statement.

[16] Gates, *The Illinois Central Railroad*, 147.

By the mid-1860's, the Illinois Central Railroad basked in the sunshine of prosperity, hauling the huge agricultural outpourings from the interior of Illinois (then the nation's grain basket) into Chicago, there to be sent eastward via the Great Lakes.

Following the pattern typical of nineteenth century American railroading, the Illinois Central's prosperity was nearly the cause of its extinction. The railroad was hounded by competitors. Eastern trunk lines quickly caused the diminution of the lake trade and seriously cut into the Illinois Central's earnings in the interior of Illinois. By the late 1870's the Illinois Central's main line was tapped by rival roads at no less than forty-nine different points.[17] The fierce intensity of this competition, coupled with the panic and depression after 1873, made for a grave situation. Harassment by Illinois' "granger laws" and the failure of the Iowa and Illinois wheat crop in 1876 added to the road's troubles. Stock values and dividends declined drastically. "The financial distress," recounted President Stuyvesant Fish in later years, "was such at that time that after all the assets in the Company's treasury had been hypothecated some of the directors had to come to the rescue by pledging their individual credit on the Company's notes."[18] Credit for saving the road must be attributed to William H. Osborn, president of the Illinois Central during the prosperous 1860's and one of the leading directors thereafter. His visit to New Orleans during the winter of 1871-72 convinced him that the future of his railroad lay in the southern trade, particularly in the port of New Orleans.[19]

[17] *Commercial and Financial Chronicle* (New York), Feb. 10, 1877, p. 134; March 19, 1881, p. 302.

[18] Stuyvesant Fish to Robert W. Patterson, Jan. 17, 1894, Fish Letters; William K. Ackerman, *Historical Sketch of the Illinois Central Railroad* (Chicago, 1890), 105-109.

[19] Stover, *Railroads of the South*, 166; Corliss, *Main Line of Mid-America*, 171-173; Ackerman, *Historical Sketch of the Illinois Central Railroad*, 114, 124-127.

Osborn's idea must have been born of faith, for even by the early 1870's the port of New Orleans did not have an attractive future. For a number of years before the Civil War, a dangerous sand bar had been piling up at the Mississippi's only navigable entrance way, causing the port to depend upon a tugboat association to keep commerce moving. As the bar and the ocean-going boats increased in size, dredging had continually to be carried on. The destruction of many of the city's shipping facilities as a result of the Civil War very nearly put the quietus to the Crescent City as a port. Yet, with all this Osborn received the cautious assent of the Illinois Central's Board of Directors to invest in two very unstable southern roads that would give the Illinois Central an operational link between New Orleans and Cairo. These two roads, the Mississippi Central and the New Orleans, Jackson and Great Northern, were an accumulation of earlier railroads that began at New Orleans and worked their way north through central Mississippi, western Tennessee, and Kentucky to Cairo. Like the Illinois Central this route was the product of Lakes-to-Gulf visions during the late 1840's. But unlike the Illinois Central the patchwork of railroads that made up the New Orleans to Cairo line suffered from a number of dramatic transformations resulting from chronic shortages of cash, too much speculation and tampering with management, and war.[20]

The Mississippi Central and the New Orleans, Jackson and Great Northern were not prospering when the Illinois Central made its investment in them. They were in worse condition after the depression of 1873. But the Illinois Central was also hard hit by the depression, which on top of the growing competition from other railroads in Illinois as well as political complications, justified the argument for retrenchment

---

[20] A vivid and lively account of the prewar rail system from Cairo to New Orleans in Thomas D. Clark, *A Pioneer Southern Railroad from New Orleans to Cairo* (Chapel Hill, 1936) ; Stover, *Railroads of the South*, 156-180.

and withdrawal from investment in the unstable conditions of southern railroads. On the other hand a number of factors favored increased investment in the South. Most important was the knowledge that without gambling on expansion there could be no increase in earning power, which was the only thing that could save the Illinois Central from being snuffed out by competition. Secondly, the depressed conditions of the Mississippi Central and the New Orleans, Jackson and Great Northern (conditions verging on bankruptcy) made possible their purchase at bargain rates. And lastly, there was a strong possibility that the port of New Orleans would be resurrected to its prewar greatness through the engineering genius of James B. Eads, whose plan to devise a system of jetties would cause the Mississippi River to scour its own channel thus allowing the largest ocean-going vessels to enter the port without the expensive necessity of constant dredging or the help of tugboats to pull them over the bar.[21]

Confronted by all these conditions, expansion to the south was the only reasonable course. It was supported further by the historical argument that the origins of the Illinois Central in the late 1840's lay in the idea of creating a trunk line railroad from the Lakes to the Gulf, thus re-enforcing with iron rails the natural unity of the Mississippi Valley. In 1877, the Illinois Central, chief creditor of the Mississippi Central and the New Orleans, Jackson and Great Northern, pressed the two roads into receivership and promptly purchased them at auction. Consolidated and greatly improved, they were renamed the Chicago, St. Louis and New Orleans. Fittingly enough, William H. Osborn was named its first president. With improvements, new management, and the support

[21] Florence Dorsey, *Road to the Sea: The Story of James B. Eads and Mississippi River* (New York, 1947), 166-217; Elmer L. Corthell, *A History of the Jetties at the Mouth of the Mississippi River* (New York, 1880), 25-49 and passim; *New York Tribune*, Feb. 11, 25, March 27, April 13, 1879.

of ample funds, the success of the Chicago, St. Louis and New Orleans was ensured and was stimulated further by the return of national prosperity beginning in 1878. Within the short space of three years after its formal incorporation, the value of traffic on the Illinois Central's southern division from New Orleans to Cairo increased sixfold. Declared by the Illinois Central Board of Directors in January 1881 to be "an absolute success,"[22] the extension in Fish's words, "proved to be the salvation of the property."[23]

With such importance attached to its southern division, the Illinois Central could ill afford to permit serious competition from the Louisville, New Orleans and Texas Railroad. In 1889, in an attempt to prevent hostility, Richard T. Wilson and Stuyvesant Fish, the new president of the Illinois Central, concluded a gentleman's agreement whereby each promised not to interfere with the vital interests of the other.[24] But the L.N.O. & T.'s very presence was a threat to the Illinois Central. By 1890, for example, the L.N.O. & T. was doing a greater amount of traffic in cotton and grain into New Orleans than the Chicago, St. Louis and New Orleans. Moreover, even while Wilson and Fish were agreeing on the "impropriety" of building "unremunerative lines," and conceding that competition between them would be a "waste of capital," the L.N.O. & T. was expanding its branch lines within the Yazoo Delta, producing the effect of drawing away the volume of traffic on the Illinois Central's southern division. Fortunately for the Illinois Central, the L.N.O. & T.'s foundation was a shaky one. This foundation was Collis P. Huntington's vast rail and shipping combine, the Newport News and Mississippi Valley Company, of which the L.N.O. & T.

<hr />

22 Illinois Central Railroad, Report of the Directors, Jan. 26, 1881, Feb. 1, 1877, Illinois Central Railroad Archives.
23 Stuyvesant Fish to Robert W. Patterson, Jan. 17, 1894, Fish Letters.
24 Richard T. Wilson to Stuyvesant Fish, July 9, 1890, *ibid.*

was a part, and whose large outstanding debt overwhelmed its relatively meager earnings making inevitable, by 1888, a reorganization of Huntington's interests. One by one, Huntington was forced to part with the pieces of his short-lived empire.[25] Thus, for the Illinois Central the solution of the L.N.O. & T. question was made easy. In 1892, under the urging of Stuyvesant Fish, the Illinois Central purchased the L.N.O. & T. for $25,000,000, quickly incorporated it into the Illinois Central system, and renamed it more appropriately the Yazoo and Mississippi Valley Railroad.[26]

A more satisfactory purchase had never been made. Throughout the 1890's, in the midst of one of the nation's most severe depressions, the Yazoo and Mississippi Valley Railroad continued to make money despite the fact that it made no extensions in track mileage. From 1892 to the end of the depression in 1898 gross receipts per mile rose from $4,111.55 to $5,901. This latter figure, Stuyvesant Fish proudly related to Huntington, "was more than the Illinois Central taken as a whole, earned in any year from 1887 to 1890 inclusive." During the decade of the 1890's gross receipts on the Yazoo and Mississippi Valley increased by 51 per cent, with the year 1897-98 being in Fish's words, "the most profitable in the history of either [the Illinois Central and the Yazoo and Mississippi Valley]." Not without a note of self-praise for having urged the purchase of the L.N.O. & T., Fish congratulated Huntington on the "intelligent foresight which induced you and Mr. R. T. Wilson to build the Louisville, New Orleans and Texas Railroad."[27]

25 Evans, *Collis Potter Huntington*, II, 578-584.
26 *Commercial and Financial Chronicle*, June 11, 1892, p. 939 (see also, Investor's Supplement, Nov. 1892, p. 66); Open Letter to Stockholders, May 31, 1892, Fish Letters; Hunter C. Leake, comp., *Illinois Central and Yazoo & Mississippi Valley Railroad Co. v. Wirt Adams, Briefs* (Jackson, 1908), Brief VII, Department of Archives and History, Jackson, Miss.
27 Stuyvesant Fish to Collis P. Huntington, July 13, 1898, Fish Letters.

What Fish wanted most was to avoid a repetition of the competition the Illinois Central had encountered in Illinois, competition that nearly extinguished it. Saved by the decision to expand southward and resuscitated by its southern division, the Illinois Central had been fortunate in nipping in the bud the serious competition presented by the L.N.O. & T. But wrapped up in the Illinois Central's decision to eradicate this competition was an awareness of the profits capable of being made from the trade of the Yazoo Delta. As Fish pointed out in his arguments in 1892 to purchase the L.N.O. & T., "The rapid development of the local interests, principally agricultural, which resulted in the opening of the L.N.O. & T. may be measured by the increase in local traffic, which shows a gain of 117.2 per cent in three and one-half years."[28] Looked at as both sides of the same coin these two factors, the avoidance of competition and the desire to reap increasing profits from the expanding economy of the Yazoo Delta, were the touchstone of Illinois Central policy in the South. The expressions of that policy were protection and expansion. And everything the Illinois Central did in Mississippi worked toward the same end, monopoly.

Achieving this monopoly involved nailing down forever the north and south route as the Delta's main channel of trade. The only challenge was the old route of the Greenville, Columbus and Birmingham Railroad. When, in 1881, this local road, which extended at that time about half way across the breadth of the Delta, was purchased by the Georgia Pacific, General Gordon, its leading owner, promised to complete the route the planters had sought—a through line eastward from Greenville across the state of Mississippi to Birmingham and beyond. But it was not until 1889 that the last spike in this railroad was driven and the Delta planters were connected on an east and west line to the Atlantic

[28] Open Letter to Stockholders, May 31, 1892.

coast.[29] By this time, however, it was too late to change the dominant north and south orientation of the Delta's trade, which resulted from the aggressiveness of the L.N.O. & T. Not even with the incorporation in 1894 of the Georgia Pacific into J. P. Morgan's colossus, the Southern Railway Company, could much be done to change that orientation. As Fish later reminded a prominent planter, "it is to the indomitable pluck and perseverance of Mr. Huntington and Mr. Wilson that the development of the existing railroad system in the Delta is due. For it can be said without fear of contradiction that the main business is on the north and south lines which connect the Delta with its natural markets, Memphis, Vicksburg and New Orleans, rather than on the east and west line operated by the Southern Railway from Greenville across the Delta eastward."[30]

From the moment after the purchase of the L.N.O. & T., the minds of Illinois Central officials were dominated by the single purpose of maintaining and extending their monopoly in the Yazoo Delta. They achieved this goal, but the price was the alienation of the people their railroad served. To the people of Mississippi monopoly was bad enough, but the Illinois Central's means of strengthening and extending it exacerbated the situation. No sooner had the news of the Southern Railway's formation reached Stuyvesant Fish than he moved to make certain that there would be no effect on the precious north and south orientation of the Delta's traffic. In 1895, Fish secured a gentleman's agreement with Samuel Spencer, president of the newly formed Southern Railway. Under its terms (wholly in violation of the Sherman

29 Georgia Pacific Railroad, *Annual Report, 1888* (Birmingham, Ala., 1888) ; *Railway Review*, XXI, 507; McCain and Capers, eds., *Papers of the Washington County Historical Society*, 325; *Commercial and Financial Chronicle*, June 22, 1889, p. 828; Fairfax Harrison, *History of the Legal Development of the Southern Railway* (Washington, 1901), 420-422.
30 Stuyvesant Fish to Charles Scott, June 21, 1904, Fish Letters.

Antitrust Act of 1890) each was to divide the Delta trade as it was already divided, both roads agreeing not to antagonize any part of their respective territories. The depression momentarily safeguarded this arrangement. But with the return of prosperity in 1898 and the eagerness to take advantage of increased earnings, the two giant corporations quarreled over the Yazoo and Mississippi Valley's secret assumption of a small railroad built by a Chicago land speculator interested in developing his lands in the eastern areas of the Delta. Spencer denounced this purchase as violating his gentleman's agreement with Stuyvesant Fish, for the acquisition in question paralleled a 33-mile north and south branch (called the Itta Bena-Webb extension) of the Southern Railway's main line through the Delta. Fish suspected Spencer of attempting to extend this branch northward into Illinois Central territory around Memphis and so had acted first to checkmate Spencer.[31]

Petty though this argument was, the resolution of the quarrel dramatized the growing public hostility to corporate monopoly. It is doubtful if Spencer ever entertained any ideas of challenging the Illinois Central. By the turn of the century, the Yazoo and Mississippi Valley's (or Illinois Central's) hold on the Delta trade was so complete as to be irrevocable. Everyone in Mississippi knew this, and so did Spencer. Indeed, in 1901, realizing that the Itta Bena-Webb branch was a financial liability, he urged Fish to take it off his hands—something Fish was delighted to do.[32] Only the law stood in the way, for according to the Mississippi Constitution, as amended by the State Code of 1892 and reinforced by a subsequent law in 1898, competing railroads were strictly

[31] Stuyvesant Fish to J. T. Harahan, April 8, 12, 1898; J. T. Harahan to Stuyvesant Fish, March 26, 28, 1900; Samuel Spencer to Stuyvesant Fish, Oct. 19, 1900; Stuyvesant Fish to Samuel Spencer, Nov. 10, 1904, *ibid.*

[32] Stuyvesant Fish to J. T. Harahan, March 22, 1901, *ibid.*

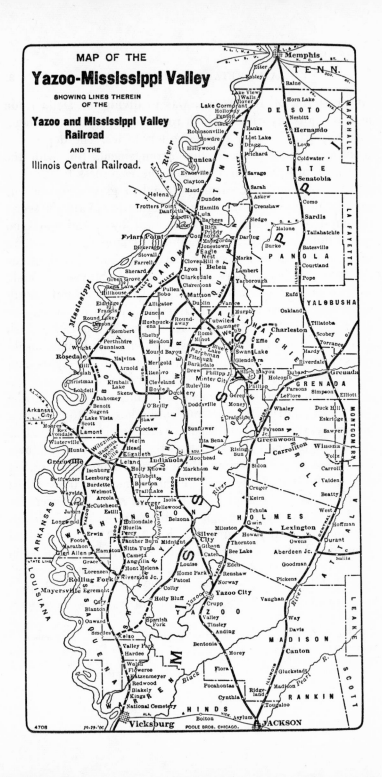

# MAP OF THE
# Yazoo-Mississippi Valley

SHOWING LINES THEREIN
OF THE

## Yazoo and Mississippi Valley Railroad

AND THE

## Illinois Central Railroad.

prohibited from purchasing or leasing one another. Never-theless, with the help of a friendly governor, the state rail-road commission, and some nimble political footwork, a special act was slipped through the state legislature legalizing the sale.[33] But the railroad overplayed its hand. Seeking to ensure the constitutionality of the enabling act, it brought a test case to the Mississippi Supreme Court where the act was promptly nullified on the grounds that "any act of the legis-lature to suspend the operation of a general law for the benefit of any individual or private corporation or association will be void, as being directly in the face of the constitution."[34]

That the Yazoo and Mississippi Valley was unable finally to purchase the Itta Bena-Webb branch was immaterial. But the fact that the Illinois Central felt it had to legalize this purchase first through legislation and then through the courts reveals the sensitivity of its officers to hostile public sentiment, which was reflected in the law and the court's decision. The question of controlling competing railroad lines, in the opin-ion of the Illinois Central's chief counsel, was an acute one in Mississippi. "We do not want to violate the law," he ad-vised, "and besides we do not want to run the risk that will be incident to violating the law." This is why he urged settling the issue before the courts.[35]

Certainly by the time of the abortive attempt to purchase the Itta Bena branch line, all Mississippians were united against corporate monopoly. This included even the Delta planters who had most to gain from the strength of the

[33] Stuyvesant Fish to Samuel Spencer, April 17, 1901; Fish to James M. Dickinson, Aug. 7, 1901; J. F. Wallace to J. T. Harahan, July 30, 1901; Stuyvesant Fish to J . T. Harahan, Aug. 9, 1901; J. M. Dickinson to Stuyvesant Fish, Aug. 23, 1901; J. M. Dickinson to Stuyvesant Fish, Feb. 8, 1902; same to Hon. J. B. Chrisman, Feb. 13, 1902; A. H. Longino to Stuyvesant Fish, May 27, 1902, ibid.

[34] Yazoo and Mississippi Valley Railroad vs. Southern Railway Company in Mississippi, 83 Miss. 773.

[35] J. M. Dickinson to Mayes & Harris, March 27, 1902, Fish Letters.

Illinois Central in their midst, but who at the same time, fearing the end of competition, were responsible for the law of 1898, which strengthened earlier prohibitions against competing railroads from purchasing or leasing one another.[36]

Fears of corporate monopoly brought with them a re-examination of the basic assumptions about northern capital, or more specifically, whether that capital was a force for good or evil. Earlier, leaders of the New South argued that capital was the key to prosperity and opportunity. It had made the North rich and victorious. Were the South, with its favored climate and natural resources, to attract sufficient capital, then the South could easily duplicate the North's achievement. But, for whatever reasons, the sanguinary hopes of New South leadership failed to materialize. Instead, the years since the Civil War were years of continual agricultural decline. In Mississippi, with the exception of the Yazoo Delta, economic conditions never returned to the normalcy associated with antebellum days. Mediocre soils were continually being depleted—a condition caused by ignorance of good farming methods and overcropping the land with cotton—and ignorance and overcropping were the two breeding grounds for the alarming increase in tenancy.[37] Tenancy was a treadmill

[36] Yerger & Percy to James Fentress, Feb. 8, 1898, *ibid.*

[37] The period 1880 to 1900 saw a sharp rise in Mississippi tenancy, as revealed by the fact that the percentage of farms operated by owners declined from 56.2 to 37.6. The greatest increase in tenancy was in the "cash tenant" category; 17.1 per cent of all farmers in 1880 to 32.0 per cent in 1900. The increase in the cash tenant category is significant because it represents the marked decline in the numbers of white yeoman farmers. It was the white yeoman or the South's middle class that was in a status decline. Throughout the South a similar situation was taking place. Farm owner-operators dropped from 60.6 per cent of the whole to 48.3, with the greatest changes taking place in the "cash tenant" category (12.4 per cent in 1880 to 20.3 per cent in 1900). The numbers in the sharecropper category increased less markedly (from 26.7 per cent of the whole to 30.4 per cent in Mississippi). *Agriculture*, U.S. Bureau of the Census, *Twelfth Census*, VI (Washington, 1902), 409.

that intensified ignorance as well as making overcropping mandatory. For the yeoman white farmer, it was the first step downward to the peonage of the Negro. And with every prospect toward it, agricultural fundamentalism rose in an inverse ratio.

The basic tenet was that the yeoman farmer democrat was bound to prosper and that his prosperity was the backbone of national strength. In the dismal period of the 1880's and 1890's this faith was given renewed amplification. Jeremiads, however, gave way to the anger and suspicions inherent to fundamentalist judgment. Hard times, according to this judgment, were not the fault of the honest farmers. They were the fault of the monied interests—the conspiratorial corporate monopoly—"THE MONSTER." Thus was the evil specter of Jacksonianism resurrected. The monster's form had not changed since the days of Old Hickory. Like the Second Bank of the United States, the monopoly corporation remained something alien, a conspiracy by foreigners, for who would deny that only the conspiratorial designs of an outside force could have brought about the godless perversions that had reduced Mississippi's white yeomanry to the bottom rail? Worst of all, the evils of outside capital (or the Illinois Central Railroad) had bred class divisions, for the railroad, by quickening the pace of the Yazoo Delta's economic development and bringing to fruition the possibilities of its inexhaustible and fertile soils, had separated and divided Mississippi's farmers into planter and redneck, rich and poor, blessed and despised.

The richest corporation in Mississippi, a monopoly, and the purveyor of class divisions; these were the sins of the Illinois Central. Hostile public feeling was not altogether unknown in the Illinois Central's history. The so-called granger ferment in Illinois during the 1870's, though less intense, taught most railroad managers to be cautious in their dealings with matters of public interest. It was, therefore, imperative, advised the general solicitor of the Illinois Central after the purchase of the Louisville, New Orleans and Texas in 1892, that there be "no shock to the public; nothing to call their attention to the matter or to suggest litigation." All the legal arrangements of sale and transfer of property, he warned, should be done in such manner as "to let the public mind come to quiet consideration of the change of ownership."[38] For this purpose the Illinois Central devised an explanation: Its officers in 1882 had toyed with the idea of building a branch road northwestward through the Yazoo Delta from the state capital at Jackson on the Chicago, St. Louis and New Orleans main line. To do this a charter was granted by the Mississippi legislature creating the Yazoo and Mississippi Valley Railroad and giving it leave to develop the territory between the Yazoo and Mississippi rivers. But this branch road, which, railroad lawyers argued, had a separate legal existence from the Illinois Central, never went beyond Yazoo City, the easternmost edge of the Yazoo Delta. Ten years later, when the Yazoo and Mississippi Valley purchased the Louisville and New Orleans and Texas, it argued that it had always intended to extend its line through the Delta to Memphis, as its charter had given it the privilege of doing. But before it could do this, the Louisville, New Orleans and Texas, a non-Mississippi corporation, usurped the territory originally granted to the Yazoo and Mississippi Valley Railroad. Thus, so went the argument, when the Yazoo and Mississippi Valley purchased the Louisville, New Orleans and Texas Railroad, it was not the case of an alien corporation expanding its power but rather the case of a native Mississippi

[38] James Fentress to Stuyvesant Fish, Oct. 31, 1892, June 20, 1892, Fish Letters.

corporation restoring to itself what had been earlier granted
to it by the sovereign state of Mississippi.[39]

This argument could hardly be taken seriously. Everyone
knew that the Illinois Central owned the Yazoo and Mississippi Valley Railroad. Even the officers were identical. Moreover, when the sale of the Louisville, New Orleans and Texas
was first announced, it was hailed in business circles as a
wise investment for the Illinois Central, and held up as
another glowing example of northern capital's continuing
interest in southern development.[40] Yet the Illinois Central
continued to maintain the façade. It did so because it knew
of no other way to soft-pedal the fact that as the "foreign"
monopolizer of Delta trade it was virtually the sole recipient
of valuable profits from the richest part of the state.

Ironically, the Illinois Central had not sought this position.
When it first entered Mississippi during the 1870's it did so
to connect Chicago with New Orleans in the cheapest and
shortest way possible. Little thought was given to developing
Mississippi as a source of new freight and passenger earnings
as the Illinois Central had done in Illinois. But with its entrance into the Yazoo Delta a change in policy was dictated.
There were good profits to be made on expanding Delta trade.
But every dollar spent on developing the Delta's rail traffic
made the Delta just so much richer than the rest of Mississippi
and widened further the gulf between Delta and hill. Indeed,
the differences were so marked that many Mississipians
felt that the Delta was not part of their state since they saw
no benefits accruing to them from the increasing wealth of
the Delta planters. Thus was the Illinois Central condemned
as the tool of avaricious Delta planters. But the planters

[39] Memorandum of Agreement between Parties: L.N.O. & T. and Y. & M.V.,
*ibid.*
[40] *Commercial and Financial Chronicle*, June 11, 1892, p. 939.

had no love for the Illinois Central either. To the dismay of railroad officialdom, the planters often joined in the chorus against the railroad for its monopolistic fixing of freight rates. Despite the fact that the Illinois Central was caught in this cross fire of interests, profits from the Yazoo Delta were too good to be sacrificed on the altar of public opinion, and it was to these complicated and conflicting conditions that the Illinois Central had to adjust itself.

# CHAPTER 5

# With a View to Upbuilding the Country

To BE SURE there were other enterprises with monopolistic characteristics, but to Mississippians the Illinois Central was something different. First, it was the biggest and richest corporation in the state. Secondly, it monopolized the carrying trade of the richest part of the state. And lastly, it was a non-Mississippi corporation whose headquarters were in the city of New York. Thus decisions affecting the economic welfare of the state of Mississippi were made in a northern city by northerners. But these were not the only factors that put the Illinois Central on the defensive. More important were the challenges of New South rhetoric; for according to the logic laid down by men like Henry Grady and General James B. Gordon, railroad entrepreneurship represented the kind of development capital needed by the South to keep up with the rapid economic progress being made by the rest of the nation. The belief that northern capital would uplift and enrich the South was shared by all southerners. It was held by the wealthy and potentially wealthy because they looked upon northern capital as giving them the support necessary to make the most of their opportunities. It was held by the poor and those rapidly slipping into poverty because there was little else for them to hope for. The Illinois Central faced the dilemma of having to reconcile its profit motives with the anticipations and great scope of expectations of hungry southern agrarians. This dilemma was irreconcilable (especially in the face of such ill-defined expectations), and deep and bitter were the disappointments.

The people of Mississippi were not the only ones trapped by the logic of the New South. Officials of the Illinois Central shared the belief that their railroad would uplift and enrich the South. Repeatedly they told one another that "this Company is doing more to send population and wealth into the State of Mississippi than any other agency within its borders."[1] As an example of its development activities the Yazoo and Mississippi Valley railroad in 1903 credited itself with having established along its line seventy-four new industries, employing 3,596 people.[2]

The railroad's president, Stuyvesant Fish, went further. He viewed the Illinois Central's relationship with Mississippi as an indissoluble and permanent partnership for material progress. The bond of this partnership was, of course, the profits made by his railroad out of the Mississippi trade, especially the trade of the Yazoo Delta. Of all the railroads operating in Mississippi the Illinois Central was dominant, doing the most volume of business and reaping the greatest profits. Naturally it sought to continue and enlarge its earnings.[3]

One method of cementing this bond was through political action. This was accomplished by the time honored method of

[1] James Fentress to Mayes & Harris, Feb. 6, 1896, Stuyvesant Fish Letters, Illinois Central Railroad Archives, Newberry Library, Chicago.

[2] *Manufacturers' Record*, XLIV (Nov. 5, 1903).

[3] Thus, as Fish stated, this railroad was, had "been for years, and always will be, more largely interested in the development of the State of Mississippi than any other person or corporation in or of that State. Everything affecting the State for good or evil affects us in like manner, and this for all time." Fish to Jerome Hill, Feb. 15, 1900, Fish Letters.

giving key politicians a personal stake in the economic welfare of the Yazoo Delta. In 1902, for example, Fish organized
a very profitable 10,000-acre Delta cotton plantation in Coahoma County called the Roundaway Manufacturing Company. Included among the owners were not only the leading
directors of the Illinois Central but politicians who might
prove useful. And Fish never went after lesser men. Two of
the most powerful politicians in the country were made part
owners of the Roundaway Company. These were Senator William B. Allison of Iowa, Chairman of the Senate Committee
on Appropriations, and "Uncle Joe" Cannon, of Illinois,
Speaker of the House and Chairman of the House Appropriations Committee. Fish used the influence established with
Allison and Cannon to secure in 1902 a new United States
Court House, long desired by the city of Memphis. Partly as
a result of his influence with Speaker Cannon he was responsible for the appointment in 1903 of Benjamin Grubb Humphreys of Greenville to the House Committee on Rivers and
Harbors.[4] This was no mean achievement, for Humphreys,
besides being a freshman Congressman (which invariably
means last place in committee assignments), was also a Democrat in a congress dominated by the Republican party. Humphreys' appointment to the Rivers and Harbors Committee
was vital to the interests of his district, the Yazoo Mississippi
Delta, which depended upon continuing appropriations for
river improvements. Moreover, as a member of this committee
(and later the Committee on Flood Control) Humphreys had
easy access to the Mississippi River Commission and could
thus oversee its work in furthering his district's levee system.
Indeed, Humphrey's twenty-year tenure on the House Rivers
and Harbors Committee made him a legend in the Yazoo

[4] Stuyvesant Fish to Joseph G. Cannon, March 19, 1902, Nov. 25, 1905;
Stuyvesant Fish to James T. Harahan, May 29, 1902; Stuyvesant Fish to LeRoy
Percy, Nov. 28, 1905; J. W. Cutrer to Stuyvesant Fish, [late 1903], *ibid.*

Delta and resulted in a long lasting precedent that there would always be a seat reserved on committees dealing with public works for the Congressman from the third congressional district of Mississippi.[5] To a large extent, therefore, Humphrey's appointment and the many advantages that accrued to the Yazoo Delta as a result of it may be attributed to Stuyvesant Fish and his desire to create a two-way bond between the state of Mississippi and the Illinois Central Railroad.

But this kind of bond was too subtle for Mississippi's public, imbued as it was with the slogans of the New South that the largest northern corporation in the state should uplift and enrich all the people. More tangible contributions were demanded. Most familiar and most profitable to the railroad and the people of Mississippi alike was the infusion of immigrants into the state. In a vague way southerners looked upon an infusion of new blood as important to the revitalization of the southern spirit. But there were important reservations. To be acceptable to the South, the new immigrants had to be white, of Anglo-Saxon origins, and yeoman farmers.[6] This kind of immigrant, it was reasoned, could be attracted to the South if plenty of good lands were made available at low rates. The Illinois Central, as everyone knew, had the opportunity to fulfill this southern view of immigration, for, like the Evers-Watson group, it owned several hundred thousand acres of land in the Yazoo Delta. It received these lands in 1892 as part of its purchase of the Louisville, New Orleans and Texas Railroad whose owners, in turn, acquired them

---

[5] In 1962, as a result of the reapportionment of Mississippi's representatives in the U.S. Congress, the third congressional district was abolished and incorporated into the second congressional district, joining the Yazoo Delta with hill country to the east and giving it a minority position in an expanded district. Thus was the Yazoo Delta wiped out as a separate entity in Congress.

[6] Governor John M. Stone of Mississippi to Edward F. McSweeney, Oct. 27, 1894, in U.S. Immigration Service, *Report of the Immigration Committee to the Secretary of the Treasury* (Washington, 1895), 141-142.

ten years earlier when they bought out the franchises of the Memphis and Vicksburg Railroad. The latter's owners purchased them, as Evers had done, as a result of the court decree in the key case of Gibbs *vs.* Green. Under identical arrangements and at the same time as Evers acquired his lands, the Memphis and Vicksburg was sold 774,000 acres of tax delinquent lands in what amounted to a virtual donation by the state of Mississippi.[7]

By the 1890's, as we have seen, the lands of the Watson syndicate were, disappointingly, still wilderness and unpeopled. It was on these grounds that the Evers-Watson speculation was condemned. Likewise, it was as a large landholder that the Illinois Central would be judged by the people of Mississippi. As Americans, Mississippians shared the general view of what should be done with vast amounts of land. From the beginning America's wealth was her lands; there was seemingly no limit to their extent. Jefferson confidently expressed the public mind when he said Americans possessed "a chosen country, with room enough for our descendants to the thousandth and thousandth generation."[8] Given this condition, and having little or no reserves for capital, it was no wonder that most Americans were physiocrats. Quesnay, founder of the eighteenth century French school that held that all wealth originated with the land and only agriculture could multiply that wealth, did not have to be explained; the head right, the soldier's land warrant, and the sale of public lands for government revenue were all established American practices. The culmination of these practices was the federal land grant first given in 1850 to the promoters of the Illinois Central Railroad. For the next quarter century thereafter (until

[7] Green *vs.* Gibbs, No. 326, Chancery Court, Hinds County (Jackson, Miss.), 1st District *Minutes,* II, 579.

[8] James D. Richardson, *Messages and Papers of the President* (Washington, 1897), I, 323.

public disgust with the corruption engendered by land grants put an end to them) millions upon millions of acres were given away primarily to help build western railroads. (Other land grants were given to establish institutions of higher learning and to clear swamp and overflow lands in the lower Mississippi Valley.) Always, these grants were premised upon the belief that the best interests of the recipients would see to it that the lands involved would be sold, cleared, and cultivated. To do so would give the lands higher value and thus provide greater sources of capital for investment. In the case of the railroads, lands in cultivation along the railroad route would produce freight and thereby earning power for the road. This was especially true for railroads attempting to build through lightly inhabited areas where there was no established trade. But the recipients of the land grant were not the only benefactors, for if the basic assumption was true that America's land could create new wealth in the form of agricultural products, then the recipients' encouragement of the sale and cultivation of their land grant favored the entire populace. Thus, in theory at least, the land grant was a practical solution for an economy long on land and short on cash, and for a people groping for a compromise between private interest and public benefit.

Even though the Illinois Central inherited its Yazoo Delta lands third hand, the association of the private land grant with public duty remained, for it was on the basis of this association that the owners of the Memphis and Vicksburg Railroad were first offered the lands. The offer, made in 1873 and patterned after the grants previously made by the federal government, consisted of the odd numbered sections or parts of sections lying ten miles on either side of the projected railroad route at a price of two cents an acre. The lands were those that had fallen into state hands for nonpayment of taxes, and which had become part of the state of Mississippi's public domain. As the number of these lands was increasing at an alarming rate the legislature sought to turn a bad situation into something beneficial. It offered to sell the lands at a price tantamount to giving them away. This was not only a quick and decisive solution to the problem of mounting tax lands, but their sale and placement on the tax rolls would continually bring in badly needed revenue to the state treasury. Their sale would also be of benefit to the Delta planters who had to pay proportionately higher taxes because the surrounding forfeited lands were nontaxbearing. Moreover, the legislature realized that a significant part of the future of the state's economy lay with the development of the Yazoo Delta and was eager to do what it could to promote the Delta's prosperity by encouraging the building of a railroad. What the legislature also intended was to breathe some life into the Memphis and Vicksburg railroad which, although chartered three years earlier, had yet to build a foot of track. The land grant had been for the national government a successful spur in railroad building. Why not, the legislature reasoned, use the same device for Mississippi? Besides, the empty state treasury was incapable of making a sufficient money subsidy. And the sale of these fertile Yazoo Delta lands by their new owners would easily provide an adequate supply of capital for building the road. Profiting from the national government's experience with the land grant, the Mississippi legislature hoped to avoid the worst aspects of speculation as well as to ensure certain social benefits. Were the owners of the Memphis and Vicksburg to buy these lands, they were to set aside at least one-quarter of them to be sold to actual settlers in tracts not exceeding 160 acres and at a price not more than $1.25 per acre. In addition, the purchasers were to build one schoolhouse every six miles along the railroad route and to maintain the schools for ten years thereafter.[9] Thus was the offer a catch-all designed to alleviate Mississippi's fiscal tax problems, promote the general economy of the Yazoo Delta, and at the same time pass on all the costs to the purchasers of the land.

This scheme presupposed that the purchasers were able (as well as willing) to undertake all these burdens. Certainly, the owners of the Memphis and Vicksburg Railroad were not. They were Delta planters seeking in the charter of their railroad a cheap franchise that might some day prove lucrative. As we have already seen, the planters at this time had their hands full merely managing their own estates. Were they to take up this offer, they could not hope to pay the accrued taxes on these lands, many of which had been accumulating taxes for more than a decade. Moreover, the onset of the depression in 1873 and the continually depreciating land values made the whole scheme futile and unrealistic. But the attempt did have an important effect, for it introduced Mississippians to the concept of the land grant scheme and provided the lands in question with a baggage of public responsibility that future owners would have always to carry with them.

The Illinois Central did not consider this baggage a burden. On the contrary, its large landholdings in Illinois proved to be its greatest asset, fulfilling every expectation of the men who guided the land grant idea through Congress. The sale of the Illinois Central's two and one-half million acres to immigrant homesteaders provided the source of cash to build the roadway, and these new farmers provided a continual source of freight and passenger earnings. Certainly anyone looking at the Illinois Central's history in the 1890's would have to admit that as the recipient of the first of the great

[9] Mississippi, *Laws, 1873*, Ch. CCXCIII.

federal land grants, the Illinois Central was one of the most successful. When in 1892 the Illinois Central took possession of 546,628 acres of Yazoo Delta lands, it was natural that its officials would want to follow the same land policy that had worked so well for them in Illinois and which they were confident would be equally successful in Mississippi.[10]

As in Illinois during the 1850's, the policy was to sell lands to actual settlers who would produce revenue for the railroad in the shipping of freight. Selling lands to big farmers in large lots was frowned upon, for the big farmer was too independent; in bad years he could afford to reduce his crop acreage (though he rarely did). Speculators likewise were shunned. They not only held land out of cultivation (a deterrent to freight income) but encouraged competing railroads to enter their lands in order to drive up land values. The ideal purchaser of railroad lands was the small farmer, the man whose precarious livelihood compelled him to grow as much as possible. As President Stuyvesant Fish forcefully declared, "the policy of the Company is to restrict its land sales to actual settlers . . . with a view to upbuilding the country."[11] So adamant was he on this subject that he was willing to see these Delta lands sold to small farmers and cultivated "even at a sacrifice."[12] This liberal land policy, emphasizing the introduction of immigrant yeoman farmers, was in harmony with southern demands for new blood. It was also in accordance with the land grant idea that characterized the offer of these lands to the Memphis and Vicksburg Railroad. Most of all it was a policy that afforded spokesmen of the New South

[10] Paul W. Gates, *The Illinois Central Railroad and Its Colonization Work* (Cambridge, Mass., 1934) ; J. M. Dickinson to Stuyvesant Fish, Dec. 16, 1901, in Papers Supporting Minutes of the Board of Directors, Office Box No. 32, Reel No. 9,367, Illinois Central Railroad Archives.

[11] Stuyvesant Fish to John D. Filley, Dec. 30, 1901, Fish Letters.

[12] Fish to John C. Welling, Aug. 14, 1902; Edward P. Skene to J. C. Welling, Oct. 3, 1896; Stuyvesant Fish to J. C. Welling, Oct. 9, 1896, *ibid.*

an opportunity to show dramatically, and in a way that everyone could see, that northern capital was willing to "do something" for the southern economy.

A liberal land policy such as that envisioned by spokesmen of the New South had one other important advantage for officials of the Illinois Central. It would soothe popular fears about the Illinois Central Railroad as the largest and most powerful northern corporation in Mississippi. These fears could not be taken lightly in view of the strong anti-corporate overtones of Mississippi's 1890 Constitution. Mississippians eyed the Illinois Central's key economic position as entailing a public reponsibility. As C. C. Harvey, vice president of the Alabama and Vicksburg Railroad and a member of the Board of Directors of the Alabama Great Southern Railway Co., Ltd., warned Fish, Mississippi's public felt "that the railroads are there only for the benefit of the people and that bondholders and stockholders have no rights in the premises."[13] Fish could hardly be expected to concede this point to public opinion. In his view, when responsibility to stockholders came into conflict with public service, it was the latter that had to give way. "Railroad property," he wrote, "cannot go out of existence. If it cannot be made to pay on the basis of giving certain service, that service must be reduced."[14] His statement indicated the grounds upon which the Illinois Central's land policy would be determined. To be sure, while earnings from the Delta trade were rising, expenditures for settling white yeomen on small plots of the Illinois Central's Delta lands was a luxury that could be indulged in. But, were the costs of this policy to impede ever so slightly upon profits, that policy would be abandoned regardless of southern sentiments on the subject.

[13] C. C. Harvey to Fish, Jan. 29, 1894, *ibid.*
[14] Fish to Robert Patterson, Jan. 17, 1894, *ibid.*

An example of this attitude was the treatment by the Illinois Central of its lands in Sharkey and Issaquena counties. Amounting to 187,000 acres, they represented 35 per cent of the total railroad landholdings in the Delta. But these lands were largely worthless. Low lying and poorly drained, they were a malaria infested swamp. Adding to their undesirability was the fact that they were yet an impenetrable wilderness whose thick cover of virgin timber was mainly sweet gum, a tree not then in demand by timber merchants. But with the rapid exploitation of southern timber during the 1890's, railroad officials hoped that these lands might some day prove valuable. For this reason they decided to keep them if local taxes were kept to a minimum.[15] But this could not be done. Because of the wild nature of these lands, Sharkey and Issaquena were sparsely settled counties. The only way of increasing their population (and thus the number of taxpayers) was to drain and clear the lands and thus make them attractive for settlement. This required increased taxes on present landowners. The Illinois Central Railroad, the richest corporation in the state and the largest landowner in both counties, was a fair target.

Soon after the railroad took possession of its lands in Sharkey and Issaquena counties the county boards of supervisors undertook a new levee program, and increased the assessed value on all lands for this purpose. Railroad officials protested and threatened to abandon the lands regardless of their possible future worth. But fear of aggravating public opinion and bringing on reprisals made Illinois Central officials soften their threats by transferring ownership temporarily to a dummy corporation. This, it was believed, would give county officials time to "come to their senses, and put

[15] George W. McGinnis to Edward P. Skene, Sept. 20, 1893; James T. Harahan to J. C. Welling, Oct. 13, 1893; McGinnis to Skene, Oct. 23, 1893, Welling Letters, Illinois Central Railroad Archives.

the valuation at a figure that will be right and proper."[16] However, the boards of supervisors remained adamant. Taxes from railroad lands represented the only hope of raising enough money to make improvements on the lands, invite settlers, and in time do away with dependence upon the railroad for county funds. Only after some legal subterfuge and more threats did tax authorities in Sharkey County, where railroad landholdings amounted to 138,000 acres (or about half the county) decide to reduce their assessment. But over 30,000 acres of land in Issaquena County were abandoned "as the authorities of that county," Fish explained, "have shown a determination to tax us out of the property."[17] Eventually the lands in Sharkey County were sold or leased, at good profits, to timber companies. And the lands, once cut over, thereafter became valuable for settlement and cultivation.[18] This long-range outcome was beneficial to the Delta's growth but the singular lack of generosity on the railroad's part was not the kind of treatment the New South expected of rich northern capital. Filled with New South rhetoric, as well as the warm expressions of support given by the railroad, the people of Mississippi expected the Illinois Central to take a more active role in developing the Yazoo Delta lands. But was this not expecting too much? The Illinois Central was not a land company. It was a railroad and it would undertake development only where costs were low and there was reason to expect benefits on the balance sheet.

[16] Skene to Welling, Sept. 25, 1893; Yerger and Percy to James Fentress, Jan. 26, 1895, *ibid.*

[17] Telegram from Stuyvesant Fish to J. C. Welling, Feb. 24, 1898; Edward P. Skene to J. C. Welling, Feb. 18, 1898, *ibid.*

[18] Most were sold to the George T. Houston Lumber Company at $1 per acre. J. C. Welling to Stuyvesant Fish, Feb. 23, April 16, 1901; Stuyvesant Fish to Board of Directors, April 17, 1901; George T. Houston & Co. to E. P. Skene, March 13, 1902, Fish Letters. Timber Contracts, Illinois Central Railroad Collection, Land Office Storage Room, Dearborn Street Station, Chicago. Washington County, Mississippi, *Deed Book*, vol. 159, pp. 186-188. Stuyvesant Fish to Sir Edward Lawrence, Oct. 5, 1900, Fish Letters.

The Illinois Central confidently believed that some expenditures for immigrant settlers to the railroad's remaining Delta lands would enlarge profits. The successful settlement of the Illinois prairies was held as a model of what could be done. There was one great similarity between the Illinois prairie lands and the lands of the Yazoo Delta; both were distrusted by prospective settlers. Just as it was believed in the 1850's that nothing could grow on tough treeless sod, so skeptics in the 1890's pointed out the difficulties of surviving in swamps inhabited by "niggers and alligators." Northerners, particularly those from the Middle West, were reluctant to emigrate to a country where their children would have to associate with the very heavy concentrations of Negroes who had moved into the Delta during the 1870's and 80's. In addition, the violence of reconstruction and the instability of southern state governments since the Civil War engendered further fears over the South as a place to live.[19]

The Illinois Central's land commissioner, Edward P. Skene, was confident he could overcome these obstacles just as his predecessors had done in Illinois. On all railroad circulars advertising the Illinois Central's Mississippi lands, he changed the name of the "Yazoo Delta" to read "Yazoo Valley," believing that the term "Delta" had connotations of a place continually flooded. He urged that Dutch, English, and German stockholders quietly pass the word among immigrant agents in their respective countries that the Yazoo and Mississippi Valley Railroad was not just another American fly-by-night corporation but an important segment of the Illinois Central system, one of America's most stable corporations.[20] But these gestures did little to change either general conceptions about Mississippi or, more important, the grudging

[19] Edward P. Skene to J. C. Welling, Dec. 17, 1904; Benjamin G. Humphreys to Fish, [probably 1903], Fish Letters.

[20] Edward P. Skene to J. C. Welling and J. C. Welling to Stuyvesant Fish, Dec. 14, 1893, *ibid.*

attitude of Skene's own land agents, who saw few commissions in hawking lands in the Yazoo Delta and because of this actively worked against their chief. Moreover, Illinois Central officials, uncertain and fearful over the implications of the recently passed Sherman Antitrust Act, worked against the latter of Skene's activities by time and again publicly asserting the independent character of the Yazoo and Mississippi Valley Railroad.

But these obstructions alone would not have prevented a duplication in Mississippi of the earlier Illinois land sale policy. More fundamental to Skene's inability to follow the pattern in Illinois was a difference in the source of immigrant settlers. In the 1850's the Illinois Central appealed heavily to immigrants from northern Europe, spending much money and effort to attract them to the Illinois prairies. But for the railroad's Mississippi lands little money was expended to attract these same immigrant groups, so favored by southern officials. To do so would have involved much greater efforts because northwestern railroads, since the 1870's, had taken over the northern European immigrant market, funneling immigrants to the northern prairies and at the same time, according to Skene, discouraging people from settling in the South by spreading "libelous reports" about the region. What effect, if any, these reports had upon retarding a flow of northern European immigrants to the South is difficult to say. But statistics alone reveal the enormous efforts that would have to be made by the Illinois Central to reverse the trend. Of the eight million people entering the United States from 1892 to 1906 only 2,697 claimed the state of Mississippi as their destination.[21]

Cut off thus from the older immigrant sources, Skene turned his attention to attracting disgruntled farmers of the

---

[21] Skene to Welling, May 2, June 6, 1894, Welling Letters; U.S. Commissioner-General of Immigration, *Annual Reports, 1893-1907* (Washington, 1894-1908).

Midwest. Times were propitious to do so. Depressed farm prices and drought combined during the late 1880's and 1890's to cause an uproar among the farmers of the northern great plains states beyond the Mississippi. The Populist fever was in full rage, and numbers of farmers, according to one of Skene's lieutenants in 1894, showed interest in moving to southern lands. Skene hurried to exploit the situation by fitting out an exhibition car with the products of Delta soils and sending it on tour. In addition, he encouraged, through the medium of the free pass, excursion parties to view the railroad's Delta lands. "Seeing is believing," he wrote "[and] if the farmers we are trying to induce to go down there can see with their own eyes what the country will produce, it will go a great way to offset what they read in the newspapers and hear from the Agents of the Northwestern Railroads and large Land Companies."[22] Again the northwestern roads were interfering with Skene's plans. In the midst of the depressed conditions of the 1890's and pinched by a general decline in freight and passenger earnings, the northwestern railroads naturally were eager to prevent a general exodus from areas they had worked so hard to populate and that now formed so valuable a part of railroad income.

Skene complained of unfair practices. The northwestern railroads owned the newspapers and filled them with stories detrimental to the Yazoo country. "You cannot hardly pick up a paper in any of the Northwestern States that has not a squib speaking disaparagingly of our section of the country."[23] Moreover, many of the roads, he claimed, in a desperate attempt to keep settlers where they were, threatened to double or triple rates to any points east or south. A proposal in 1895 by some northwestern roads to fix high passenger rates through a railway rate pool was summarily rejected by

---

[22] Quotation from letter of Skene to Welling, July 2, 1895; same to same, May 2, 1894, Welling Letters.
[23] Skene to Welling, July 2, 1895, *ibid*.

the Illinois Central on the grounds that it would work against its interest in attracting farmers from the northwestern plains states to the South.[24] The expected exodus, however, did not take place. By the end of 1896, after two years of free passes, excursions, and exhibition cars, Skene reported that only 270 farmers from the northwest had taken up the railroad's lands in the Yazoo Delta.[25] Actually the exodus from the plains states during these depression years was very small. It was magnified out of all proportions by newspapers and contemporary journalists and since has become part of American folklore. By the winter of 1896-97 rain and prosperity returned to the plains and ended further hopes of the Illinois Central to capitalize on unhappy farming conditions beyond the Mississippi.

The trouble was that Skene and other railroad officials were operating on an erroneous assumption. Hard times elsewhere would not necessarily drive people into the Delta. Indeed, unhappy economic conditions defeated one of the most successful methods of settling railroad lands. This was the colonization method whereby groups of ten to fifty families would settle in one township. Under this arrangement large acreages were purchased at one time by the combined financial resources of a whole group. This was an advantage for the railroad because the pooled resources and natural homogeneity of a group prevented cancellations and thus kept the lands settled and cultivated for the benefit of the railroad's freight and passenger earnings. Officials of the Illinois Central had no reason to expect any different results from the colonization method in Mississippi than in Illinois.[26] But here again they were disappointed. Upon hearing reports in the

[24] Skene to Welling, June 13, 1895; General Passenger Agent to T. J. Hudson, June 1, 1895, *ibid.*

[25] I.C.R.R., *Annual Report, 1896*, p. 9, Illinois Central Railroad Archives.

[26] Gates, *Illinois Central Railroad and Its Colonization Work*, 227-236; Skene to Welling, May 31, 1894, Welling Letters.

spring of 1894 that Dutch immigrants were unhappy with their lot in Michigan, Skene traveled to Grand Rapids, Benton Harbor, Muskegon, and St. Joseph to try to wean the Dutch away from the cold climate and closed factories to the warmer climates and fertile lands of the Yazoo Delta. The Dutch, it was reasoned, were excellent prospects. Not only were they acceptable to southerners as Anglo-Saxons but they were also used to flooded lands and how best to live on them. But the unsettled state of business conditions in Michigan prevented their migration. "They were anxious to get away from the cold climate," Skene reported, "but business was so stagnant, that they could not get rid of the little properties that they owned, and . . . it would not pay them to move to some other locality so long as they held the property that they had."[27]

Hard times likewise worked against successful colonization by spiritually and socially motivated groups. Just as in the depression of the 1930's, there arose during the 1890's a "back to the farm" movement. The Roman Catholic Church was particularly interested in this movement. It was deeply concerned about the deep sufferings among the mounting numbers of unemployed Catholic immigrants in the northern cities. Cities, it was believed, caused moral contamination. In Chicago one of the leaders of the movement was Father Thomas F. Cashman, who, animated by the spirit of the founders of colonial Maryland, wanted to "bring the discontented from the cities, the industrious and intelligent toilers who desire to remove their children from moral contamination to the blessings of a country home and religious association and example."[28] The Marquette Colonization Company was formed for this purpose and received land sale offers from a number of western and southern railroads. Skene succeeded in "fighting off other railroad companies," and

27 Skene to Welling, May 2, 1894, *ibid.*
28 *Northwestern Chronicle* (St. Paul, Minn.), Jan. 25, 1895.

signed a contract with Father Cashman for options on 119,000 acres of Illinois Central Delta lands at $7 an acre under three-year credit terms. But the poor financial resources of the Marquette Colonization Company were not equal to the task, and severe floods and an outbreak of yellow fever during 1897 frightened away prospective settlers. Moreover, prosperity and jobs had returned. Failure of these efforts at colonization led Illinois Central officials to discourage further colonization schemes by other groups.[29] In addition, by the end of the 1890's it became clear to railroad officials that the old formulas for settlement used so effectively in Illinois did not apply to the lands of the Yazoo Delta.

The old formulas did not apply because farming in the Yazoo Delta was unlike farming in most areas of the country; it was a state of mind. No sooner did a man set foot into the Yazoo Delta than "his eyes . . . opened upon the fair prospect." His farmer status was left behind and he quickly succumbed to the heady myths and pretensions of king cotton, the overlordship of Negro tenants and the imagery of an antebellum southland that never was. This was the infection of the Yazoo Delta: more than a place to earn a better living it represented an opportunity to attain the very heights of the South's agricultural social status—to be a planter. Expansion was the password. Every demand for it was based upon the confident belief that the Delta's inexhaustible soils could absorb the cost of expansion and yield a rich return as well. Clearing, draining (which included levee taxes), and finding suitable tenant or wage labor to perform these tasks was a necessary prerequisite to begin operations in the Yazoo Delta. To

[29] E. P. Skene to Stuyvesant Fish, Aug. 13, 1895, Fish Letters; *The Outlook* (New York), April 10, 1897, p. 964, Sept. 18, 1897, p. 155; Illinois Central Railroad, *Annual Report, 1899*; Y & MVRR Land Office Records, Individual Accounts, Sales of Land, 1893-99, Dearborn Street Station, Chicago; Dr. Paul Pollack to Stuyvesant Fish, March 12, 1898, Fish to E. P. Skene, March 17, 1898, and same to same, Oct. 6, 1902, all in Fish Letters.

this extent, Delta lands were more expensive to farm than else-where. The high initial outlay of cash thus put added pressure on the land's earning capacity even before the first crop was planted. Pressure was increased by the local method of bor-rowing. The interest rate on loans in the Yazoo Delta during this period was quoted by the Illinois Central's legal depart-ment to be 10 per cent, not an exorbitant figure in view of the risk. But hidden charges and the method by which the loan was negotiated doubled the initial rate. In the spring, say March 1, the planter borrowed $10,000 from his factor giving a note payable the following January 1. In fact, the planter did not receive cash, but rather a credit for $9,000, the interest being deducted immediately. The 10 per cent was deducted on the basis of one year even though the loan was for ten months, thus making the actual interest rate slightly more than 13 per cent. As a condition of the loan the planter was required to grant a $2\frac{1}{2}$ per cent commission on each and every purchase and sale of the crop to the factor. This com-mission charge was not extravagant, but it added up because of the frequency of sales and purchases. In total, railroad lawyers in Mississippi estimated that the planter paid each year 20 per cent or higher in interest and commission charges. By any standard this was a heavy load for the lands to bear. Regardless of this, however, living on credit was the custom of the Delta. The Illinois Central was well advised of this situation. It was warned by its Mississippi lawyers that unless the avenue to borrow and borrow heavily was left wide open the railroad would be unable to make any sales of its Delta lands.[30]

The Illinois Central was proud of its record of liberal credit, and its policy in the Yazoo Delta was no exception.

[30] James Fentress to J. C. Welling, June 13, 1895, and Skene to Welling, July 13, 1895, Welling Letters; Memorandum to the President, Oct. 19, 1900, Fish Letters.

Prices were advertised to sell from $7 to $15 per acre according to location and physical condition. The terms were one-fifth down and the balance payable in from two to five years at 6 per cent. As an extra inducement a person buying anything more than 160 acres received reimbursement of full railroad fare made to view the lands. More important, on the basis of a mere down payment a purchaser was given a warranted title deed.[31] This was the one important difference between land policy in Illinois and in Mississippi. In Illinois the purchaser of railroad land on credit received a bond; and the title only after the land had been fully paid for. Because Illinois Central lands were exempt from local taxation in Illinois, it was common to defer final payments as long as possible (and thus delay receiving title) in order to avoid paying taxes.[32] But the Delta lands were not exempt from local taxes. As we have seen, in the less cultivated lower Delta counties of Sharkey and Issaquena, taxes from the Illinois Central's large landholdings made up a significant, if not the major part, of county revenue. It was, therefore, to the railroad's advantage to give a title deed as soon as possible and avoid paying the taxes. It was also an advantage for the planter and would-be planter whose thirst for credit and the opportunity to expand far exceeded his desire to escape taxes. With a title deed in his pocket he found it easier to raise large amounts of cash by mortgaging his land rather than by tenuous crop liens or personal cognizance. Because the Illinois Central was not in the business of making loans to its purchasers the mortgage was always to another party

[31] Illinois Central Railroad, *Annual Reports, 1894-1906*; Illinois Central Railroad, *600,000 Acres of Railroad Lands for Sale Owned by the Yazoo and Mississippi Valley Railroad Company in the Famous Yazoo Valley of Mississippi* (Chicago, 1896).

[32] Leslie E. Decker, *Railroads, Lands, and Politics: The Taxation of the Railroad Land Grants, 1864-1897* (Providence, R.I., 1964), 13.

(usually a New York, New Orleans, or Scottish bank) in the form of a deed of trust.[33]

The deed of trust, while satisfying the Delta planter's insatiable desire for more and more credit, made difficult the Illinois Central's small farmer land policy in the Yazoo Delta. Under the terms of a deed of trust, land mortgaged for a loan was deeded to a third party, a trustee, "through whom the rights of the creditor are exercised." Under the law, the trustee was empowered in the case of default on the loan to enter the land of the borrower, sell and dispose of the premises, and, in short, take over all the rights, title benefits, and equity of redemption as if the land were his. Moreover, the rights of this third party were by Mississippi law, according to the Illinois Central's legal department, paramount over any other lien including the railroad's vendor's lien. Time and again the railroad found itself effectively barred from any title claim to lands that had not been paid for and that rightfully belonged to it. Skene deplored the consequences of granting title to lands upon mere receipt of down payment, not only because the railroad was being cheated out of its rights to the lands but because the trustees were local cotton factors or planter-merchants whose interests in the lands worked against the railroad's policy of settling its lands with small farmers. "The chances are nine to one," Skene wrote, "that the party who loans the money will own the land eventually. This is what this Company does not want. It rather wants the land to be owned by the small farmer, so that he will produce revenue in the shipping of freight."[34] He urged that the company return to the bond system used in Illinois and was supported in his plea by the railroad's legal depart-

[33] I have made extensive use of the Washington County, Mississippi, *Deed Books*, which are full of examples of deeds of trust.
[34] Edward P. Skene to J. C. Welling, July 12, 1895, Welling Letters.

ment, then plagued with litigation asserting the railroad's vendor's lien to lands conveyed to others on deeds of trust. In 1896, the Illinois Central adopted the bond method of selling its lands.[35]

At the time the change met with little objection. The Delta, like every other area, was in the midst of depression. Cotton prices in 1898 hit their lowest point in the entire nineteenth century.[36] As a result, expansion was slowed, even in the Yazoo Delta. But because of the so-called world-wide "cotton famine" beginning in 1898, high cotton prices and prosperity returned. The demand for expansion and more credit was renewed with greater energy than ever before. Land values were on the rise and planters wanted more lands to use as security for greater loans, without which it was impossible to expand cotton cultivation and capture the profits that were coming. It was, therefore, impossible after 1900 for the Illinois Central to prevent a return to giving warranted title deeds on down payments. When on July 1 of that year it reestablished the old practice, it found that it, too, could join profitably the wave of expansion. Not only did the railroad sell its lands on credit but it also began granting loans and securing deferred payments on its lands with a deed of trust.[37] Thus the Illinois Central took on the combined role of seller, usurer, and trustee.

In one sense this was the ideal role for northern capital as envisioned by spokesmen of the New South. But in another, larger sense, it was a disappointment. The results of the Illinois Central's land policy did not promote the interests of the yeoman farmer either in the Yazoo Delta or outside of it.

[35] James Fentress to Yerger and Percy, May 4, 1896; James Fentress to Jacob M. Dickinson, January [?], 1900, ibid.

[36] Cotton Production and Distribution, U.S. Department of Commerce and Labor, Bureau of Census Bulletin 134 (Washington, 1916), 51.

[37] Illinois Central Railroad, Annual Report, 1901, "Report of the Vice-President."

In practice, the railroad's land policy enlarged the opportunities of the Delta planters to make greater profits from their favored lands. The Yazoo and Mississippi Valley land books and Delta county deed books are replete with examples to show that the purchasers of Illinois Central lands were not new emigrés from the North but Delta people, speculating in timber or in new lands in order to raise more credit to enlarge their cotton specialization. The railroad's policy of granting a warranted title deed encouraged the ambitions of the Delta planters. This acquiescence in the "custom" of the Delta, in addition to the railroad's failure to people its Delta lands according to popular notions about the public responsibilities of large landholders, further increased public resentment against the Illinois Central. For it was now believed that the Illinois Central, the greatest symbol of northern capital in Mississippi, was in league with the rich Delta planters for their mutual profit. To be sure, the railroad acquiesced in the planter's ambitions, but this was because it favored its balance sheet. This acquiescence, however, was fortuitous, an adaptation to the facts of Delta life. These facts, and not prior policies, fanciful theories, or rhetoric, were responsible for the Illinois Central's policy in the Delta. They were equally responsible for the general feeling about the inevitability of the Delta's wealth which, contrasted to the poverty of non-Delta Mississippians, made more bitter the growing separatism between the sections.

# CHAPTER 6

# A Twentieth Century Cotton Kingdom

W HILE THE Illinois Central Railroad was midwife to the Yazoo Mississippi Delta, it had no hand in making the region's character. That character was described with succinct finality during the 1930's: "The Yazoo-Mississippi Delta area is one of the most highly specialized cotton-producing areas in the world."[1] This was not a new finding. During the 1890's the desire for intense cotton specialization among Delta planters was the greatest fact facing the Illinois Central, forcing the mighty symbol of northern capital to redirect its policies to conform with local conditions. By the decade before the outbreak of World War I (when this study ends), every element of Delta life was affected by cotton: the land and its rehabilitation, the motives of its people, the landholding forms and methods of plantation operations, land values, profits and wealth, and social organization. The region's course as a cotton kingdom was recognized from the very beginning of settlement early in the nineteenth century. But by the end of that century, with less than one-third of its land

[1] E. L. Langsford and B. H. Thibodeaux, *Plantation Organization and Operation in the Yazoo-Mississippi Delta Area*, U.S. Department of Agriculture, Technical Bulletin 682 (Washington, 1939), 1.

in cultivation, the Yazoo Delta had yet to fulfill the grand potential extolled by successive generations of boomers, proven by high yields per acre, and recognized by a first-class rail network. Then, suddenly, at the dawn of the twentieth century, the Delta's economy was infused with a new spurt of energy. The result coalesced all elements of Delta life and created a new class of sectional wealth in Mississippi that stood in marked contrast to the sinking poverty surrounding it.

The acceleration of the Delta's economy came with a sudden world-wide demand for more cotton. This demand had been gaining momentum during the last third of the nineteenth century. It was the result of a significant increase in the world's population and the opening up of new markets by imperialist powers. The sharp rise in the world's spindles— from 104 million in 1900 to 116 million four years later— reflected the new demand. The need for cotton to feed these spindles took the producers by surprise. Cotton growth during the last decade of the century was sluggish and tended to follow the trend of depression prices. All this changed, however, in 1899 when cotton prices began to inch upwards again, reflecting the world-wide cotton shortage. Unfavorable weather conditions and the first significant effects of the boll weevil during the 1903 season restricted the supply still further and made conditions ripe for large speculations on the cotton exchange. The so-called New Orleans "bull clique" led by Daniel J. Sully drove the price in February 1904 to a high of $17\frac{1}{4}$, cents per pound the highest figure in thirty years. In short, the turn of the century were years of a new "cotton famine" when it was confidently asserted that six- and eight-cent cotton were things of the past.[2]

2 New York Cotton Exchange, *Market Reports, 1879-1927* (New York, 1879-1927); James L. Watkins, *Production and Price of Cotton for One Hundred Years*, U.S. Department of Agriculture, Miscellaneous Series Bulletin No. 9

Official statements strengthened beliefs by cotton growers that large profits were in store for them if they were to increase their cotton production. The statistician for the United States Department of Agriculture reported that although the commercial movement of cotton in 1902-03 was the largest on record, "it is a noteworthy fact that even this crop did not begin to meet the requirements of spinners who use American cotton.[3] A few voices of restraint, including Secretary of Agriculture James Wilson, cautioned against uncontrolled expansion; it would lead to overproduction and a disastrous decline in price. Wilson attributed the sharp rise in cotton prices to speculative manipulations on the cotton market rather than to any shortage.[4] But his warnings were brushed aside. After long years of low prices it was natural that the cotton grower heeded joyfully only the optimistic voices. One of these was the powerful organ for the hopes of southern business circles, the *Manufacturers' Record,* which refuted the skeptics. "Almost universally among the best informed cotton dealers in New Orleans," it declared, "the opinion prevails that an overproduction of cotton, sufficient to produce a disastrously low price, is entirely out of the question."[5] This conclusion was buttressed the following year by the statistician of Wilson's own department: "The season (1903-4) demonstrated the fact that the world's consumption of cotton had overtaken the supply."[6]

(Washington, 1895), 18-20; *Lea's Cotton Book and Statistical History of the American Cotton Crop* (New Orleans, 1914), 33; *Manufacturers' Record,* XLIV (July 23, 1903), 2, and XLV (May 12, 1904), 363-366, 370-373; *Dictionary of American Biography* (New York, 1936), XVIII, 201-202; James L. Watkins, *The Commercial Cotton Crop of 1903-4,* U.S. Department of Agriculture, Bureau of Statistics, Bulletin No. 34 (Washington, 1905), 77.

[3] James L. Watkins, *The Commercial Cotton Crops of 1900-1901, 1901-1902, and 1902-1903,* U.S. Department of Agriculture, Bureau of Statistics, Bulletin No. 28 (Washington, 1904), 7.

[4] *Ibid.,* 8; *Manufacturers' Record,* XLIV (Oct. 15, 1903), 239.

[5] *Manufacturers' Record,* XLIV (Aug. 8, 1903), 59.

[6] Watkins, *The Commercial Cotton Crop of 1903-4,* p. 7.

As important as high prices during this period were the changes in the cotton spinning industry. These changes were fundamental and deeply affected the American cotton South. The rural southland is the epitome of American provincialism. Yet of all the rural provincialism throughout the nation only the South has mixed within it the flavor of internationalism. Cotton gave the South this curious mixture, for the South's economy, geared as it was to this staple, was more than any other section traditionally dependent upon the state of the international market. This was as fundamental a fact for the New South as it was for the Old. By the beginning of the twentieth century, for example, at least two-thirds of the world's raw cotton supply came from the southern states. The overwhelming percentage of the South's cotton was exported to the United Kingdom. Thus the fundamental changes that took place in the British cotton textile industry after the Civil War were bound to have drastic repercussions upon the future of cotton growing in the South, especially in adaptable cotton growing areas such as the Yazoo Delta. With the virtual cessation of cotton exports from the South during the Civil War, British spinners turned to new sources in India and Egypt. They continued to develop these areas throughout the remainder of the century. But this competition was hardly felt among American cotton growers. More important was the shift in the nature of British spinning. Since the peak years of 1882–1884, when Britain exported 82 per cent of the world's cotton textiles, competition from France, Germany, Japan, and the United States forced the British spinning industry to specialize in finer grades of cloth, leaving the coarser grades to the newcomers in the field.[7]

These changes account for the reaction by British spinners to this turn-of-the-century "cotton famine." Just as in the

7 Robert Robson, *The Cotton Industry in Britain* (London, 1957), 4.

earlier "cotton famine" during the American Civil War, the old cry was raised to lessen the dependence upon American cotton. New to this later "cotton famine" was the British desire to have the Americans raise the quality of their cotton both in its condition and the way it was marketed. The desire to seek new sources of cotton was premised on a belief that American optimum growth had been reached and was stabilized at about eleven million bales. (The belief that the sum of natural resources was fixed was not limited at this time to American conservationists.) To make matters worse, growing numbers of American spindles would continually restrict the amount of southern cotton available for export. Under these conditions it was not hard to see that without new sources the continuing demands for more cotton cloth in the face of a contracting American cotton supply would mean continual "famine prices" for the spinners. American observers to the annual meetings of the international congress of cotton spinners, which began in 1904 under British sponsorship, declared that the minimum price for cotton should be fifteen cents, and that unless this price were met southern cotton growers would diversify their agriculture.[8] This threat added fuel to the ardor of the spinners to break the American monopoly on the cotton supply. To some it was the only hope. "Competition in other parts of the world is the only lever we can bring to bear on America" said H. W. Macalister of the Manchester Federa-

[8] Mr. George Horwood, M.P., predicted in 1911 that in 25 years "every bale of cotton grown in America [would] be wanted in America." *Manchester Guardian*, April 10, 1911. Theodore Saloutos, *Farmer Movements in the South* (Berkeley, 1960), 153-166; "Report of the Lancashire Private Cotton Investigation Commission," quoted in *International Congress of Delegated Representatives of Master Cotton Spinners and Manufacturers' Associations, Official Report, 1907* (Manchester, n.d.), 333-353 (hereafter cited as *International Cotton Congress, Official Report, [year]*); *Second International Conference of Cotton Growers, Spinners, and Manufacturers, Held in Atlanta, Georgia, October 7, 8, 9, 1907* (Atlanta, n.d.), 38 and passim; *International Cotton Congress, Official Report, 1910*, p. 40.

tion. "We must get the Indian Government to produce more cotton in India, and the British Cotton Growing Association to increase the production in Africa."[9]

Associated with the necessity to stimulate the growth of more cotton was the problem of speculation; a problem made more sinister under the opportunistic conditions of a "cotton famine." A certain amount of speculation in the form of hedging on futures was essential to alleviate the risks involved in buying cotton. But what the spinners sought to avoid was the violent fluctuations in futures prices. The so-called "Sully Year" in 1904 was a harsh lesson. "Without in any way slackening our efforts for securing a larger cotton supply," declared the chairman of the first international spinners' congress in his opening address, "the dealing with undue inflation of prices is undoubtedly at the present time the greatest question which we have to consider."[10] Various schemes were proposed to do away with this evil, the most influential being the creation of an international cotton buying agency that would buy cotton at low prices and hold it in reserve against future price fluctuations.[11]

Delegates to these spinners' congresses quickly realized that the bleak situation facing them in the cotton market could not be attributed solely to opportunists and gamblers on the exchange. Arguments over problems of marketing and supply quickly enlarged to take on a host of related problems, which bore directly on the American monopoly of the cotton supply. The report of a private six-man commission of Manchester cotton spinners in 1905 (the Lancashire Private Cotton Investigating Commission) merely spelled out what was already

[9] *International Cotton Congress, Official Report, 1910*, p. 65.

[10] *International Cotton Congress, Official Report, 1904*, p. 14.

[11] *Ibid.*, 39-40 and passim; Henry D. Martin to Stuyvesant Fish, March 14, 1906, Stuyvesant Fish Letters, Illinois Central Railroad Archives, Newberry Library, Chicago.

well known—the archaic and slovenly methods of American cotton growers. The commission was gracious enough to explain the sad state of American cotton as the result of the vicious circle of tenancy and financing that compelled production on marginal and submarginal lands. The same factors, according to the commissioners, were indirectly responsible for the inferior product that finally landed on the Liverpool docks. The poor grade of American cotton was the result of ignorant selection of seed, too rapid ginning, poor compresses, and damp in cotton due to overexposure and inadequate storage facilities. Most infamous of all was the notorious American manner of baling, a condition derided by American cotton growers themselves. According to the commission one southern cotton grower was overheard to condemn the American bale as "a dirty, damaged, disreputable, water-soaked, wasteful, slovenly, clumsy, highly inflammable, turtle-backed package." In typical English understatement, the commissioners commented that this American "was none too severe in his indictment."[12]

High on the spinners' list of complaints against American cotton was the gross inaccuracies of the costs of cotton growing and growth estimates, both of which bore heavily on futures prices and encouraged gambling on the exchange market. Spinners long suspected that crop estimates made by the U.S. Department of Agriculture favored the growing interests; some described its system of collecting information as "guesswork." Leakage of statistical information, the underestimation of the cotton crop in 1904–1906, and a public scandal in 1905 confirmed spinner suspicions and so wrecked confidence in the

---

[12] *International Cotton Congress, Official Report, 1907*, p. 346; J. H. Clapham, *An Economic History of Modern Britain*, III: *Machinery and National Rivalries* (Cambridge, Eng., 1938), 314; Edward P. Skene to J. T. Harahan, April 18, 1906, Fish Letters.

Agriculture Department's integrity as to cause spinners to remark that "no reliance whatever may be placed upon it."[13]

The appearance at this time of the boll weevil strengthened spinner beliefs that American sources of cotton would forever remain inadequate. Indigenous to Mexico and feeding and multiplying exclusively off the cotton plant, the boll weevil crossed into Texas about 1892. Spreading north and east into the American cotton belt at an annual rate of 40 to 70 miles, it struck terror into every community that crossed its path. Cotton growers had known other parasites, but the weevil was indestructible. It could survive severe shocks of climate. It could withstand massive attacks by other parasites. And it was incredibly prolific; a single mating produced one hundred and thirty four million offspring! "The Boll Weevil," wrote W. D. Hunter of the Agriculture Department's Division of Entomology in 1903, "is undoubtedly the most serious menace that the cotton planters of the South have ever been compelled to face; indeed it is doubtful if any other insect ever caused such grave fears for an agricultural industry."[14] Losses were staggering. In the first year of its entrance into any cotton community it wiped out 50 per cent of the crop. From 1902 to 1911, the time it took to cover every inch of Texas soil, the cotton loss suffered by Texas growers amounted to twenty-seven million dollars. Total American crop losses during this period (which include crops in Texas, Louisiana, Arkansas, and Mississippi) were put at two and one-half million bales, valued at one hundred and twenty-five million dollars.[15]

[13] *International Cotton Congress, Official Report, 1908*, p. 231; Saloutos, *Farmer Movements in the South*, 160-161.

[14] U.S. Department of Agriculture, *Yearbook of Agriculture, 1903* (Washington, 1904), 205.

[15] W. H. Hunter, *The Boll Weevil Problem*, U.S. Department of Agriculture, Farmer's Bulletin 512 (Washington, 1912), 5-8; *Ravages of the Boll Weevil*, U.S. Department of Commerce, Bureau of the Census (Washington, 1914).

But neither the boll weevil, nor the archaic methods of American cotton growers and shippers, nor the market raids of the bulls and bears were as demanding on American cotton growers as the last of the spinners' complaints against their American supply. This was that American short staple cotton, after a century of being good enough, was no longer suitable for the future of the cotton spinning industry. The British were specializing in finer grades of cloth; these were the grades of the future. For over a decade, British spinners had turned with increasing interest to Egyptian Metafifi cotton whose long fibre and resilient tensile strength was more easily adaptable to mercerization than were American fibres. Metafifi seed was first introduced into the Nile Valley in 1890. Nurtured carefully under the process of irrigation (without fear of untimely rainfall that spots cotton and lowers its grade), its growth proved very satisfactory and gave every indication of ever-increasing yields. The more sanguine British spinners anticipated with hope that at long last their Egyptian supplies would relieve them from dependence upon the Americans.[16]

It was thus an accumulating list of demands that was put upon American cotton growers at the dawn of the twentieth century. For certain types of American cotton growers these demands presented opportunity. The planters of the Yazoo Delta were confident that because of the natural fertility of their lands they could remedy every complaint by the world's spinners. For years their lands had been compared with the lands of the Egyptian Nile Valley. Indeed, it was long a shibboleth among cotton men that the alluvial lands of the lower Mississippi were the world's new Nile Valley. Of the two areas, reasoned the Americans, the advantage lay with the lower Mississippi for only about 30 per cent of these lands were cultivated, which left plenty of room for expansion. With

[16] *International Cotton Congress, Official Report, 1910,* pp. 139-146.

one bale to the acre as the advertised standard yield, the boomers of the Yazoo Delta claimed that, given the opportunity, the river counties alone could equal the entire American cotton crop. Thus, it might be true that American optimum growth had been reached, but this referred only to the lands of the older cotton South.

But what of the boll weevil which was unknown in Egypt? To this challenge, Delta planters had their reply. The weevil first struck the Yazoo Delta in 1908. Six years later the entire area, as well as the whole state of Mississippi, was infested. During these years, however, cotton production in the Yazoo Delta was not retarded. On the contrary, it rose by 20 per cent, from 376,042 bales in 1909 to 452,064 in 1915. The crippling effect of the weevil on the rest of Mississippi can be seen by contrast; the latter statistic represented half of the state's entire cotton crop.[17] The explanation for the Delta's survival and growth was presented by two prosperous Delta planters, Alfred H. Stone and Julian Fort, who in 1910-11 toured over 1,500 miles of weevil devastated lands in Mississippi, Texas, and Louisiana. Their findings as to why Delta lands survived and prospered and other lands did not were in accord with the U.S. Department of Agriculture's notion that only certain areas in the southern cotton belt could best continue growing cotton under boll weevil conditions. One of these areas was the Yazoo Mississippi Delta. In large part, it was the superiority of Delta geography, Stone and Fort concluded, that made the difference. Although yearly statistics showed only minute changes in temperature and rainfall between the Yazoo-Mississippi Delta and the weevil devastated cotton kingdom south of Vicksburg around Natchez, the Yazoo Delta's favorable dew moisture, vegetation, and soil conditions

[17] *Cotton Production and Distribution, 1915-1916,* U.S. Department of Commerce, Bureau of the Census, Bulletin No. 134 (Washington, 1916).

accumulated over countless centuries, endowed Delta lands with an inherent resiliency to the boll weevil. For Stone and Fort nature played but one part in overcoming the problem of the weevil, man another. "The weevil has never yet, anywhere or at any time, rendered impossible the production of cotton. Beyond question, it has in some places rendered the growing of certain types of cotton apparently impossible [but] the problem of boll weevil cotton production . . . is no longer that of determining whether cotton can or cannot be grown. It is simplified to one of merely determining where it may be grown to the best advantage, what varieties of cotton are best adapted to certain conditions of soil and climate, and what methods and practices will give the best and most profitable results." Success in cotton growing, despite the boll weevil, was like anything else, "a matter of intelligent human effort."[18] In short, intelligent plantation management combined with improvements in physical condition would enable the planters of the Yazoo Delta to survive the effects of the weevil.

As Stone and Fort were writing, Delta planters were embarked upon a program of improving their land's physical condition. Higher cotton prices and the threat of the boll weevil combined to produce an enthusiasm for organized land drainage. The development of drainage expressed the planter's confidence in the profitable expansion of his cotton specialization. Moreover, the drainage movement was evidence to the world's spinners that Delta planters were capable of responding to criticisms of American cotton growing.

To a large extent the Illinois Central Railroad was responsible for the introduction of drainage into the Yazoo Delta. Railroad officials experimented with well-type drainage and in 1895 unsuccessfully proposed a drainage law before the legislature. It was not until 1906 that a drainage law, popu-

[18] Alfred H. Stone and Julian Fort, *The Truth About the Boll Weevil* (Greenville, Miss., 1911).

larly known as the Alcorn Law, was passed. Supported by the Illinois Central, it was copied after the Illinois Drainage Law of 1879. The Alcorn Law provided for the incorporation of drainage districts through local courts and county boards of supervisors. Whenever a majority of the landowners representing one-third of the lands in a proposed district wished to form a drainage district, they could, after the proper legal proceedings, organize. All the landowners in the district would then be assessed to build and to maintain the canals and laterals. Assessments would be based on the possible benefits that each landowner would derive from his membership in the district. But all did not run smoothly. Problems arose over those planters whose lands were drained naturally and who saw no need to pay taxes while not receiving any greater benefits. There were complaints of excessive assessment for drainage tax purposes and complaints of unfair compensation for damages done to lands by the building of the ditches. Inadequate administration failed to settle conflicts between adjacent counties over control of main drainage canals. Accompanying charges of mismanagement led cynics to declare that all one needed to create a drainage district in Mississippi was a crooked stream, a crooked lawyer, and a crooked engineer. What was sorely needed was coordination, for the nature of the Delta's surface water demands the systematization of drainage. An attempt to create this was made in 1908 when the Mississippi legislature, in hopes of relieving the splintering effects of the Alcorn Law, created the Tallahatchie Drainage District, which encompassed the northern third of the Delta. Despite the support given it by the U.S. Department of Agriculture, this over-all drainage program met stiff opposition from many planters who feared the loss of their power within the local district, suspected centralization, and frowned on the higher taxes that would accompany the district's expensive and ambitious building projects. Parochialism triumphed, and the Tallahatchie Drainage District was repealed in 1912, its program to be revived at federal expense after the great flood of 1927.[19]

All these troubles did nothing to retard the drainage movement. Few doubted the wisdom of it; higher yields (and thus greater profits) were always the result. Within a decade after the Alcorn Law, drainage districts dotted the Delta's landscape. In this respect the Yazoo Delta was in the vanguard of the drainage movement that swept many agricultural communities during the 1920's and 1930's. For the Delta the benefits of drainage were incalculable. Indeed, without it there would have been no cotton kingdom. Drainage helped rid the Delta of malaria and yellow fever. It alleviated the worst effects of the boll weevil, for the weevil did not thrive under hot and dry conditions. The most far-reaching effect of drainage was the control it offered over growing conditions. This control allowed planters to experiment with new varieties of seed, thus

[19] Preceding discussion of drainage based on: Mississippi, *House and Senate Journals, 1906-1920*; Mississippi, *Laws, 1906*, Ch. CXXXII; Mississippi, *Code, 1917*, Ch. 99; Illinois, *Revised Statutes, 1880* (Springfield, 1880), Ch. 42; *The Daily Democrat* (Greenville), 1906-1920; *The Tallahatchie Herald*, 1908-1910 (available at Miss. Department of Archives and History); *The Delta Register* (Clarksdale), 1908; *Friars Point Coahomian*, July 29, 1911 (available at Clarksdale Public Library). Briefs and Files of: Mississippi *vs.* Crenshaw (Miss. Supreme Court File No. 15703); T. G. James *vs.* Tallahatchie Drainage District (Miss. Supreme Court File No. 14386). A significant amount of material on the Tallahatchie Drainage District and drainage in Mississippi can be found in the Agricultural Division, National Archives, Washington, D.C. Also, see, *Minutes*, Chancery Court, Washington Co., Miss.; Correspondence of the Bogue Phalia Drainage District Files No. 1-7 (July 1912-June 1915) of Leroy Percy in law office of Farrish, Keady and Campbell, Greenville, Miss.; *Minute Books of the Drainage Commissioners of Coahoma County, Miss.*, 4 vols., in office of Harding Corley, Clarksdale, Miss.; U.S. Congress, House, *Yazoo River, Mississippi*, 67th Cong., 4th Sess. (1923), House Doc. 597, Serial 8215; U.S. Department of Agriculture, *Department Bulletin*, No. 1207, p. 1224; Bernard A. Etcheverry, *Land Drainage and Flood Protection* (Stanford, 1940); Stuyvesant Fish to J. C. Welling, Dec. 14, 1895, and James Fentress to Mayes & Harris, Dec. 16, 1895, Fish Letters; Edward P. Skene to J. C. Welling, Dec. 17, 1895, Welling Letters; J. B. Harris to Yerger & Percy, Feb. 18, 1896, Fish Letters.

meeting spinners' complaints about the ignorant seed selection of American cotton growers. Delta planters were convinced that this control combined with their land's proven fertility and the encouragement of high prices would enable them to grow the kinds of long fibers required by British spinners. At the international spinners' congress in 1910 these views were presented in a report by the director of Mississippi's experiment stations, Jessie W. Fox. He found that Delta soils were perfectly capable of growing Egyptian varieties without significant reductions in unit yields.[20]

Fox's report came at a period of great anxiety for the world's spinners. After 1904, the somber predictions of a continuing cotton famine failed to materialize. Despair gave way to unrestrained optimism. Bumper crops in America and Egypt from 1905 to 1908 encouraged English spinners to expand. But a severe drought in Texas in addition to the cumulative effect of the boll weevil made the 1909 crop smallest since the "famine" six years earlier. The precipitous drop in 1909 of three million bales from the previous year was reflected in the market price, which rose to a high of $19\frac{3}{4}$ cents per pound, a figure not reached since 1874. By the end of 1909, Manchester mills were again working half and quarter time.[21] And, as the spinners' congress met in 1910, the assembled delegates heard their chairman gloomily declare: "The Seventh International Cotton Congress takes place at a most critical period in the history of the cotton industry. The years 1909 and 1910 will long be remembered as disastrous."[22] For the British the situation was made worse by the fact that their Egyptian supply of long fibre was also dis-

[20] *International Cotton Congress, Official Report, 1910*, pp. 150-152.
[21] *Cotton Production, 1909*, U.S. Department of Commerce and Labor, Bureau of the Census, Bulletin No. 107 (Washington, 1910), 9, 11, 27, 48; *London Times*, Nov. 2, 1909; *Cotton Production and Distribution, 1915-1916*, p. 51.
[22] *International Cotton Conference, Official Report, 1910*, p. 20.

appointing. Although larger crops were being produced, the unit yield was decreasing and reached a new low in 1909. The previous belief that the Nile Valley was the new source for British spinners now turned to discouragement, made darker by the failure of the American supply of normal length cotton.[23]

It was on this note that the British fine cotton spinners picked up in earnest the old idea of a cotton buying agency. There were now, however, some added features. The new agency would not limit itself to acting as a sort of market granary, but would be actively engaged in growing the cotton itself. Ever since the visit of the Lancashire Private Cotton Investigating Commission in 1906, English spinners had toyed with the idea of investing directly in American cotton lands. Fox's report, added to the favorable accounts of the Yazoo Mississippi Delta brought back by the commissioners, focused attention on the alluvial lands of the lower Mississippi Valley. Their thinking was aided by a group of Delta merchants, cotton factors, and planters led by a Yazoo Delta land speculator, Lant K. Salsbury. A Michigan born timber merchant, Salsbury was one of the many northern timbermen who turned to the South at the end of the nineteenth century. After years of successful dabbling in southern land and sawmills, he began buying and selling fully developed Delta plantations with a view to reaping large profits from rapidly rising land values. By 1910, Salsbury reportedly either owned or held options on thousands of acres of highly developed plantation lands.[24] At this time, as we have seen, the British were excellent prospects for a sale. Early in 1911, several leading directors of the Fine Cotton Spinners' and Doublers' As-

23 *Ibid.*, 139-146.
24 *Tennessee: The Volunteer State, 1769-1923* (Nashville, 1923), III, 197-199; *Memphis Commercial Appeal*, July 13, 1934; *Friars Point Coahomian*, Feb. 26, 1910.

sociation, a large Manchester holding company, came to America to view Salsbury's holdings and were persuaded to purchase them. The details of the transaction are not known, but it was the biggest sale ever seen in the Delta up to that time. Estimates of the amount of land sold range from 30,000 to 40,000 acres, while the price paid for them varies from two to three million dollars. Two operating plantations were formed, each with a paid-in capital of $1,500,000. Both were leased to a third company, the Mississippi Delta Planting Company, whose capital stock, owned completely by the Fine Cotton Spinners' and Doublers' Association, was one million dollars.[25] In 1919, in the face of popular attacks on alien landholding, the company escaped restrictions on its size by clothing itself with the defunct charter of Thomas Watson's Delta and Pine Land Company.[26]

For many years thereafter, Delta and Pine Land Company cotton was sold on the open market to whomever would buy. The English fine cotton spinners did not use a pound of their Delta cotton. Delta fibers, it was soon discovered, could not compete with the long fibers grown on irrigated soils in Egypt or on the cotton lands in the American Southwest. Egyptian cotton made a swift recovery just prior to World War I, and the cheapness of Egyptian labor made for far lower costs of production than any cotton produced in the United States.[27]

[25] Oscar Johnston, History of the Delta and Pine Land Company, Delta and Pine Land Company Office, Scott, Miss.; Wirt A. Williams, ed., *History of Bolivar County, Mississippi* (Jackson, 1948), 249-253; *The Daily Democrat*, Oct. 17, 1911; *Fortune* XV (March 1937), 125-132, 156, 158, 160.

[26] Mississippi, *Laws, 1912*, Ch. CLXII; Mississippi, *Code of 1906*, sec. 2768; *The Daily Democrat Times* (Greenville), July 9, 1919; Johnston, History of the Delta and Pine Land Company.

[27] U.S. Congress, Senate, *Production and Marketing of Egyptian Cotton*, 63d Cong., 1st Sess. (1913), Senate Doc. 113, Serial 6536, pp. 4-5; Thomas H. Kearney and William A. Peterson, *Egyptian Cotton in the Southwestern United States*, United States Department of Agriculture, Bureau of Plant Industry, Bulletin No. 128 (Washington, 1908); Thomas H. Kearney, *Breeding New Types of Egyptian Cotton*, U.S. Department of Agriculture, Bureau of Plant Industry, Bulletin No. 200 (Washington, 1910).

But this did not mean that the English had made a bad investment in Yazoo Delta cotton lands. An assured supply of adequate fibers was their alleged motive, but it is certain that Salsbury and his Delta associates did not leave the English visitors unaware of the profits afforded by Delta plantations. To be sure, Delta soils were attractive; the yields were unequaled anywhere in America, and there was certainly a great deal of room to expand cultivation. But the main thing impressed upon the English spinners was the efficient organization of farming that leading Delta planters had perfected. As much a recognition of the Delta as a reliable source of cotton, the English investment in 1911 was a recognition of a superior type of farm organization. The plantation dominated all other types of agricultural organization in the Delta and was, in the opinion of the United States Bureau of the Census in 1910, "more firmly fixed in the Yazoo-Mississippi Delta than in any other area of the South."[28] The English investment was a tribute to the kind of plantation management whose efficiencies assured profits without exception. For despite all the complaints about the American supply and the measures suggested to reform it, the English investment in these Delta plantations was no different from most other European adventures in American enterprise. The motive was always the same—stock dividends. Were these to arrive regularly, the English fine cotton spinners would rest content, regardless of whether they used their cotton or whether they ever exercised any control.

The Delta merchants, cotton factors, and planters who organized this plantation empire were now given the opportunity to enlarge their operations on a scale never before dreamed of. They were confident that their English backers would not be disappointed, for profits from Delta plantations by this time were a matter of course. Not long after the

[28] *Agriculture*, U.S. Bureau of the Census, *Thirteenth Census*, V (Washington, 1913), 884.

English embarked on their American scheme the U.S. Department of Agriculture's Office of Farm Management published a study of tenant systems in the Yazoo Delta. The report revealed that Delta landlords were assured of returns of from not less than 6 per cent to three times that amount.[29] So secure were profits from Delta plantations that money was made even during the bleak years of the 1930's. A later study of twenty-four representative Delta plantations revealed that in 1932, the bottom of the agricultural depression, Delta landowners still came out in the black; net profits averaged $615. And in the succeeding four years, reinforced by New Deal price supports, average net profits were $9,870.[30]

To be a successful plantation owner required great skill in buying, selling, and financing. It required an ability to adapt to the violent fluctuations in the market. But with agriculture, as with any other enterprise, high yields per acre combined with low unit costs determined the margin of profit. Delta planters excelled in reducing their costs to a minimum. The Delta's alluvial soil gave them a natural advantage over other Mississippi farmers. Cotton yields vary from plantation to plantation and from year to year. But in the period before World War I, the average yields per acre in the Yazoo Delta varied from lows of slightly more than one-third of a bale to highs of two-thirds of a bale. In contrast, average yields for cotton on non-Delta lands as reported by the census of 1910 ranged from a low of .06 bales per acre in Adams County (Natchez), which had just been ravaged by the boll weevil, to anywhere from less than a quarter to slightly more than one-third of a bale per acre. These figures included the rich black

[29] Ernest A. Boeger and Emanuel A. Goldenweiser, *A Study of the Tenant Systems of Farming in the Yazoo-Mississippi Delta*, U.S. Department of Agriculture, Bulletin No. 337 (Washington, 1916), 1-2, 7.

[30] Langsford and Thibodeaux, *Plantation Organization and Operation in the Yazoo-Mississippi Delta Area*, 35-36.

prairie regions in northeastern Mississippi.[31] In terms of unit costs the wide disparity between Delta and non-Delta productivity was made greater by the fact that the Delta's higher yields were achieved with virtually no fertilizers. The Delta's expenditure for fertilizers in 1909 was only .002 per cent of Mississippi's total expenditure of $2.7 million. And the increased use of fertilizers on non-Delta lands, with corresponding increases in unit costs, was not rising fast enough to keep pace with the eroding qualities of much of Mississippi's soils. In the decade 1899–1909, amounts spent on fertilizers by Mississippi's farmers rose by 190 per cent.[32]

It took more than naturally fertile soils to make high yields and low unit costs. Delta plantation owners were unique in achieving this vital combination because of the organization and supervision of their labor. In general, tenant farms in the Delta were similar to those found all over the South, with variations from plantation to plantation (and on the same plantation). Most independent was the cash-renter. He was the tenant who contracted to work his land at a fixed rent in cash or lint cotton. The landlord gave the cash-renter a house free of charge and fuel; the tenant provided the labor, workstock, feed for the workstock, tools, seeds, and fertilizers. When the harvest was over, the tenant received the entire crop. (If a fixed amount of lint cotton was contracted in lieu of a money rent, so much cotton was deducted from the cash tenant's harvest.) Less independent was the so-called sharerenter. Having no money to pay a cash rent, he promised to pay in return for the land either one-fourth or one-third of the crop. Otherwise, the arrangement was very similar to the cash-renter. The majority of the Delta's tenants in this period

[31] Boeger and Goldenweiser, *Study of the Tenant Systems of Farming in the Yazoo-Mississippi Delta*, 4; *Agriculture*, U.S. Bureau of the Census, *Thirteenth Census*, VI (Washington, 1913), 880-887.

[32] *Ibid.*, 863.

prior to World War I were sharecroppers (sometimes known as the half-and-half system). The sharecropper came with nothing but his labor and was dependent upon his landlord for just about everything. In return for sharing the crop on an equal basis, the landlord provided the sharecropper with land, a house free of charge, tools, workstock, seed, and fuel. Two other arrangements were especially suited to itinerants who could not be depended upon as tenants. Under the first form, the laborer was employed to plant a crop and work it to the time it was ready for picking. This he did at a fixed wage per acre, usually five dollars depending upon the character of the land. During picking time the laborer would be paid additional wages for harvesting. Under this system the landlord provided everything to the laborer as in the case of the sharecropper. The lowest form of labor was the drifting laborer (in greatest demand at harvest time) who was paid by the hundredweight of cotton picked and who usually received seventy-five cents to a dollar per day. Where he lived was usually his own business.[33]

Every form of labor was accompanied by landlord paternalism. More than a romantic residue left over from antebellum times, paternalism was an important feature of plantation life in the New South. It softened the cold impersonality of the contract. No tenant was allowed to go naked for long, if only for the reason that the planter was hard up for his labor and took care of the workers he did have. If the tenant or wage laborer wanted a few human amenities, the landlord furnished them from the plantation store (owned by the landlord), the cost being deducted from the tenant's account. Medicine and doctor's care were likewise provided by the landlord, under the same terms. Special arrangements were

[33] Boeger and Goldenweiser, *Study of the Tenant Systems of Farming in the Yazoo-Mississippi Delta*, 6-7; Allen Gray to C. B. Phipard, June 29, 1904, Fish Letters.

made in certain cases, depending upon the character of the tenant and the temperament of his landlord. But paternalism was indulged in not so much because it eased the conditions of the labor contract as because it was a means which emphasized the social gulf between planters and poorer white men. The planter spoke of "my tenants" or "my laborers." Appearing before the local court to plead bail for one of his habitually unruly tenants, the planter was heard to lament, with sighs and pious hand-wringing, the heartaches and costs into which "my tenants" had enslaved him. His laments were acknowledged by the local white citizenry, whose sympathies for the planter's problems were as much a subtle acknowledgment of their inferior status toward him as they were a sign of superiority over the lowly tenant.[34]

The closer the planter's supervision over his tenants, the greater his margin of profit. The size of the farm was a determining factor in controlling what was grown and how intensively it was done. According to the 1910 census the average non-Delta tenant farm was 38.3 acres; the average Delta tenant farm was 23.1 acres. Of the typical non-Delta tenant farm only about two-thirds of the land was "improved," that is, in actual cultivation.[35] Of the three forms of tenant contracts, planters had the greatest supervision over sharecroppers, whose holdings were the smallest and most intensively cultivated with cotton. Some corn was grown but only to feed the workstock. The U.S. Office of Farm Management Study in 1913 of 878 Delta plantation records showed that 88 per cent of all sharecropped land was in cotton while slightly less on

[34] Alfred Holt Stone, *Studies in the American Race Problem* (New York, 1908); R. H. Leavell et al., *Negro Migration in 1916-17*, U.S. Department of Labor, Division of Negro Economics (Washington, 1919), 36-44. An excellent study of Negro-white and planter-tenant relations in the Yazoo Mississippi Delta is Hortense Powdermaker, *After Freedom: A Cultural Study in the Deep South* (New York, 1934), 14-110.

[35] U.S. Bureau of the Census, *Thirteenth Census*, VI, 864-871.

share-rent and cash-rent lands (77 and 81 per cent respectively). Because rents on the latter two types were fixed, the planter's greatest profits came with increased yields on share-cropped lands, where he and the tenant divided the increase. But differences in control over all three was a matter of degree hardly affecting the planter's average return on his investment, which the Office of Farm Management study reckoned at 10.6 per cent.[36]

The planter's profits were determined not only by the small size of the tenant holding but by the availability and submissiveness of his labor force. Fully 92 per cent of all farmers in the Yazoo Delta in 1910 were tenants. Of these, close to 95 per cent were Negro.[37] The Negroes began flocking into the Yazoo Delta at the end of the 1860's. Uprooted by the dislocations of war and reconstruction they came from many parts of the older South. They were enticed to the Delta by the planters who, eager for labor, filled the Negroes with ideas about the ease with which Delta lands could provide a living. In their drive for cheap black immigration the planters had the sanction of the state government; the Mississippi Bureau of Immigration, headed in this early period by a Delta Negro, worked hard to bring Negroes into Mississippi and direct them to the fertile river counties. During the 1880's, while a revamped state board of immigration struggled vainly to populate declining hill lands with whites, the planters turned successfully for help to land agents of the Louisville, New Orleans and Texas Railroad.[38] By 1890, the Yazoo Mississippi

[handwritten margin note: work force shaped settlement population]

[36] Boeger and Goldenweiser, *Study of the Tenant Systems of Farming in the Yazoo-Mississippi Delta*, 12-18, see especially, p. 7, table IV.

[37] *Ibid.*, 3.

[38] "Report of the Commissioner of Immigration," in Mississippi, *House Journal, 1874*, Appendix, 538; Emmie E. Wade, The Office of Commissioner of Immigration and Agriculture in Mississippi from 1873 to 1890 (unpublished M.A. thesis, University of Mississippi, 1940); Vernon L. Wharton, *The Negro in Mississippi, 1865-1890* (Chapel Hill, 1947), 103-104, 111.

Delta was the nation's and Mississippi's new "black belt." Of the 742,559 Negroes in Mississippi in that year approximately one-quarter made their homes in the Delta. The average ratio black to white was 6.7 to 1, with one county (Issaquena) having a ratio of 15.7 to 1. In 1900, seven Yazoo Delta counties were among the dozen counties in the nation having the highest percentage of Negroes (from 88 to 94 per cent).[39]

During the late 1860's and early 1870's a large part of the Negro work force entering the Delta came from the Carolinas, Georgia, Alabama, and as far off as Virginia. This stream ended when these states restricted out-of-state labor agents from carrying off their labor force. By the end of the 1870's and thereafter the Yazoo Delta's labor agents turned with great success to Negroes from the southern and eastern areas of Mississippi, where poor crops and depleting lands were in sharp contrast with the Delta's fertile soils and the promises of better tenant relations. By the mid-1880's a pattern of Negro migration within Mississippi had been formed with the lands of the Yazoo Delta becoming a sort of prolonged way station for Negroes moving west and north. This pattern persisted into the twentieth century. For some whites in those areas, losing their Negroes was good riddance. But others saw that the Negro was an irreplaceable work force whose exodus not merely accelerated their own economic decline but enriched the economy of the Yazoo Delta; sufficient labor was the key to success. It was not the Negro who was cursed for his leaving but the Delta planters who, it was charged, were monopolizing the all essential labor force and thus enriching themselves at the expense of the rest of the state.[40]

[39] Stone, *Studies in the American Race Problem*, 84-85; *Negroes in the United States*, U.S. Department of Commerce and Labor, Bureau of the Census, Bulletin No. 8 (Washington, 1904), 23.

[40] Wharton, *The Negro in Mississippi*, 107-116; R. H. Leavell et al., *Negro Migration in 1916-17*, pp. 16-19.

Even convict labor was monopolized by the Delta planters. Indeed, it was the Delta planters who during the unsettled period of the late 1860's first originated this system of forced labor in Mississippi. Again, they had the sanction of successive state administrations, which consistently leased out convict labor on contract to leading Delta planters. Despite protests against it, an occasional scandal, and repeated legislative investigations, the convict lease system continued.[41] Denunciations of it, however, were not predicated on its barbarity, but rather on the Delta planters' monopoly over it. Having come to power partly as a result of his exposure of corruption and favoritism in the State Penitentiary Board of Control, Governor James K. Vardaman expressed public sentiment when he said in his annual message in 1906: "While the State has realized a very considerable revenue from the work of the convicts, it has also contributed a very large revenue—the products of the convicts' toil—to swell the fortunes of favored private individuals. It is an easy matter to make money planting cotton in the Yazoo-Mississippi Delta when you own the labor, pay no taxes or interest, and the products sell for a good price."[42]

By the time of Vardaman's message the Delta had become an enclave in Mississippi. Unlike its neighbors to the east and west, the state possessed no mineral resources; it had no foundations for industrialism. It was an area destined for agriculture. But its poor soils, seriously depleted by overcropping and poor farming, made it one of the poorest states in the unoin even though it specialized in cotton, one of the

[41] Testimony of Edmund Richardson in *Testimony in the Impeachment of Adelbert Ames, Governor of Mississippi* (Jackson, 1877), 126-128; "Report of the Committee to Investigate the Penitentiary," in Mississippi, *House Journal, 1886*, pp. 600-605; Jacob M. Dickinson to Stuyvesant Fish, Jan. 10, 1902, Fish Letters; Albert D. Kirwan, *Revolt of the Rednecks* (Lexington, 1951), 167-175.

[42] Mississippi, *Governor's Messages, 1906* (James K. Vardaman), 8, Department of Archives and History, Jackson, Miss.

nation's leading commercial exports. Measured against a booming and productive twentieth century America, Mississippi was less than an underdeveloped area. It was a land that nature had largely by-passed and that man had quickly exhausted. The Yazoo Delta was Mississippi's exception. Its lands, as we have seen, were naturally fertile and periodically refurbished by the floods of the Mississippi River. The advantage of its alluvial lands can be measured in terms of the Delta's proportion of Mississippi's wealth. In 1910 the total value of all crops in this predominantly agricultural state amounted to $147,315,000, of which $83,148,000 represented the value of cotton grown. Nine Delta counties measuring one-eleventh of Mississippi's land area, accounted for 28 per cent of the total cotton value, or a fraction less than 18 per cent of the state's total crop value.[43]

Because of the Delta's ability to grow a cash crop in abundance, it attracted and monopolized the best part of the state's Negro labor supply. The Delta had the advantages of a national railroad system that covered the entire region, gave its products swift and reliable outlets to markets, and indirectly provided capital support. It also had the recognition of capitalists and speculators who believed the area had a future and were willing to place their money in it. The combination of all these factors accounted for the fact that in the Yazoo Delta, unlike most other parts of Mississippi, specialization in cotton produced surplus capital for reinvestment. This was reflected in the contrast of land values, the true measure of agricultural economies. The average value of farm land outside the Delta ranged from a low of $5.88 to a high of $21. But not a single Delta county had an average land value as low as the highest values outside the Delta. The lowest average land value among the Delta's nine counties was

---

[43] *Agriculture*, in *Thirteenth Census*, V, 799-800.

$31.67, and the highest average was $47.76.[44] By every factor of reckoning, the Yazoo Delta in the period prior to World War I was superior to the economy of the rest of the state. Moreover, it had the potential for pulling away from the rest of Mississippi's economy at a faster and faster rate. The Yazoo Delta alone, of all the sections in Mississippi, could take advantage of the opportunities that world demands for cotton had precipitated. It alone had entered the twentieth century. But it was still of Mississippi and the South, a fact proved by the hopelessness of some planters' attempts to dissassociate themselves from the restraining vestiges of southern life.

[44] *Ibid.*, VI, 864-871.

# CHAPTER 7

# The End of Immigration
# to the Cotton Fields

IN THE PRE-CIVIL WAR PERIOD few immigrants to the United States settled in the South. Post-reconstruction leaders urged the promotion of immigration, which they considered essential, if the southern states were to match northern industrial achievement.[1] But these attempts to attract a larger share of the immigrant tide in the latter part of the nineteenth and early years of the twentieth centuries are well-known chronicles of failure,[2] reflecting an inability to rise above the South's dominant agriculturalism. As a result, the South remained a

[1] See *Proceedings of the Southern Interstate Immigration Convention*, convened in Montgomery, Alabama, Dec. 12-13, 1888 (Dallas, 1888); *Proceedings of the First Annual Session of the Southern Immigration Association of America* (Nashville, 1884); John C. C. Newton, *The New South* (Baltimore, 1887); Atticus G. Haygood, *The New South: Gratitude, Amendment, Hope* (Oxford, Ga., 1880); John C. Reed, *The Old and New South* (New York, 1876); Paul H. Buck, *The Road to Reunion* (Boston, 1937), 151-152.

[2] Walter L. Fleming, "Immigration to the Southern States," *Political Science Quarterly*, XX (June 1905), 276-297; Bert J. Lowenberg, "Efforts of the South to Encourage Immigration, 1865-1900," *South Atlantic Quarterly*, XXXIII (October 1934), 363-385; Rowland T. Berthoff, "Southern Attitudes Toward Immigration, 1865-1914," *Journal of Southern History*, XVII (August 1951), 328-360; C. Vann Woodward, *Origins of the New South, 1877-1913* (Baton Rouge, 1951), 297-299.

second-class section, geared to the decisions of northeastern capitalism.

Xenophobia has been given as the chief reason for the defeat of southern efforts to attract immigrants.[3] Though playing its part, this reason alone is confusing: Why should the South, with an insignificant minority of foreigners, echo the sentiments of northern immigration restrictionists? More fundamental reasons for the defeat of southern efforts lay in confusion over ends. Post-reconstruction leadership based its calls for increased immigration to the South on the illusory belief that factories would follow labor. By the dawn of the twentieth century, however, the South was far from becoming an industrial section. Compared with the Northeast, the number of factories in the South was negligible. There was no real need for an industrial labor force. The remaining avenue for immigration, one closer to the agrarian nature of the southern economy, was farming. There was, however, little room for an influx of immigrant yeoman farmers. On the contrary, the southern economy already suffered from an overabundance of yeomen increasingly sinking into tenancy on overcropped soils. Immigration, therefore, might be advantageous only if it could be used as a cheap agricultural labor force. This involved the channeling of white immigrants not to their own plots of land as yeomen but as laborers to the large and fertile plantations already flooded with the older source of southern labor—the Negro.

By the end of the nineteenth century, the Yazoo Mississippi Delta was a leading plantation area where the introduction of immigrant labor would further benefit its cotton-dominated economy. The extraordinarily rich soils of this area, reclaimed as a result of the post-Civil War leveeing of the

[3] John Higham, *Strangers in the Land: Patterns of American Nativism, 1860-1925* (New Brunswick, 1955), 169-171; Berthoff, "Southern Attitudes Toward Immigration," 360.

Mississippi River, had created a new planter class specializing in the large-scale production of cotton, possessing a highly developed and nationally integrated rail network, and utilizing the highest concentration of Negro labor in the nation. The ambitions of the Yazoo area planters encompassed the full cultivation of the Delta's four million acres, of which fully two-thirds remained in virgin wilderness in 1900.[4]

According to the planters, only the insufficiency of labor stood in the way of capitalizing fully on their opportunities.[5] The demands for more Negro labor for the Delta's cotton fields were meeting stiff competition from other areas of the South's economy. Cotton mills, phosphate mines, double tracking of railroads, cotton oil mills, saw mills, and the increased building of roads and levees were drawing heavily upon the available labor supply and retarding the normal flow of Negro labor westward from the worn-out lands of the seaboard states.[6] The new values placed upon Negro labor led these older areas to enforce laws preventing Delta labor agents from "kidnapping" their Negroes.[7] To make matters worse, James K. Vardaman's demagogic campaign for the governorship of Mississippi during the summer of 1903 inflamed the delicate state of racial tensions. The resultant intimidation put Delta Negroes in fear for their very lives. They were thus particularly susceptible to inducements that might be made to them by labor agents from the western South

[4] Lee J. Langley, "Italians in the Cotton Fields," *Manufacturers' Record*, XLV (April 7, 1904), 250; Allen Gray to C. B. Phipard, June 29, 1904, Stuyvesant Fish Letters, Illinois Central Railroad Archives, Newberry Library, Chicago; Charles Scott to Stuyvesant Fish, April 5, 1902, *ibid.*; Edmondo Mayor des Planches, *Attraverso Gli Stati Uniti* (Torino, 1913), 134.

[5] Langley, "Italians in the Cotton Fields," 250; Scott to Fish, Dec. 3, 1903, Fish Letters.

[6] *Manufacturers' Record*, XLV (June 2, 1904), 437; Woodward, *Origins of the New South*, 117-140; Berthoff, "Southern Attitudes Toward Immigration," 329, 335.

[7] Edward P. Skene to J. C. Welling, Dec. 17, 1904, Fish Letters.

—Texas, Indian Territory (Oklahoma), Arkansas, and Missouri.[8]

Greater than the complaints over inadequate numbers was planter frustration and disgust with Negro labor in general. Despite the confining characteristics of tenant forms and the relatively high agricultural day wages (as much as seventy-five cents),[9] planters were unable to maintain a stable Negro agricultural labor force. Why, they asked, were Delta Negroes so poverty-stricken and in a state of peonage while working the most fertile soil in America? The tenant system, they argued, offered the unskilled generous opportunities. During his apprenticeship as a cropper, it protected him from the winds of destitution, hard times, and occasional crop failures. With the exercise of thrift and the application of skills employed on bounteous soils, planters reasoned, a man could easily rise on the graduated scale from cropper to renter to outright landowner. But, as Alfred H. Stone of Greenville explained, the Negro's innate laziness, inefficiency, and lack of thrift had squandered the advantages offered to him. Stone and other Delta planters complained bitterly of the Negro's reaction to growing indebtedness. He literally walked away from it, shiftlessly drifting from one plantation to another or to new adventures in one of the Delta towns.[10]

[8] Edward Atkinson to Fish, Sept. 23, 1903, *ibid.*; Albert D. Kirwan, *Revolt of the Rednecks* (Lexington, 1951), 145-148; Woodward, *Origins of the New South*, 351.

[9] E. L. Langsford and B. H. Thibodeaux, *Plantation Organization and Operation in the Yazoo-Mississippi Delta Area*, U.S. Department of Agriculture, Technical Bulletin 682 (Washington, 1939), 5; Allen Gray to C. B. Phipard, June 29, 1904, Fish Letters.

[10] Alfred H. Stone, *Studies in the American Race Problem* (New York, 1908), 102, 115-123; David L. Cohn, *Where I Was Born and Raised* (Boston, 1948), 121-141; William A. Percy, *Lanterns on the Levee* (New York, 1941), 282-284; Ray S. Baker, *Following the Color Line* (New York, 1908), 57-58, 77; clipping from Memphis *Commercial* (n.d.) enclosed in letter from W. G. Yerger to Fish, Dec. 2, 1893, Fish Letters; Scott to Fish, Jan. 6, 1905, *ibid.*; Scott to John C. Burrus, Jan. 29, 1906, Burrus Papers, Mississippi Department of Archives and History, Jackson; Langley, "Italians in the Cotton Fields," 250.

The alternative to Negro labor was the large-scale utilization of immigrants pouring into the United States at the end of the nineteenth century and continuing in increasing numbers during the first decade of the twentieth century. This new supply of cheap labor had its source in southern and eastern Europe, especially in Italy. In 1898-99, the number of Italians entering the United States totaled 77,419. The following year this figure had increased to 100,135, and the year after that it reached a high of 135,996.[11] Deprived of the large quantities of Negroes they wished for and thoroughly dissatisfied with the Negro labor they already possessed, the Delta planters indulged in wild hopes of tapping this rich source of immigrant white labor.

Years before this great human flood made its way to the United States, a tiny trickle of Italian immigrant labor appeared in the Yazoo Delta. In the early 1880's *padrones* had been active in bringing laborers from northern cities to work on the Mississippi levees.[12] Some of these laborers might have formed the nucleus of the Delta's first Italian agricultural settlement at Friar's Point (Coahoma County) in 1885.

The successful use of these Italians at Friar's Point stimulated planter dissatisfaction with Negro labor. Planters were now able to contrast the efficiency and value of the two types. The facts of comparison, the planters believed, were self-evident, and were published by Alfred H. Stone in 1893. The Italians at Friar's Point, he maintained, had made full use of the opportunities presented to them by the tenancy labor system. Quickly and without indebtedness they had risen from mere agricultural laborers to self-sufficient renters. "Contrast this," he added, "with the appearance of indolence, squalor, thriftlessness and decay which characterizes the house of the average Negro tenant ... The secret of the differ-

---

[11] U.S. Commissioner-General of Immigration, *Annual Reports, 1889-1901.*
[12] *New York Tribune,* Jan. 2, 1884.

ence in favor of the Italian lay in the fact that he had laid
away from the previous year everything he needed, while,
as he always had done and will do, the Negro raised nothing,
but relied on the planter to support him. The one did as much
work as was possible, the other did only what constant watch-
ing compelled him to do."[13]

Addressing the American Economic Association in 1905
Stone, himself a leading Delta planter by that time, returned
to his earlier theme. The southern Negro as a cotton laborer
and renter was a failure, especially when competing with
white labor. Large-scale Italian immigration into the Delta,
he predicted, would result in the eventual displacement of the
Negro by the white in the cotton fields. This was a revolu-
tionary belief, for it had always been taken as an article of
faith that the Negro was both supreme and essential in cotton
growing.[14]

By 1905, Stone's beliefs had gained widespread support
among Delta planters. This was due to the good fortune
(after a faltering start) of the Italian colony of Sunnyside,
Arkansas. In 1895, Austin Corbin, New York banker, railroad organizer, and speculator in southern lands, embarked
upon a scheme to settle his vast Arkansas estates with one
hundred Italian families. In this endeavor, he had the support
of Prince Ruspoli, the mayor of Rome. Lying on the western
bank of the Mississippi River opposite Greenville, Corbin's
lands were, for the most part, low-lying, undrained swamps,
reeking with yellow fever and malaria. These unfavorable
conditions, combined with the depressed cotton prices of
1895, defeated the efforts of the Italian colonists, who were
inexperienced in cotton growing and alien to the dangers of

---

[13] Clipping from Memphis *Commercial* (n.d.), enclosed in letter from W. G.
Yerger to Fish, Dec. 2, 1893, Fish Letters; U.S. Immigration Commission Re-
ports, *Immigrants in Industries, Senate Docs.*, 61st Cong., 2d Sess. (1911),
No. 633, Part 24, *Recent Immigrants in Agriculture*, vol. I, Serial 5682, p. 308.

[14] Stone, *Studies in the American Race Problem*, 188-208.

the Mississippi's alluvial lands. In 1896, many of them, under the valiant leadership of their priest, Father Pietro Bandini, moved in a band to the western part of Arkansas to found the village of Tontitown.

These disastrous beginnings, however, did not reflect the final outcome of Corbin's enterprise. In the first two years a good portion of the lands had been cleared and drained. Upon Corbin's death in 1897, the executors of his estate leased the Sunnyside lands to O. B. Crittenden and Company of Greenville, Mississippi. Crittenden and his partner, Leroy Percy, had long experience in the precarious operation of cotton growing. Their skills in plantation organization and management proved decisive in the eventual success of the Italian colony. The remaining Italians were encouraged to stay at Sunnyside and urged to send for their relatives and friends in Italy. Experienced Negro tenants were introduced on a segregated basis among Italian tenants. Despite the disappointment of rock bottom cotton prices in 1898,[15] the experiment survived. In following years higher cotton prices and the introduction of efficient methods of production and sale transformed the Sunnyside plantation into a model colony for Italian agricultural labor.[16]

Under Percy-Crittenden management a simple crop-rent system was adopted. Each tenant was charged an annual

[15] On October 15, 1898, cotton on the New York Cotton Exchange hit the lowest point in its history, dropping to 4 and 15/16 cents per pound (middling inch). That year marked the absolute low point in the history of American cotton prices. *Cotton Production and Distribution*, U.S. Department of Commerce and Labor, Bureau of Census Bulletin 134 (Washington, 1916), 51.

[16] For the Sunnyside operation see: *Recent Immigrants in Agriculture*, I, 319-337; Langley, "Italians in the Cotton Fields," 250; Alfred H. Stone, "Italian Cotton-Growers in Arkansas," *Review of Reviews*, XXXV (Feb. 1907), 209-213; Stone, *Studies in the American Race Problem*, chs. 3-5 and passim; *Review of Reviews*, XXXIV (Sept. 1906), 361-362; Mayor des Planches, *Attraverso Gli Stati Uniti*, 137-145; Robert F. Foerster, *The Italian Emigration of Our Times* (Cambridge, Mass., 1919), 368; Fleming, "Immigration to the Southern States," 293.

seven-dollar-an-acre rental. Household supplies as well as doctor's care were furnished by the plantation store and charged to the tenant's account. When the crop was harvested, Percy and Crittenden bought the entire crop, deducting rents and amounts owed to the company. The difference went to the tenant, whose margin of profit was determined by his ability to reduce costs to a minimum. In this, the Italians were very successful, devoting as much land as possible to cotton but cultivating small truck gardens to cut down purchases at the plantation store. This practice was in accord with their Old World backgrounds. Italians were at home in the Delta's share-crop or share-tenant system. These and other variations of tenancy had existed for centuries in the ungenerous lands of central and southern Italy. Absentee landlordism and the intense cultivation of minute plots of land by an agricultural proletariat characterized Italian farming. To every peasant in Italy each foot of earth was precious; to extract the most from it meant survival in life's precarious struggle. These values were transferred and applied to the fertile and vast acreages of the lower Mississippi Valley.[17] The result was a belief on the part of the planters in the innate superiority of the Italian because he possessed what the Negro lacked—frugality and zealousness.

Italian tenants contrasted sharply with Negro tenants on the same plantation. In 1903, there were fifty-two Italian families on the Sunnyside plantation. Percy and Crittenden claimed to have paid them a total of $32,000 over and above their rents and expenses. In other years, Italian families were reported to have saved from $350 to $1,400 a year. As far as plantation finances were concerned, Percy estimated that

[17] Joseph E. Haven and Alan T. Hurd, " 'Share' System in Italian Agriculture," *Monthly Labor Review*, XXVII (July 1928), 31-32; Carl T. Schmidt, *The Plough and the Sword* (New York, 1938), 7-13; Foerster, *The Italian Emigration of Our Times*, 51-105.

for every dollar a Negro made on a crop the Italian made five. Investigating the 4,000-acre Sunnyside plantation in 1909, the Federal Immigration Commission substantiated planter beliefs about the inferiority of the Negro when placed in direct competition with white labor. Under almost identical conditions, the commissioners reported, the Italians raised nearly 40 per cent more cotton per working hand than the Negro. In value produced per working hand, the Italian exceeded the Negro by 85 per cent. The commission concluded, "Every comparison that can be drawn points clearly to the superiority of the Italian."[18]

The experience at Sunnyside convinced the planters that Italian immigration would eventually relieve their reliance upon the Negro. "If the immigration of these people is encouraged," declared Leroy Percy in 1904, "they will gradually take the place of the Negro without there being any such violent change as to paralyze for a generation the prosperity of the country."[19] The replacement of the Negro in the cotton fields by a more efficient labor force would do more for the planters than increase their profits. It would alleviate their anxieties in having such a heavy concentration of Negroes surrounding them. Apprehensions for "the conservation of our institutions" echoed earlier fears voiced during the 1880's when the Delta was becoming the nation's blackest belt.[20]

At the turn of the century both racial and economic solutions seemed possible. In the 1880's planter appeals for white immigration had fallen on the skeptical ears of Mississippi's legislators. During the latter part of that decade and thereafter, the political situation had turned skepticism into hos-

[18] *Recent Immigrants in Agriculture*, I, 326; James F. Merry to J. M. Dickinson, March 28, 1905, Fish Letters; Langley, "Italians in the Cotton Fields," 250; Foerster, *The Italian Emigration of Our Times*, 368.

[19] Langley, "Italians in the Cotton Fields," 250.

[20] Statement by William L. Nugent of Jackson, Mississippi, in "Joint Committee to Investigate Public Offices," Mississippi, *House Journal, 1886*, p. 576.

tility toward both the planters and their schemes for mixing the blood of Mississippi with foreign immigrants. The planters had then turned to securing the powerful support of the Illinois Central Railroad whose own best interests, it was thought, favored the promotion of immigration into the Delta.

Delta planters and Illinois Central railroad officials clashed, however, over the ulterior ends of immigration policy. The railroad's objective was to fill the Delta lands with yeoman farmers with a view to increasing freight volume. The planters, on the other hand, sought immigration as a source of cheap labor, not as a means of creating more landowners. Appeals to the Illinois Central's president, Stuyvesant Fish, for his support of the planters' position first met with a polite but negative reply. "Without pretending to any familiarity with the subject," wrote Fish in 1893, "the pressing need seems to me to be to encourage the black labor which you have, to habits of frugality and thrift, and to protect them from the 'sharks' of one kind and another who prey upon their simplicity and childlike appetites for sweets and gewgaws."[21]

Disappointment arising from the failure of the railroad to achieve the ends of its land sale policy did not dim increasing satisfaction over the value of the Delta's freight and passenger earnings. Yazoo Delta trade took on added importance in the railroad's balance sheet. The passing years thus drew tighter the common economic bonds between railroad and planter and eroded some of the hard-shelled self-interest of railroad officialdom. In addition, the winning charm of leading Delta planters supplemented economic bonds with personal class ties. The conscious ideals of the Delta's new gentleman planter class—wealth, honesty, paternalism, and moral integrity—were shared by higher officials of the railroad and were a refreshing relief to the base personalities of

21 Fish to W. G. Yerger, Nov. 16, 1893, Fish Letters.

"bottom rail" southern politicians. Charles Scott of Rosedale, owner of 30,000 acres, was a leading figure of this new Delta planter society. An eminent Delta lawyer, banker, railroad promoter, cotton planter, sportsman, philanthropist, and personal friend of important public figures, Scott skillfully combined the appeals of the southern romantic past with the successful business virtues of the twentieth century.[22] For this he was rewarded with the sufferance of northern high society.

Scott's friendship with the president of the Illinois Central Railroad allowed for a more intimate presentation of the planters' labor problem. Writing to Fish at the end of 1903, Scott suggested a personal conference between them. In the meantime, he reminded Fish that a large part of the Delta was still in forest, and the best interest of both railroad and planters was to bring this valuable land under the plow. "At present," he claimed, "we are without sufficient labor to work that which is already cleared. The fact is that on many of the larger plantations a considerable quantity of land lies fallow each year for the want of labor sufficient to work it. These conditions grow more and more acute each year, and as we can no longer bring Negroes from Georgia, Alabama and the Carolines we must turn elsewhere for a new supply of farm laborers." He concluded by asking the railroad's help in securing Negroes from Puerto Rico, or white laborers from Portugal and Italy.[23]

By the time of Scott's request, a number of circumstances had modified the railroad's earlier policy of getting more Delta lands under the plow. Virtually all of the railroad's Delta lands had been sold. Moreover, the Illinois Central

---

[22] *The National Cyclopedia of American Biography*, XVII (New York, 1920), 231; Wirt A. Williams, ed., *History of Bolivar County, Mississippi* (Jackson, 1948), 507-511 and passim.
[23] Scott to Fish, Dec. 3, 1903, Fish Letters.

monopolized the Delta's rail network. Yazoo and Mississippi Valley Railroad gross profits were very satisfactory, but operating costs were increasing yearly. Further expenses incurred by promoting immigration would eat up the margin of net profit.

All these considerations boiled down to the question of whether an increase in cotton freight would warrant additional expenditures by the railroad. In his reply to his friend Charles Scott, Fish gently tried to make this clear:

> What I want to present to you, in all candor, is that the success of the railroad is no longer dependent upon bringing in increased acreage, from year to year, under the plow, however much we might like to see this happen. What I want you to understand is that it is hardly the function of the railroad to furnish agricultural labor to till the fields in the country through which it runs, and in the management of a railroad we must be selfish to a certain extent.[24]

He hastened to assure Scott and other Delta planters that the Illinois Central had not abandoned them. Rather, the railroad's interest "was necessarily less than it had been." Agricultural products, he explained, no longer formed a very large percentage of railroad freight. The Illinois Central was profiting greatly from a vigorously developing southern lumber trade. Lumber and coal had replaced cotton as the chief item of freight. Cotton freight on the Illinois Central and Yazoo and Mississippi Valley railroads did not yield "anything like one-half as much gross revenue as coal . . . and barely one-third as much as lumber. Add to this that there has been in recent years a very large increase in the revenue from passengers, and a greater increase in the revenue from that source than in the revenue from freight, and you will see why it is we have not at this moment the same motive of direct

24 Fish to Scott, Dec. 9, 1903, *ibid.*

self-interest to import labor into the Delta that we had when offering lands for sale, and when the Y & MV Co. was dependent almost entirely upon cotton for revenue."[25]

Within six months Fish had changed his mind. Repeated counterarguments from Scott denying the belief that coal and lumber-freight could be isolated from the economy of the Delta were supported by other high officials of the Illinois Central. Edward P. Skene of the land department and James F. Merry, assistant general passenger agent, both tried to convince Fish that the introduction of immigrant labor, particularly Italians, would in the long run prove beneficial to the railroad. Philanthropy joined in the pressure. The noted New England economist Edward Atkinson, another personal friend and adviser of Fish, thought it urgent that the railroad help to move Italians from Boston's deplorable slums to the railroad's southern lands in the Yazoo Delta.[26]

The most influential source of pressure, however, came from southern business circles. For them, 1903 was more than just another boom year. The South, they believed, was at last on the threshold of a prolonged era of happy prosperity. The cotton situation was especially encouraging. A short supply was riding a rising demand curve. The resultant rise in prices would provide the opportunity to expand cotton cultivation. In turn, the opening up of new agricultural areas would mean an enlarged market for consumer goods and would lead to increased demands for new southern industries and manufactures. In the expansion of the cotton fields, so reasoned southern businessmen, lay the South's hope for keeping pace with the advancing industrialization of the rest

[25] Fish to Scott, Dec. 21, 1903, *ibid.*
[26] Scott to Fish, Dec. 17 and 30, 1903, and Skene to Welling, Dec. 17, 1904, *ibid.* James F. Merry sent numerous articles to Fish about Italians in the Delta. Merry to Fish, April 13, 1904; Fish to Merry, April 14, 1904; Edward Atkinson to Fish, Dec. 17, 1903; Fish to Atkinson, Dec. 21, 1903, *ibid.*

of the nation. In this manner was king cotton resurrected.

The editor of the *Manufacturers' Record,* speaking on behalf of southern business circles, challenged the railroads to support the planters' vital search for more labor:

Are the railroad people interested in the development of the South and Southwest equal to such an occasion? Are they broad enough to grasp the opportunity? These are the questions which they must meet. If they let this opportunity pass because of any pretense of financial inability to carry out this work on a scale many times larger than they have ever considered theretofore, they will fail to utilize the one great chance—in fact, the only great chance which has come to the South in a century—for attracting a heavy movement of population southward.[27]

Once committed, Fish responded with characteristic decisiveness. He directed James F. Merry to entertain suggestions from the Delta's three leading planters, Leroy Percy, John M. Parker, and Charles Scott. Assuring Scott of his personal support in securing Italian labor for the Delta, Fish promised to "leave no stone unturned in that direction." And to Frank P. Sargent, United States Commissioner General of Immigration, he wrote, "If at any time you have good farm laborers coming in at Ellis Island, whom you do not know what to do with, I would be very glad to take the matter up with you, not only to supply Mr. Scott's wants, but those of others."[28]

His efforts culminated in the visit of the Italian ambassador to the lower Mississippi Valley as guest of the Illinois Central and other railroads. In the winter of 1904-05, Baron Edmondo Mayor des Planches was invited to inspect personally the numerous Italian colonies scattered throughout the South.

[27] *Manufacturers' Record* XLV (June 2, 1904), 438.
[28] Fish to Frank P. Sargent, Jan. 3, 1905; Fish to Scott, Jan. 3, 1905; Fish to Merry, May 5, 1904, Fish Letters. Scott was also interested in getting Chinese and Japanese labor. Scott to Fish, Jan. 6, 1905; Fish to J. A. Harahan, Jan. 10, 1905; Scott to Dickinson, Feb. 1, 1905, *ibid.*

By this method, planters and southern industrial interests hoped to assure the ambassador that his countrymen were receiving favorable treatment. The end result of the visit, it was hoped, would be Mayor des Planches' decisive support in influencing the immigration of Italians to the southern states.[29]

Mayor des Planches had already acquainted himself with the condition of Italian immigrants in other parts of the United States. In the summer of 1904, he had been authorized by his government to make a coast to coast inspection tour of Italian immigrant communities. This first trip took him through the cities of San Francisco, Los Angeles, El Paso, San Antonio, Houston, and New Orleans. His second trip, to be taken in the spring of 1905, would provide him with an intensive examination of conditions in agricultural communities of Texas, Louisiana, Mississippi, and Arkansas.

As a guest of the Southern Railroad in April 1905, Mayor des Planches traveled westward across the breadth of the Yazoo Delta from Greenwood to Greenville, where he crossed the Mississippi to make a hasty inspection of Crittenden and Percy's Sunnyside plantation. After visiting numerous settlements on the western side of the Mississippi River, the ambassador was transported to St. Louis where he was greeted by several officials of the Illinois Central Railroad. From St. Louis he was conducted southward on the Illinois Central line to Memphis, and was transferred to the Yazoo and Mississippi Valley Railroad.

Upon his arrival in the Yazoo Delta, he was never lacking for company. His official host was Jacob M. Dickinson, former Assistant Attorney General of the United States and then

<hr>

[29] Fish to Dickinson, April 10, 1905, and Dickinson to Fish, April 10, 1905, *ibid.*; Frederick B. Stevenson, "Italian Colonies in the United States: A New Solution for the Immigration Problem," *Public Opinion*, XXXIX (Sept. 30, 1906), 456.

general counsel for the Illinois Central Railroad. But others joined and left him throughout the trip. From Clarksdale to Rosedale the ambassador was accompanied by Charles Scott, eager to make Mayor des Planches' acquaintance before setting sail for Italy where he hoped to interest Italian emigration officials in channeling Italian peasants to his own Delta plantations. At Greenville, the ambassador was joined by Leroy Percy and William R. Campbell. Leaving the Delta, he was escorted to Jackson and introduced to Governor James K. Vardaman, Thomas C. Catchings, and other influential lawyers and politicians.[30]

For the moment, at least, the ambassador's trip seemed to justify the railroad's invitation. Dickinson, instrumental in urging the undertaking upon Stuyvesant Fish, was particularly satisfied. "He made a delightful impression upon everyone he met," wrote Dickinson to his superiors. "I believe that the Company acted wisely in inaugurating and carrying out this trip, and that it will bear substantial results."[31] The ambassador had done his part well by urging the Italians living along the Illinois Central rail line to become American citizens, property owners, and home builders. Moreover, he had reported favorably on conditions in Mississippi and Louisiana to the Italian Bureau of Emigration in Rome.[32]

Optimism was short-lived. Even as Mayor des Planches was visiting New Orleans in May 1905, yellow fever was appearing in the Crescent City and was in full rage by August. The cause of this disease had been isolated a few years earlier, and after strenuous and cooperative efforts on the part of

---

[30] Mayor des Planches, *Attraverso Gli Stati Uniti*, 129-136, 250-256; Dickinson to Signor E. Mayor des Planches, March 28, 1905, Fish to Dickinson, April 25, 1905, and Fish to Henry White, Aug. 14, 1905, all in Fish Letters. Mayor des Planches wrote several letters of introduction for Scott to leading emigration officials. Mayor des Planches to Dickinson, July 19, 1905, *ibid.*

[31] Dickinson to Fish and Harahan, May 24, 1905, *ibid.*

[32] Mayor des Planches to Dickinson, July 10, 1905, *ibid.*

its citizenry, New Orleans was enabled to contain it by the fall of 1905. For the first time in its long history this disastrous plague had not been allowed to run its deadly course. For Delta planters, however, New Orleans' triumph had been a Pyrrhic victory: Italian immigration was discouraged. Once again, the Delta, though relatively untouched by this latest epidemic, was haunted by its age-old reputation as an unhealthy disease-ridden swamp.[33] All the efforts devoted to the successful visit of the Italian ambassador had been undone.

In Rome, Charles Scott was a discouraged witness to the fears engendered among Italian emigration officials. During the early summer of 1905, Scott, armed with introductions from Mayor des Planches, visited the Italian commissioner general of emigration in Rome. He believed he had convinced the commissioner of the wisdom of settling Italians on southern farms and away from the wretched life of the cities. No sooner had his interview ended than news of the outbreak of yellow fever in New Orleans alarmed the emigration officials. Thereafter, Scott complained, Italian officials turned their attention to settling emigrants in Texas.[34]

More subtle factors defeated southern hopes for a significant share of cheap Italian labor. Foremost among these were the powerful reasons every Italian had for leaving his past behind him. In the late nineteenth century, Italy was for the first time undergoing the strains of modern industrialization, setting loose the inevitable movement of population from farm to city. This was accentuated in southern Italy and Sicily by disenchantment with unification and declining agricultural prices. Dispossessed, a great flood of drifting farm labor

[33] Eleanor McMain, "Behind the Yellow Fever in Little Palermo," *Charities*, XV (Nov. 4, 1905), 152-159; Samuel H. Adams, "Yellow Fever: A Problem Solved," *McClure's Magazine*, XXVII (June 1906), 178-192; Fish to Harahan, July 26, 1905, Fish Letters.

[34] Scott to Fish, Oct. 30, 1905, Fish Letters.

sought escape in the higher wages of factory life and crowded into cities unprepared to absorb them. In this sense, the flood tide of Italian immigration to the United States was an international projection of similar population movements occurring within Italy.

Everywhere, this movement was looked upon as temporary. The sole object was to save some money and return to the native land. This motive guided the actions of great numbers of Italian farm laborers who sought high wages in the industrial cities of the United States.[35] A mere perusal of wages offered by industry in the northern and north central states during 1903 reveal their marked superiority to the forty to seventy-five cents per day offered to farm laborers by Yazoo Delta planters.[36] The long period needed to accumulate significant savings as an agricultural tenant offered little more.

In addition, the plantation-tenant system itself tended to repel the uprooted immigrant farming classes. Why, they asked, undertake the expense and hazards of a 5,000-mile journey to exchange one type of tenancy for another? Although planters widely claimed that a laborer could rise from tenancy to outright ownership, neither Scott nor the owners of Sunnyside would allow tenants to purchase any of their plantation lands.[37] Sound reasoning supported this policy. The plantation was a business system representing the integrated sum of all its parts—lands, gins, houses, stores, barns, tools, equipment, warehouses. Naturally enough, the piecemeal sale of any of these parts, especially the lands, meant an end to the plantation. This situation thus reveals

[35] Foerster, *The Italian Emigration of Our Times*, 342-362, 416-430.

[36] *Nineteenth Annual Report of the Commission of Labor, 1904*, 58th Cong., 3d Sess. (1904) House Doc. No. 428, Serial 4861, pp. 233-434; James H. Blodgett, *Wages of Farm Labor in the United States. Results of Twelve Statistical Investigations, 1866-1902*, U.S. Department of Agriculture, Bureau of Statistics, Miscellaneous Series Bulletin No. 26 (Washington, 1903), 18-19.

[37] Mayor des Planches, *Attraverso Gli Stati Uniti*, 138, 253.

the incongruities of planter claims about tenant opportunities. Having once entered the plantation system, the tenant was more an employee of a coordinated business enterprise than an apprentice who, by thrift and hard work, could some day own the land he worked. For the tenant, the plantation could only be a manner of living. It could not possibly be a means to economic independence or social mobility.

For the Italian, this type of enforced tenancy was entirely unsatisfactory. Coming from a land where property ownership, however small, meant great social prestige, he was not destined to remain a mere agricultural worker or tenant for long. The Immigration Commission predicted in 1910 that "where land is cheap and where opportunities for economic and social advancement are many the Italian rural laborer for wages will not outlast the first generation . . . The Italian seems destined to become a property owner, rather than an agricultural laborer."[38] Neither cheap land nor opportunities for economic and social advancement were available for Italians in the Yazoo Delta.

The isolation of the plantation from other economic outlets also inhibited Italian tenancy in the Delta. In theory, the tenant was free to sell his cotton to whomever he wished. In fact, however, he had no choice but to sell to the plantation company. The company owned the nearest practicable gin, compress, and warehouse. It had the factoring connections with the outside world. For the tenant to transport his products to competitors would raise his operating costs, something he could not afford to do. Isolation also brought on tenant suspicions about the good faith of the plantation company store. Immigrants overheard by the Italian ambassador at Sunnyside grumbled about the company store selling its goods for higher prices than the shops in Greenville.[39]

[38] *Recent Immigrants in Agriculture*, I, 244.
[39] Mayor des Planches, *Attraverso Gli Stati Uniti*, 143-144.

Lastly, a haphazard immigration system led to inevitable charges of peonage, exploitation, and mistreatment. For example, in the Yazoo Delta at a place called Marathon, the Italian ambassador was met by an angry crowd of Italians claiming betrayal. Enticed by glowing pictures of a southern paradise, they were discouraged by impure water and unhealthy living conditions. Already, they complained, the fever had carried off a dozen of their number. Moreover, they had been assured before going to Marathon that work was available. But upon their arrival they learned that the harvest had already taken place. They were thus left to drift for themselves in a primitive country and among a hostile people whose language they could not understand.[40]

Mayor des Planches continually emphasized the necessity for orderly and planned immigration. Spontaneous migration had the virtues of individualism but led to the exploitation of immigrants by *padrones*. The most satisfactory migration, the ambassador believed, was by groups. The movement of whole colonies would necessarily require planning, coordination, and agreement among all the parties concerned. Climate, pure water, nutritious food, proximity to transportation, and the stability of the immigrants would have to be accounted for in advance. Above all, clear contracts were essential. These would outline the specific rights and duties of both planter and immigrants. "Under these conditions," the ambassador declared, "Italian migration can come and will come to the South. Otherwise, no."[41]

No one was more willing to meet these requirements than the Delta planter. Bringing in whole colonies was for him the most efficient and economical way of making tenant contracts. By happy coincidence it satisfied the immigrants too. Homogeneous ethnic groupings eased the burden of being alone

[40] *Ibid.*, 253-256.
[41] *Ibid.*, 256.

among completely foreign surroundings. In their desire to contract entire colonies the planters had the support of the Italian emigration office in Rome. American cities were believed detrimental to the physical and moral health of the immigrants. Despite the outbreak of yellow fever, officials in the emigration office were still willing to direct Italian emigrés to the southern states, if it could be done in an orderly, clearly defined way.[42]

But it could not be done. Neither the apparent need for orderly group migration nor the planter willingness to bring it about had any effect on loosening the tight restrictions of the American anti-contract labor laws. These strictly forbade the advance contracting of labor in a foreign country, even by mere advertisement. By the beginning of the twentieth century, American immigration officials were attempting to give these laws greater enforcement. In its efforts to safeguard their nationals from exploitation by planning for their employment in advance, the Italian government found the American anti-contract labor laws "an almost insuperable obstacle."

To overcome these legal and other barriers, planters sought the aid of the Italian government in contracting whole groups of Italians upon their arrival in the United States. Support for this scheme was not forthcoming from officials of the Italian emigration office. Remembering the unfortunate experience at Marathon, they feared the uncertainties of these arrangements. Once in America, the immigrants were no longer under the protective and guiding care of the emigration office. The American ambassador to Italy, Henry White, explained the position of the Italian officials: "They cannot well assume the responsibility of advising their people to pro-

[42] *Ibid.*, 279, 284; Scott to Fish, Oct. 30, 1905, Fish Letters; G. E. Di Palma-Castiglione, "Italian Immigration into the United States, 1901-1904," *American Journal of Sociology*, XI (Sept. 1905), 202-206; Frank P. Sargent to Fish, Jan. 10, 1905, Fish Letters.

ceed to places at which the latter cannot be certain before leaving home of finding employment."[43]

One remaining factor provided the final blow to the declining hopes of the Delta planters. This was the resentment of the immigrants by native Americans. The Italian's inability to adjust to familiar southern patterns of behavior marked him as un-American. "Sin" played its part. Southern evangelicalism was particularly disturbed over the strange Catholicism, the incomprehensible language, and the Babylonian wine drinking, music, and dancing. Worst of all, the Italian's exclusiveness and the mystery of his ways were too reminiscent of the Negro.

A distinction was made among southern Italians (including Sicilians) and northern Italians. The latter, it was generally believed, were capable of being assimilated into American society and were thus the more desirable. Southerners had their doubts about the others. Representative Adam Byrd of Philadelphia, Mississippi, echoed these beliefs in Congress:

> I have witnessed the degradation of certain of this foreign element in my own section, who prefer a hut to a home, who believe not in the American idea of home comforts, who prefer a monkey and an organ to a piano, who pack their children away like sardines in their crowded huts. In other words, most of them live a life of utter degradation, and I am not one to make the honest yeomanry of my section labor in competition with such people.

Byrd claimed not to be against those Italians who made efforts to be Americans. He himself had supported former Governor Andrew H. Longino who was of Italian descent. But Longino was of north Italian extraction; the "Dagoes" of

[43] White to Fish, Oct. 14, 1905, Fish Letters. Apparently, the Foran Anti-Contract Labor Law of 1885 did have an effect upon Italian emigration officials even though, as Charlotte Erickson points out in *American Industry and the European Immigrant, 1860-1885* (Cambridge, Eng., 1957), 170-176, it was easily evaded by American labor agents.

southern Italy, Byrd believed, would never assimilate. "Hundreds of them," he exclaimed, "may be seen in New Orleans today, three generations from Italy, still pushing carts, yelling 'Banans,' 'Banans,' 'Banans'!!"[44]

Discrimination was accompanied by lynchings and threats of violence. The gruesome record began in 1891 when eleven Sicilians, being held for trial on charges of murdering the New Orleans police chief, were taken from prison and hanged by a mob. The following year, six Italians, charged with murder at Hahnsville, Louisiana, were taken from the parish jail by an unidentified mob and three of the prisoners were hanged. In 1899, five Italians were lynched in Tallulah, Louisiana, in a dispute over the wounding of a native American physician. In the summer of 1901, Vincerrzo Serio and his father were shot and killed at Erwin, Mississippi, not far from Greenville. And in 1907, Frank Scaglioni, a crippled shoemaker and leader of the Italian colony at Sumrall, Mississippi, was severely beaten and threatened with hanging if he persisted in his efforts to protect his fellow Italians from discrimination. Official protests by the Italian government against these offenses went unheeded. Local sentiment against Italians made it impossible to prosecute the offenders.[45]

The Italian immigrants failed to see the reason for these attacks. Language and customs notwithstanding, they had proved themselves reliable, efficient, and thrifty workers. Were not these virtues in the very best of yeoman farmer traditions and what the planters themselves desired in their

[44] 60th Cong., 1st Sess. (Jan. 20, 1908), *Congressional Record*, XLII, 884-885; *Recent Immigrants in Agriculture*, I, 244; Merry to Fish, July 5, 1904, Fish Letters.

[45] Senator Augusto Pierantoni, "Italian Feeling on American Lynching," *The Independent*, LV (Aug. 27, 1903), 2040-2042; Mayor des Planches, *Attraverso Gli Stati Uniti*, 255; *The Outlook*, LXII (Aug. 5, 1899), 735, and LXXXVII (Nov. 16, 1907), 556-558; Berthoff, "Southern Attitudes Toward Immigration," 343-344.

tenants? The planters' insistence upon bunching all the Italians into isolated colonies retarded the immigrants' assimilation into the rest of society. Their seclusion on the plantation meant that little or no provision was made for the American education of their children, and violence served only to pull the immigrants even closer together for security.

The planters were admittedly not interested in the assimilation of their Italian tenants. Washing their hands of personal relationships, the question of immigrant labor was for them "purely one of abstract economics."[46] Planter attitudes left the white Italian isolated within white society and not fully accepted by it. The result was his categorization with the nonwhite labor groups—Chinese, Mexicans, Indians, and Negroes. This treatment seemed more offensive to Italian officials than the beatings and lynchings. The Italian was being considered by the planters and railroad magnates as nothing more than a more efficient replacement for the Negro. "The company," commented Mayor des Planches on the Sunnyside operation, "is a company of speculation. From the settler it tries to draw the greatest profit without caring about his well-being. The Italian at Sunnyside is a human machine of production. Better than the Negro, a more perfect machine [than the Negro] but beside him a machine nevertheless."[47]

The identification with nonwhite labor, especially the Negro, robbed the Italian of his status as a white man. This status decline was reinforced by the servility associated with working on the plantation. In the Delta, no self-respecting white man labored on the huge cotton plantations. This was Negro's work. It was the badge of his inferiority. By replacing the Negro in the same type of work and under the same conditions, the Italians assumed the status of Negroes. One

[46] Stone, *Studies in the American Race Problem*, 198.
[47] Mayor des Planches, *Attraverso Gli Stati Uniti*, 145, 287.

blended into the other, and southern thinking made no effort to distinguish between them.[48]

Italian emigration officials were aware of the motives behind planter designs to bring more of their citizens to the South. The Italian ambassador understood why he had been treated with such courtesy by all the rich planters, eminent politicians, and railroad magnates—those groups were convinced that white immigrant labor would bring the southern economy into the twentieth century and somehow rid the South of its race problem. But unless the Italian immigrant received the recognition of a white man in a white man's society, these theories would never be tested.

The conditions of labor under the plantation system and the patterns of racial identification combined and interacted to frustrate the sanguine hopes for new sources of non-Negro labor. Significant numbers of Italians never made their way to the lower South. The high water mark of Italian immigration into the Delta was reached in 1910 when the number of Italians there was 1,167, a mere 2.3 per cent of the small total white population.[49] Thereafter, their numbers declined

[48] *Ibid.*, 138. The unwillingness of the white man to do what was considered Negro's work was, in the opinion of the Illinois Central Railroad's industrial commissioner, the chief reason for the failure to develop cotton spinning mills in the Yazoo Delta. "The average white citizen of Vicksburg," said the industrial commissioner, "would look upon it as an insult to be requested to work in a cotton mill. This is the situation in the larger cities in the Delta. In the country the white men will not work in the field and all the work is done by the Negro." George C. Power to Fish, Feb. 26, 1900, Fish Letters. See also, Paul S. Taylor, *Mexican Labor in the United States, Demmit County, Winter Garden District, South Texas* (Berkeley, 1930).

[49] *Population*, U.S. Bureau of the Census, *Thirteenth Census*, II (Washington, 1913), 1044-1062; *Population*, in *Fourteenth Census*, III (Washington, 1922), 543. In 1910, foreign born in Texas, Arkansas, Louisiana, and Mississippi represented an average of 2.7 per cent of the total population of those states. Texas and Louisiana showed the highest percentages, 6.2 and 3.2, respectively. Of the 8,924,493 people in those four states, only 31,259 were Italian-born and two-thirds of these lived in Louisiana, primarily in New Orleans. *Population*, in *Thirteenth Census*, II, 113, 773, 799, 1039.

and the concentrations of Italians in Washington and Bolivar countries were scattered throughout the rest of the Delta. The Negro remained, as ever, the sole source of plantation labor.

In 1907, the boll weevil first entered the state of Mississippi in the area around Natchez, causing havoc among a Negro labor force already impoverished by deteriorated soils. Delta planters made the most of this opportunity. Laying aside their ideas for Italian labor, planters brought the forsaken Negroes into the Delta by the wagon load.[50] This action, taken when hopes of immigrant labor were dimming, symbolized the planter's final surrender to the Negro. Predictions foretelling of his eventual displacement had come to nothing. The Delta's cotton fields, for better or worse, were left in the hands of the Negro tenant, and the earlier declaration of Frederick Douglass that the dependence of planters, landowners, and the old master class upon the Negro "is nearly complete and perfect"[51] rang true with greater authority.

[50] Alfred H. Stone and Julian Fort, *The Truth About the Boll Weevil* (Greenville, 1911).
[51] Frederick Douglass, *Life and Times* (Hartford, 1881), 438.

# CHAPTER 8

# A Reckoning with the Railroad

T HE NEW SOUTH'S HISTORY is that of a section powerless before the control of outside capital investment. Thoughout the last third of the nineteenth century, capitalists naturally sought out areas in the South that would bring them the greatest returns. Thus, railroads and mineral exploitation favored some areas with growth while others, equally in need of outside help, were neglected, and as a result passed into decline. Side by side, the fruits of the New South period left extremes of prosperity and poverty, the prosperity of the Yazoo Delta and the poverty of the rest of Mississippi, for example. Decisions by outside capitalists (such as the owners and managers of the Illinois Central Railroad) to venture south were not based on southern necessities, but rather, these decisions were geared to northern objectives. The resulting accentuation of sectionalism within the South, dividing rich and poor, and the milking of southern resources, lie at the heart of southern political reactions to capitalism. These reactions produced railroad regulatory commissions, laws against alien ownership, and restrictions on monopoly growth —legislation associated with the period of Populism and

Progressivism that swept the country at the turn of the twentieth century.

To be sure, these reforms against the evils of capitalism appeared at the same time, North, South, and West. But the impulse for Progressivism was not everywhere the same. Had southern Progressivism possessed a humanizing spirit the treatment of the Negro and non-Anglo-Saxon foreigner (indeed, the structure of southern state government itself) would have been different. Rather, the impulse to reform for southerners was fear; a negative fear whose scapegoat was the Negro, the non-Anglo-Saxon foreigner, and the corporation. The first two were treated in summary fashion; the former was disfranchised, and the latter discouraged from entering the South by intimidation and a lack of opportunity. The corporation, which in southern thinking meant northern capital, was a more complicated problem. By the turn of the twentieth century, northern capital was responsible (with the notable exceptions of the tobacco and textile spinning industries) for the major part of what wealth the South produced. For this very powerful reason, no one seriously urged getting rid of it, even if it were possible to do so. Regardless of its advantages, however, it was cursed by the swelling numbers of the South's poor, whose road to peonage and servility was paved by capital's neglect of them. Similarly, it was feared by those who benefited from it; northern investment usually represented monopoly control that snuffed out competitive enterprise.[1] Thus, like the poorer elements,

---

[1] Wilbur J. Cash, *The Mind of the South* (New York, 1941), 156-185; C. Vann Woodward, *Tom Watson: Agrarian Rebel* (New York, 1938); C. Vann Woodward, *Origins of the New South* (Baton Rouge, 1951), 371-382; Arthur S. Link, "The Progressive Movement in the South, 1870-1914," *North Carolina Historical Review*, XXIII (April 1946), 172-195; Daniel M. Robison, "From Tillman to Long: Some Striking Leaders of the Rural South," *Journal of Southern History*, III (Aug. 1937), 301, 305. There are a number of state studies of the Populist movement in the South. See Alex M. Arnett, *The*

even the blessed were threatened with servility, albeit a more comfortable one. These feelings, fanned by hard times and a long-held suspicion of anything Yankee, were channeled by politics into a pervasive belief that northern capital had divided the South and had robbed it of the best part of its natural wealth. Born of fear and disillusion, southern Progressivism transformed earlier encomiums of northern capital into a lingering conspiratorial cloud that threatened to smother the South with the kind of colonialism of which Calhoun and his followers had warned.

For Mississippians at the end of the nineteenth century, the Illinois Central Railroad was the incarnation of northern capital. It was natural for a people becoming progressively poorer to conclude that the Illinois Central's wealth and size made it corrupt; its favored position was based on unnatural tax privileges that enhanced its wealth and power. Devastated by war, without credit or cash, and holding lands whose worth was unrecognized or depreciated, Mississippi's reconstruction governments had sought to attract outside capital by granting liberal tax exemptions. For railroads, the standard form, written into legislative charter grants, was the privilege of creating a thirty-year reserve fund composed of all taxes the railroad should have paid to the state. From this fund, the railroad could pay its construction costs and other initial liabilities. If, however, railroad net profits allowed it to pay annual dividends of more than 8 per cent above its debts and liabilities, the tax exemption would cease. Counties and mu-

*Populist Movement in Georgia*, in Studies in History, Economics and Public Law, CIV, No. 1 (New York, 1932), 49-74; Roscoe C. Martin, *The People's Party in Texas*, in The University of Texas Bulletin No. 3308 (Austin, 1912), 48, 52-53. For Mississippi, see Albert D. Kirwan, *Revolt of the Rednecks* (Lexington, Ky., 1951), 49-57; William D. McCain, The Populist Party in Mississippi (unpublished M.A. thesis, University of Mississippi, 1931). If I have leaned heavily on the records of the Illinois Central Railroad for the material in this chapter, it is because there are no other primary source materials available.

nicipalities followed the state's example by offering other forms of tax benefits. Although not granted to the Illinois Central's main line in Mississippi (the Chicago, St. Louis and New Orleans Railroad), tax exemptions allegedly were granted to the Louisville, New Orleans and Texas Railroad and were therefore included in the sale to the Mississippi Valley Railroad, which was owned and controlled by the Illinois Central.[2] In this way, more than half the Illinois Central system in Mississippi, the wealthiest corporation in the state, was tax-exempt. Even if, it was believed, these tax exemptions had not been first granted as a result of corruption, to insist upon their continuation when they were no longer needed perverted the spirit behind the exemptions. Charges of corruption thus completed the list of complaints against northern capital.

Attacks against it were staged initially in the local courts, or more specifically, the jury trial courtroom. In rural areas, the jury courtroom is not merely a place where facts are determined. As the arena of community gossip, it is a made-to-order oratorical stump for aspiring country lawyers. In this setting, the Illinois Central was a natural target. It was the largest corporation, nonsouthern and rich, an all too tempting combination for a legal brotherhood made lean by accumulating years of general economic decline. As one Illinois Central lawyer explained it, the proliferation of personal injury suits against his railroad in Mississippi was caused by "the general shortage of pasturage for lawyers in any other

[2] See Section 21 of Act of Incorporation of Mobile and Northwestern Railroad in Mississippi, *Laws, 1870*, Ch. CIV; *Laws, 1870*, Ch. CXIII; *Laws, 1882*, Ch. DLV; Yazoo and Mississippi Valley Railroad *vs.* Wirt Adams, in Hunter C. Leake, comp., *Illinois Central and Yazoo & Mississippi Valley Railroad Co. v. Wirt Adams, Briefs* (Jackson, 1908), Department of Archives and History, Jackson, Miss., hereafter cited as Leake, *Briefs*; Mayes & Harris to R. T. Wilson, March 13, 1895, Stuyvesant Fish Letters, Illinois Central Railroad Archives, Newberry Library, Chicago.

field of litigation."[3] His reasoning was supported by statistics. In 1900, for example, no less than half the Illinois Central's 1,193 cases were in Mississippi.[4] This situation did more than offer a living to Mississippi's lawyers. In hot pursuit of a lucrative judgment, it was too easy to set the alien railroad leviathan against the helplessly injured railroad employee or the poor farmer whose only mule had ill-advisedly strayed across an unfenced railroad track. The juries, stirred to the proper pitch of righteous indignation by the impassioned harangues of tomorrow's member of the legislature, made their awards worth the candle. Hostile local sentiment thus built up against the railroad was inadvertently aided by the Illinois Central's policy of promoting the best members of Mississippi's bar to high salaried positions with the Illinois Central. With few other opportunities left to them, lawyers not so annointed with lucrative railroad positions were left in the jury courtroom, there to vent personal resentments against the Illinois Central upon primed ears eager to hear more.

In time, local sentiment oozed into state government policy. Here, too, hostile attitudes toward the rich railroad corporation were motivated by economic considerations. At the outset of the 1870's, New South leadership premised its demands for home rule and the Democratic party on the alleged waste and corruption of "Black Republicanism." The return to the "wise and frugal administration" of the Democratic party in 1875 signaled drastic reductions in state social services with a corresponding cut in taxation, especially on lands, the base of the state's tax structure.[5] For landowners, tax relief

[3] Mayes & Harris to Jacob M. Dickinson, Nov. 7, 1901, Fish Letters.

[4] Jacob M. Dickinson to Mayes & Harris, March 16, 1900, and Stuyvesant Fish to Jacob M. Dickinson, Nov. 12, 1902, Fish Letters; "Report of the General Solicitor," in Illinois Central Railroad, *Annual Report, 1897*.

[5] James W. Garner, *Reconstruction in Mississippi* (New York, 1901), 314-324.

was especially welcome. But the return in 1878 of a modicum of prosperity and its accompanying wave of optimism about the future raised irresistible demands, particularly among Yazoo Delta planters, for more roads, bridges, courthouses, and other capital improvements, without which the opportunities presented by high prices would be squandered.

Eager to meet these demands, yet fearing to open itself to the same charges leveled recently against reconstruction leadership, Mississippi's New South governments, after 1880, resorted to floating bond issues rather than making any distasteful increases in taxation. The result of this policy was increasing treasury indebtedness, by 1895 reckoned at over three million dollars. Persisting for more than a decade, indebtedness threatened seriously to undermine the state's credit (already tarnished by its repudiation, during the 1840's, of state bank bonds) and to make new bond issues impossible. Moreover, the specter of faster growing indebtedness became ominous by the 1890's as a result of widespread declines in agricultural prices. By mid-decade, the worst depression in history had settled upon the state. For the state treasury this meant a sharp decrease in tax income as new quantities of land were forfeited for nonpayment of taxes. Neither were these difficulties confined to the state level. County and municipal governments, even with services cut to a minimum, were also pinched by the squeeze of declining tax revenues.[6]

Desperate, Mississippi's state government searched for ways to raise additional revenue with the least pain for its suffering populace. In January 1894, Governor John M.

[6] Mississippi, *Biennial Reports of the State Treasurer, 1882-1897* (Jackson, 1882-1897); Mississippi, *Biennial Reports of the State Land Commissioner, 1892-1897* (Jackson, 1892-1897); Charles H. Brough, "History of Banking in Mississippi," *Publications of the Mississippi Historical Society*, III (Oxford, Miss., 1900), 327-339; Robison, "From Tillman to Long," 300.

Stone unrealistically urged the authorization of another bond issue and a general increase in taxation. Both measures were impossible for legislators harassed by the economic laments of their constituents. Instead, an abortive attempt was made by the legislature to skirt the problem by issuing state warrants as legal tender. Because of their similarity with federal notes, these warrants were confiscated by the federal government, and Mississippi's governor, treasurer, and auditor were momentarily arrested by United States secret service agents on charges of counterfeiting. The charges were quickly dismissed by a grand jury[7] but the incident highlighted the financial plight of the state government and made clear the need for more careful action.

Popular sentiment against the Illinois Central Railroad opened the possibility of a solution to the treasury problem, but success in this direction would not be easy. In 1892, the railroad cleverly made a shambles of the state railroad commission's attempt to bring in more revenue by reassessing railroad property. Railroad lawyers proved by the public testimony of no less an official than the state auditor that property in Mississippi, regardless of the constitutional injunction that it be assessed at full cash value, was by long practice assessed at about one-half of its actual cash value. Were the commissioners to insist upon the reassessment, the railroad would retaliate by demanding the reassessment of all property in Mississippi on an equal basis of full cash value.[8] This was something Mississippi's landowners obviously would not tolerate. Both sides felt it unwise to press too far. Their compromise increased the tax burden for the

---

[7] Mississippi, *House Journal, 1896,* pp. 17-21; J. G. Carlisle to U.S. Attorney General [Richard Olney], Aug. 18, 1894, and Robert N. Niles to Hon. Judson Harmon, Dec. 20, 1895, in Justice Division File 9149-9194, National Archives, Washington.

[8] James Fentress to Stuyvesant Fish, Sept. 9, 1892, Fish Letters.

Illinois Central's main line (Chicago, St. Louis and New Orleans). But it was far below popular expectations, and wholly insufficient to meet the needs of the state and county treasuries.[9]

Blocked at every turn and goaded by Populist sentiment sweeping the South and West, Mississippi's government decided to undermine corporation tax privileges. Although demagoguery and high-pitched public emotion were always present, it must not be thought that the state of Mississippi embarked precipitously upon this course of action. The assault on corporation privilege was a slow, if relentless, movement through the courts as well as the legislature. Its purpose was to make northern capital contribute more to the public treasury without discouraging its desire to further investment. The chief target was the Illinois Central's most profitable property in Mississippi, the Yazoo and Mississippi Valley Railroad. Were the state government successful in this cause, the Delta planters would be the chief benefactors, for it was through the Delta counties that most of the railroad ran. Regardless of who was to benefit, public sentiment generally favored this course of action. For what could be done against the Yazoo and Mississippi Valley Railroad might be done against lesser, but still privileged, corporations in other parts of the state. There were, however, some important reservations. No one wished to delete further the state's credit by opening it to charges of repudiation. The tax exemptions were clearly written into the corporation charters. They were to run for a specified term of years. Both these facts led to the assumption (championed without letup by most officials of the Illinois Central) that the exemptions amounted to a contractual relationship between the state of Mississippi and these corporations. That there was reluctance

[9] *Clarion-Ledger* (Jackson), Sept. 23, 1892.

by Mississippi's officials to overstep the bounds of possible contractual relationships with capitalist interests is shown by the state's strategy. Its object was to prove not that the granting of the exemptions was illegal or unjustified and should be repealed, but rather that past actions of the corporation had violated the conditions of its tax privilege. The corporation would thus be sued for back taxes, "illegally withheld." Moreover, once the state proved that the corporation had violated the conditions in the past, it would follow that the corporation's future exemptions would also be forfeit. With jury courtroom feelings running high against the Illinois Central in particular and all corporations in general, proof of these charges was not expected to be difficult.

Thus was the Illinois Central propelled into Mississippi politics. Railroad officials often disclaimed any political intentions; they were, they said, merely trying to run a railroad. But having contributed decisively to the growth of Mississippi's wealthiest section and having profited handsomely because of it, the Illinois Central was automatically involved in the state's political affairs. Southern politics, they quickly learned, had an entirely different flavor than the kind they were used to in Illinois. Lacking the discipline that comes from a competitive two-party structure, southern politics revolved more outwardly around personalities and personal ambitions. The back tax struggle that was about to begin provides a rare insight into the inner workings of Mississippi politics during this period. More pertinent to this study, however, is the naïvete it reveals of leading railroad officials who believed that the Illinois Central's economic interests in the Yazoo Delta could be divorced from their political consequences.

The burden of proof for the charges against the railroad fell upon the state revenue agent, Wirt Adams, Jr., whose office was given new legal powers by the legislature to go after back taxes and tax exemption privileges. Personal incentives were added. Win or lose, administrative and court costs were to be borne by the state. Adams' salary and those of his staff would be paid solely from the 20 per cent commission on all collections of back taxes received from delinquent taxpayers. No longer appointive, his office was now made elective.[10] His tenure would thus be dependent upon his success. Adams succeeded beyond all expectations. At the time of his death in 1914, after twenty-eight consecutive years in office, he was responsible for wresting from numerous corporations in Mississippi an estimated seven million dollars of additional tax revenue for state and local governments. His largest haul was the judgment he received against the Illinois Central. As a result of ten years of persistent legal and political efforts, he gathered from the railroad, one and a half million dollars in back taxes, and he forced it to forfeit an additional million dollars in future tax exemptions. As a result of this victory Adams was credited with having provided the state with money enough to build a badly needed new state capitol without the necessity of floating a new bond issue.[11]

His course against the Illinois Central was as persistent as his arguments were simple. They appealed to the background of suspicion and jealous envy of the rich Illinois Central. First, he argued, the underhanded methods used by the Yazoo and Mississippi Valley's predecessor, the Louisville, New Orleans and Texas Railroad, in watering its stock and passing its profits to a "secret ring of alien financiers" in New York, made it virtually certain that the railroad's net profits would never exceed 8 per cent above its debts and liabilities. In this

[10] State *vs.* Tonella, 70 Miss. 701; Mississippi, *Laws, 1894*, Ch. XXXIV. See also Governor's Report (J. M. Stone), *ibid.*, 132-133.

[11] *The Official and Statistical Register of the State of Mississippi, 1904* (Nashville, 1904), 451-454; J. B. Harris to Stuyvesant Fish, Sept. 2, 1897, Fish Letters; Obituary in *Clarion-Ledger*, April 26, 1914.

way, the road had illegally maintained its tax privileges at the expense of Mississippi's taxpayers. Secondly, Adams charged, the Louisville, New Orleans and Texas had been competitors with the Illinois Central for the north and south trade out of New Orleans. Under Mississippi law it was illegal for competing railroads to combine. The Illinois Central had tried to circumvent this restriction by having its tool, the Yazoo and Mississippi Valley Railroad buy out the Louisville, New Orleans and Texas while all the time maintaining the fiction that the Yazoo and Mississippi Valley was independent. Long before the sale was made official in 1892, Adams continued, members of the Illinois Central board of directors composed the secret ring of New York financiers who were reaping the profits of the Louisville, New Orleans and Texas. The circumstances of the sale, in short, were "a sham and a fraud" designed to avoid the law and to claim undeserved tax privileges. Lastly, as a result of the sale, an entirely new railroad was created, thus abrogating any prior tax exemptions claimed by the Louisville, New Orleans and Texas.[12]

These arguments quickly caught the public imagination. James Fentress, General Solicitor of the Illinois Central, was at a loss to account for their general acceptance. "The understanding in Mississippi," he wrote, "(how it came, I do not know), seems to be very general, and to have gotten into the heads of the Judges and Legislators that a large amount of money was made in these transactions, and that the road [Louisville, New Orleans and Texas] cost very little in comparison with the securities that were issued, and that the money actually expended in its construction bore such a small

12 Leake, *Briefs*, nos. 6, 7; James Fentress to Stuyvesant Fish, Oct. 26, 1892, Mayes & Harris to Fentress, Feb. 17, March 16, 1894, Mayes & Harris to R. T. Wilson, March 13, 1895, and Edward Mayes to James M. Edwards, Dec. 11, 1895, all in Fish Letters.

ratio to what was put upon it in the share of debts for construction, that it amounted to fraud."[13] Himself a southerner from Bolivar, Tennessee, Fentress had spent many years in the Illinois Central's legal department. He was proud of the Illinois Central's reputation for honesty and integrity. "From 1876 up to the present time," he wrote in 1896, "there has been much legislation in Mississippi granted to companies connected with the Illinois Central Railroad; and, as I had charge of most of it, I can state, as a fact, that not one cent was ever offered or paid or asked, and that everything was done openly and honestly and fearlessly."[14] It seemed unjust to him that the Illinois Central should now be accused of corruption. But having spent a lifetime dealing with southern legislators, judges, lawyers, and assorted politicians, no one was more deeply conscious of the agrarian ferment sweeping the southern states or the effect it would one day have upon the railroads. Fentress foresaw a grim future in the number and severity of southern laws designed to take from the rich man's hand. The assault upon the railroads' tax privileges was just one example. "People in Mississippi," he wrote to President Stuyvesant Fish, "having made so many bad crops, are extremely hungry, and it appears we are going to have serious litigation in this matter."[15] Because of "the present temper of the Mississippi courts" he was pessimistic about the outcome.

The railroad's complicated and tortuous rejoinder to Adams' charges did nothing to reduce the general suspicions of conspiracy held against the Illinois Central. The railroad denied owning the Louisville, New Orleans and Texas Railroad before its "consolidation" with the Yazoo and Missis-

[13] James Fentress to Stuyvesant Fish, Dec. 30, 1895, *ibid*.
[14] James Fentress to Mayes & Harris, Feb. 6, 1896, *ibid*.
[15] Fentress to Fish, Nov. 29, 1893, May 6, 1896, *ibid*.; Fentress to J. C. Welling, Feb. 4, 1895, Welling Letters.

sippi Valley. A flat denial should have been enough. But rail-road lawyers went on to add that the only connection between the two roads was through the Mississippi Valley Company, a sort of holding company chartered by the Mississippi legis-lature in 1872. The Illinois Central owned "some stock" of this holding company, as did some of the members of its board of directors. The Mississippi Valley Company, railroad lawyers argued, and not the Illinois Central, bought the stock of the Louisville, New Orleans and Texas. This stock was then transferred to the United States Trust Company in New York in order to secure some bonds of the Illinois Central. Thus, there was no direct connection between the Illinois Central and the Louisville, New Orleans and Texas before or after its "con-solidation" with the Yazoo and Mississippi Valley. Because it was a consolidation rather than a simple purchase, the Ya-zoo and Mississippi Valley had every right to the tax privi-leges possessed by the Louisville, New Orleans and Texas. Railroad lawyers substantiated this argument by pointing to several Mississippi Supreme Court decisions upholding the state's right to grant tax exemptions as well as the right of the Yazoo and Mississippi Valley to inherit them from the Louis-ville, New Orleans and Texas. Moreover, these tax privileges, railroad attorneys warned, amounted to a solemn, binding, irrepealable contract between the railroad and the state of Mississippi. To abrogate this contract by attacking the Yazoo and Mississippi Valley's clear and indisputable right to its tax exemptions would blot the state of Mississippi with a fresh stain of repudiation.[16]

16 Leake, *Briefs* (see Illinois Central *vs.* Wirt Adams et al., 30-31); Mayes & Harris to Fish, Jan. 3, 1895, James Fentress to Stuyvesant Fish, Dec. 13, 1895, Fentress to Edward Mayes, Dec. 23, 1895, and Stuyvesant Fish to James Fentress, Feb. 25, 1902, all in Fish Letters. In the opinion of William Z. Ripley, *Railroads, Finance and Organization* (New York, 1915), 440, the Mississippi Valley Company was a holding company used "to promote corpo-rate secrecy." The papers of the Illinois Central Railroad bear out his descrip-

The jury trial held in January 1896 to determine the facts of these arguments aroused a new wave of public emotion on the issue and brought about the inevitable extremism on both sides. A delegation of Delta citizens, led by a one-time member of the legislature, L. C. Dulaney, lobbied for passage of a bill "to repeal all laws exempting railroads from taxes in the State of Mississippi."[17] The Jackson *Evening News* expressed their sentiments: "Why should the people be required to pay all the taxes and the railroad company go free? This railroad recently sold for $25,000,000 and is owned by fourteen stockholders making each stockholder worth nearly two million dollars . . . The way this company has escaped taxation is evidence of the great manipulation of railroad magnates . . . It is now time for the people to have a reckoning with the railroad."[18]

With the active support of other Mississippi corporations, the Illinois Central quickly and easily quashed the bill in com-

tion. In 1901, for example, the Mississippi Valley Company, though capitalized at only $300,000 held varying amounts of stock in at least 16 (and possibly more) corporations, including six railroads, Alabama coal lands and other bridge and coal companies. Memorandum, Fish Out-Letters, vol. 58, p. 12. It was true that no stock of the Louisville, New Orleans and Texas Railroad was ever registered in the name of the Illinois Central Railroad, and that the Louisville, New Orleans and Texas' shares were transferred directly to the Mississippi Valley Company. But the Mississippi Valley Company was owned by the Illinois Central. In May 1902 the Illinois Central owned 5,910 shares of the Mississippi Valley Company while the remaining 90 shares were owned by the individual members of the Illinois Central's board of directors. Stuyvesant Fish to James Fentress, Feb. 25, 1902, Fish Letters; Memorandum in Fish Out-Letters, vol. 57, p. 905. The Mississippi Valley Company was a sensitive point for the Illinois Central. When, in 1901, the Illinois Central was seeking to purchase the Southern Railway lines in the Yazoo Delta (see above, Ch. 4), General Counsellor Jacob M. Dickinson warned Fish to tred lightly on the idea that the Mississippi Valley Company should buy the Southern's lines, for it "would necessarily bring an explanation and attract attention and an inquiry in respect to the Mississippi Valley Company, and that is something which it is not desirable to push into the foreground." Dickinson to Fish, Aug. 23, 1901, Fish Letters.

17 Mississippi, *House Journal, 1896* (H.B. 358), 242.
18 *Jackson Evening News*, Feb. 3, 1896.

mittee. Buttonholing influential members of the legislature, railroad lobbyists left little doubt about their feelings on the question of repudiating tax exemptions. They emphasized the contractual relationship and the importance of not alienating the Illinois Central in its work of furthering the state's economic future.[19] The latter threat was asserted by the president of the Illinois Central, Stuyvesant Fish. "I cannot believe," he wrote, "that the people of Mississippi, in view of what we are doing for the state, have sunk so low as to repudiate their contract in regard to taxation, or to attempt to harass us with more class legislation. While it would be inexpedient, at this time, to make any threats, it is impossible to conceal the fact that legislation of this sort would both hamper our capacity, and diminish our inclination to develop the material interests in the state in the way in which we have been doing of late."[20]

Throughout the entire back tax proceedings, which lasted nearly a decade, the Mississippi legislature restrained itself from anything smacking of repudiation. Whether it was from timidity before the railroad or an inborn conservatism, a bill such as Dulaney's went too far. It would have upset the balance between capital investment and capital responsibility that the state government was seeking. But heavy-handed railroad

[19] James Fentress to William G. Herger, Feb. 6, 1896; Fentress to Mayes & Harris, Feb. 7, 1896, Fish Letters. "Our people are beginning to see that Mississippi is left behind in the march of progress . . . and we have taken pains in a skillful way to call attention to this fact . . . and to suggest that the cause must be found in the character of legislation, especially as affecting investments of capital in the State of Mississippi and the sensitiveness of capitalists to anything like hostile legislation and that the temper toward railroads the only corporation, to speak of, that we have is taken by parties who have money to invest as an indication of what the temper would be in regard to other investments of capital. We hope in this way to being [sic] about a state of feeling that will result beneficially and prevent any oppressive legislation measures going through." Mayes & Harris to Fentress, Feb. 10, 1896, Fish Letters.
[20] Stuyvesant Fish to James Fentress, Feb. 8, 1896, *ibid.*

pressure, which at times bordered on the offensive, did not make things easier. For example, in the middle of the jury proceedings in February 1896, the trial judge disqualified himself and postponed the trial on the grounds that he had accepted a high paying position with the Illinois Central.[21] Later that same year, while the case was being heard on appeal in the Mississippi Supreme Court, the railroad enticed Justice Tim Cooper, one of the associate justices, to take a top position in the Illinois Central's legal department. This highly impolitic action was impassionately denounced by the revenue agent's legal assistants as an underhanded scheme of the Illinois Central to stack the bench in its favor.[22]

If the diplomatic light touch that great power can afford was missing from the actions of the Illinois Central, neither was it the distinguishing trait of its president, Stuyvesant Fish. All along the Mississippi Valley, the Illinois Central Railroad was associated with his name. As one southerner recalled years later: Mr. Stuyvesant Fish . . . personified the road. I grew up in the South, and I know that down in Mississippi when we thought of the Illinois Central Railroad we always thought of Stuyvesant Fish."[23]

Born in 1851, Fish's American ancestry dated back two hundred years. Of English yeoman stock, the Fish family was always associated with Long Island and New York. By the mid-eighteenth century the family had achieved high social and political standing. Colonel Nicholas Fish served under Washington from the battle of Long Island through the battle of Yorktown. Later, Washington appointed him supervisor of the revenue, one of the highest posts in the United States

21 J. C. Welling to Stuyvesant Fish, Jan. 17, 1896, *ibid.*

22 R. C. Beckett to Anselm J. McLaurin, Nov. 24, 1896, McLaurin Papers, Mississippi Department of Archives and History, Jackson.

23 Testimony of Waddil Catchings in U.S. Congress, Senate, *Nomination of Louis D. Brandeis*, 64th Cong., 1st Sess. (1916), Senate Doc. 409, Serial 6926, p. 343.

treasury. But Stuyvesant's father, Hamilton, achieved the greatest degree of prominence in the family's history. Governor of New York, United States Senator and Secretary of State under Grant, Hamilton Fish was a figure of domestic and international importance. His high social rank was signified by his position as director-general of the Society of the Cincinnati.[24] Family background had thus endowed Stuyvesant with traditions of family honor and public responsibility. The two traditions were viewed by generations of Fish family members as endowing them with a peculiar responsibility to constantly "be defending the principles of the Republic."[25] These same traditions were responsible for Stuyvesant's personal standards of honesty, Victorian morality, and gentlemanly honor. Upon these principles he formed loyal and unwavering friendships. And upon the same principles he developed bitter personal hatreds charged with emotional self-righteousness.

Fish's rapid rise in the hierarchy of the Illinois Central management (he became president when he was only thirty-seven years of age) was due to a combination of his family name and the fact that he was the protégé of William H. Osborn, the leading figure in the history of the railroad.[26] It was Osborn who, desperate for more capital during the mid-1870's, induced the young Stuyvesant, who already had a seat on the New York Stock Exchange, to accept a high position with the Illinois Central and membership on its board of directors. "To a young man 25 years of age," Fish later recalled, "[this] was something of a compliment."[27] Fish became associated immediately with the railroad's southern

24 New York Genealogical and Biographical Record, LIV (Oct. 1923), 324-331; Allan Nevins, Hamilton Fish: The Inner History of the Grant Administration (New York, 1936).

25 Edmund Wilson, The American Earthquake (New York, 1958), 189.

26 Carlton J. Corliss, Main Line of Mid-America, 138-139.

27 Stuyvesant Fish to C. C. Clarke, Dec. 8, 1903, Fish Letters.

division (Chicago, St. Louis and New Orleans), upon whose success the Illinois Central was able to take a new lease on life. When Osborn, in 1882, retired from active participation, Fish assumed his mantle of leadership, becoming vice president of the Illinois Central in 1884 and three years later assuming the presidency. In 1906, Fish was ousted from the presidency by a junta within the board of directors led by Edward H. Harriman. The Harriman forces complained that Fish had neglected his responsibilities to the railroad, that "he [Fish] had nothing to do with it; that he had lived in New York and Newport all the time; and the road had been run by [Vice President James T.] Harahan from Chicago."[28]

Whether or not these charges were the real reasons for Fish's dismissal, there was no denying that the Fish homes in Newport and New York were the leading centers of northeastern society. Fish and his socialite wife, the former Marion Graves Anthon, were proud of their leadership in this exclusive circle. For Fish viewed his role as president of one of the nation's largest and most successful railroads as being more than slavish obedience to the ledger book. He looked upon his presidency as a kind of stewardship for the national welfare. Family tradition gave this stewardship a special responsibility. Since man was naturally corrupt and driven by pecuniary ambitions, business was essentially a jungle. "The struggle is," he once wrote, "as usual, based on the survival of the fittest. We are and must continue to be the fittest."[29] Not by "socialistic" "Populist" regulation but only by social control could the businessman best be restrained to behave in a civilized way according to a strict code of gentlemanly honor. Fish's leadership of society, endowed to him by

[28] Illinois Central Railroad, Board Meetings, *Minutes*, VII, 110-113, Dearborn Street Station, Chicago; Testimony of Waddil Catchings, *Nomination of Louis D. Brandeis*, 343, 340, 350.

[29] Stuyvesant Fish to Robert W. Patterson, Jan. 17, 1894, Fish Letters.

his family name, was therefore essential in regulating and enforcing this code. The alternative was anarchy.

The geographical position of the Illinois Central Railroad lent an additional element to his concept of the social-leader businessman as national steward. The Illinois Central for Fish was the single great rail link tying North and South together in the heartland of America. As such it was the symbol of the lasting restoration of the Union and the essential ingredient for stability, without which there would be no national progress. Annoying legal restrictions on the railroads in general and his railroad in particular was "in many cases inconsistent with, and opposed to, good common sense and business policy."[30] The public had to be educated to the railroad's problems and its responsibilities. It had to understand, "that anything which detracts from the profitableness and efficiency of the railways injuriously affect all other interests in our common country . . . The magnitude of the interests involved are too great to allow of any other course."[31] But how to educate the public if it were continually misguided by self-aggrandizing politicians? This was the great question in Mississippi where open debate on the railroad's problems gave too many opportunities for demagogues such as Governor Anselm J. McLaurin "to seek popularity with the ignorant by making 'ad capitandum' harangues against so-called 'monopolies.' "[32] On top of this, shabby lawyers such as Adams "and his gang" were harassing the railroad with back tax suits and fights over the railroad's contractual tax exemptions only for the "prospect of recovering 20 per cent for themselves."[33] Against these attacks, Fish was determined to "fight this thing with every means in our power and to the

[30] Stuyvesant Fish to Robert W. Patterson, Jan. 17, 1894, *ibid.*
[31] *Ibid.*
[32] *Ibid.*
[33] Stuyvesant Fish to James Fentress, Dec. 23, 29, 1898, Fish Letters.

end."[34] Spurning the costs of the fight, he said verbosely, "I am determined, if possible, to prevent those who, I think, are trying through plundering us, to fill their own pockets, from succeeding."[35] To compromise with these attacks in any way would be as immoral as the attacks themselves, for it would mean that he, Stuyvesant Fish, had given way to the baser instincts of man's natural state and betrayed the public trust which society, his family tradition, and national progress had placed in his hands.

It was, therefore, a foregone conclusion that the Illinois Central would appeal the verdict of the jury trial in July 1896 to determine whether or not the Yazoo and Mississippi Valley Railroad had made dividends of 8 per cent since 1892. For the railroad, the verdict was a generous compromise which favored it with exemptions for the years 1892 through 1894 (saving it over $350,000) and awarded Adams the back taxes only for the year 1895.[36] With both sides seeking a clear decision, however, the jury's decision was appealed to Mississippi's Supreme Court. The railroad appealed because agreement to compromise would not only be immoral in Fish's eyes but would jeopardize railroad claims to future exemptions, which were supposed to last until 1907. The disappointed revenue agent appealed because he was certain that, given enough time, he could not only collect all back taxes, including those prior to 1892, but force the railroad to forfeit its future exemptions as well.

Adams' optimism grew from the conviction that popular trends against the Illinois Central would prevail because the prolonged economic depression in Mississippi was deepening and exciting demands for political action. In April 1897, for

---

34 Fish to Fentress, July 11, 1898, *ibid*.

35 Fish to Fentress, Dec. 9, 1898, *ibid*.

36 Mayes & Harris to James Fentress, July 27, 1896, and James Fentress to Stuyvesant Fish, July 28, 1896, *ibid*.

example, the ever persistent treasury problem forced another special session of the Mississippi legislature. At the same time, the most disastrous Mississippi flood in history caused widespread damage within the Yazoo Delta and reduced still further one of the state's richest sources of tax revenue. "The State of Mississippi," Fentress reported, "is in fearful condition right now, being out of money and wildly hunting for somebody to get it from." He therefore urged his Mississippi attorneys to delay the appeal of the jury verdict to the Mississippi Supreme Court until later in the year. It was his belief that "after the crop has been made and the river has gone down, things will be a little more quiet, and that under-current which influences courts as well as other people will not be so strong against releasing anything they might grab for taxes."[37] Privately, however, Fentress was pessimistic that the delay would bring any benefit to the railroad. He sensed that Adams' persistence would triumph in the long run because he felt, after a lifetime of legal experience, that southern courts were very active "in searching out some theory or stretching some rule of law beyond its legitimate scope in order to take away exemptions from taxation." "Indeed," he added, "I am not quite sure that in the long run it is of much benefit to the Railroad Company, even if it shall succeed in maintaining the exemption; for the reason that it has the state government and the people arrayed against it, as not paying its proper share of the public burden."[38]

That the judges of Mississippi's highest court would bend before the popular will was testified to in December 1897 in a subordinate attack by Adams on the Yazoo and Mississippi Valley's exemptions from municipal and town taxation between the year 1882 (when the Yazoo and Mississippi Valley

[37] James Fentress to Mayes & Harris, May 17, 1897, *ibid.*

[38] James Fentress to Mayes & Harris (no date, but probably early Feb. 1896), *ibid.*

was chartered) and 1892 (the period before its "consolidation" with the Louisville, New Orleans and Texas Railroad). By a two-to-one majority, a lineup consistently followed throughout the entire back tax episode, the Court ruled against the railroad's argument that a concluding clause in its charter exempting it from municipal taxation made the exemption perpetual. This, it held, "was a purpose most indisputably never dreamed of by the legislators."[39] The loss to the railroad of the exemptions was not so severe as the reasoning behind the Court majority. The practice of the federal Supreme Court to rule on the intent of the legislature and not the words of the law was now adopted by the highest bench of Mississippi, for without doubt, the Mississippi Supreme Court in this case was ruling on the wisdom of the 1882 legislature in so phrasing the Yazoo and Mississippi Valley's charter. "I am coming to believe that I do not understand the English language," Fentress wrote dejectedly. "I have read [the Court's] opinion, and after getting all the light I can from it, I do not see the slightest foundation for a doubt as to what the charter said in express terms."[40] It was Fish who drew the inevitable conclusion: "It is pretty evident, from this [case], that corporations have, in Mississippi, no rights which the Courts are bound to respect."[41]

On the appeal of the jury trial verdict the Illinois Central went before the Mississippi Supreme Court armed with the legal precedent of the Court itself. By the Mississippi Mills decision in 1884,[42] the Court ruled that while Mississippi's constitution declared all property liable to taxation, the state legislature could determine what property could actually be

[39] Wirt Adams vs. Yazoo and Mississippi Valley Railroad, 75 Miss. 275.

[40] Fentress to Mayes & Harris, Dec. 28, 1897, and Fentress to Stuyvesant Fish, Dec. 28, 1897, Fish Letters.

[41] Stuyvesant Fish to James Fentress, Dec. 31, 1897, ibid.

[42] Mississippi Mills vs. Cook, 56 Miss. 40. See also McCulloch vs. Stone, 64 Miss. 378 and Yazoo and Mississippi Valley vs. Thomas, 65 Miss. 553.

taxed. Obviously then, railroad attorneys argued, the legislature had the power to exempt certain property from taxation and did so in the case of the Louisville, New Orleans and Texas Railroad. Again, in the Lambert Case in 1893,[43] the Mississippi Supreme Court declared that the restrictive clauses on corporate consolidation in the State Constitution of 1890, did not apply to the tax exemption privileges of the Louisville, New Orleans and Texas. Thus it would follow that when the Yazoo and Mississippi Valley and the Louisville, New Orleans and Texas "consolidated" in 1892 the latter's tax privileges passed to the former.[44]

This barrage of prior rulings was overturned by the Court, which simply denied the fundamental propositions of the railroad's arguments. It denied that the state legislature under the Constitution of 1869 had the power to grant tax exemptions, much less irrepealable ones. It denied that the consolidation was a consolidation at all. Rather, it insisted, the sale in 1892 of the Louisville, New Orleans and Texas to the Illinois Central resulted in the formation of a new corporation to which the tax exemption claims of the former railroad could not have passed; section 180 of the State Constitution of 1890 forbade it. And (hypothetically speaking), even if the new corporation did have such a tax exemption, it was no longer valid as a result of certain enactments passed in 1884, 1886, and 1890. In short, because the Yazoo and Mississippi Valley Railroad was a new corporation after October 1892, no contract between it and the state of Mississippi existed.[45]

The decision was a cruel rebuff to years of patient efforts to secure the railroad's tax exemptions. "If," Fentress confided to Edward Mayes, one of the Mississippi railroad lawyers,

[43] Natchez, Jackson & Columbus Railroad *vs.* Lambert, 70 Miss. 779; James Fentress to Stuyvesant Fish, Nov. 29, 1893, Fish Letters.

[44] Leake, *Briefs* (see Illinois Central Railroad *vs.* Wirt Adams, 15); James Fentress to Stuyvesant Fish, June 21, 1898, Fish Letters.

[45] Yazoo and Mississippi Valley Railroad *vs.* Wirt Adams, 77 Miss. 206.

"there was anything that a prudent man could have concluded was settled, when we became interested in the Louisville, New Orleans and Texas property, it was that this contract would be observed."[46] But the Court's decision, differing little "from the morals of a highway robbery transaction," did more than take away rights belonging to the Illinois Central. By knocking "to pieces the settled law of the State," it shattered the rights of private property and "must impress people who own property in that state with the insecurity of decisions and laws upon which the community has acted for many years and which the court has held to be valid."[47] If Fentress' condemnation skirted the edges of an outright declaration of state perfidy, Fish was unrestrained in his belief that his railroad was being plundered by the corruption of Mississippi officials, from top to bottom. "The course pursued by the court, taken in connection with the large amount involved, the enormous commission to be received by Revenue Agent Adams, and some knowledge of the fallibility of human nature, convince me that either money or political aspirations have corrupted the court."[48] The issue in Fish's mind was the defense of private property from the attacks upon it by a corrupt government. The magnitude of this issue was too great to be dealt with by Mississippians. Redress, therefore, had to be to a higher authority— the United States Supreme Court, which was then deeply concerned with the sanctified nature of contractual obligations. This would not only right the wrongs suffered by the Illinois Central but by the long legal process of appeal the railroad would have time "in which to be able to prove what I believe are the facts with regard to the distribution of Wirt Adams' enormous fees."[49] "As time runs along, the people of Mississippi will begin to see that, by giving Wirt Adams 20 per cent

[46] James Fentress to Mayes & Harris, June 21, 1898, Fish Letters.
[47] James Fentress to Stuyvesant Fish, June 21, 1898, *ibid.*
[48] Stuyvesant Fish to James Fentress, July 13, 1898, *ibid.*
[49] Same to same, Dec. 7, 1898, *ibid.*

they have given him a fund which will necessarily amount to many times the entire tax levy of the state for a single year . . . Is it conceivable that frail human nature can stand the corrupting influences of such a fund in the hands of a single man and his associates, especially when they are in no way called upon to reveal the disposal which they make therefore?"[50] With time, the people of Mississippi would not only be alerted to the dangers of moral erosion that Adams and his back tax suits represented, they would also come to realize "that if the decision of the Mississippi Supreme Court stands there is absolutely nothing settled in Mississippi in the way of a right of property."[51]

Fish's legal advisers were not certain that a victory in the United States Supreme Court would have any real effect. Whatever the outcome of the federal ruling, charges of stock watering by the Louisville, New Orleans and Texas Railroad and the related questions of 8 per cent dividends would still have to be determined by a hostile local jury, certain to be angered by appeals outside the jurisdiction of Mississippi. They urged compromise, and had good reason to believe that negotiation was possible.[52] Adams, in December 1898, had offered to settle at 90 per cent of the total in back taxes, or $1,035,137. This figure, denounced as excessive by Fish, was flatly rejected at a special meeting of the Illinois Central board of directors.[53] Notwithstanding this initial failure, Fish's advisers persisted in calling for a compromise. They pointed to the fact that since Adams received 20 per cent of back taxes and nothing on forfeiture of future exemptions, it was to his personal interest to protract the litigation. Not to attempt a

50 Same to same, Dec. 29, 1898, *ibid.*
51 Same to same, June 30, 1898, *ibid.*
52 Mayes & Harris to Jacob M. Dickinson, Dec. 22, 1899, *ibid.*
53 Memorandum, Fish to Board of Directors, Dec. 23, 1898, and Fish to James Fentress, Dec. 23, 1898, *ibid.*

compromise, they told Fish, was to play into Adams' hands (or, more literally, help to line his pockets). They planned to outflank Adams by presenting a compromise in the form of a legislative enactment to the state legislature.[54] The legislators, caught in the usual bind between public outcries for action and conservative fears of alienating capital investment might prove more tractable before the pressures of a railroad lobby.

A number of other influences were persuading Fish. By 1899, prosperity had returned in the form of higher cotton prices, and with hope of money in their pockets the Delta planters might find it more profitable to join hands with the railroad in pushing the compromise through the legislature. By 1900, when the compromise would come up for consideration, the extremist McLaurin, who had been stirring up popular sentiment against the railroads, would be leaving the governorship. He was to be succeeded by Andrew H. Longino, a moderate, who railroad attorneys claimed had given them personal assurances of his favoritism toward corporations and, according to one of the lawyers, would "do what can lawfully and properly be done in advancement of any amicable settlement."[55] Part of Longino's successful bid for the governorship was based on his promise to provide a new state capitol building. For this he needed funds, which a compromise with the railroad might provide. Moreover, by May 1899 Fish had what he believed to be his trump card. This was the federal Supreme Court's acceptance of the appeal from the ruling of Mississippi's high court.[56] Fish's faith in the power

---

[54] J. B. Harris to Stuyvesant Fish, Jan. 6, 1898, and James Fentress to Stuyvesant Fish, Dec. 26, 1898, *ibid.*; Mississippi, *Code of 1892*, Ch. 36, Sec. 1572.

[55] Mayes & Harris to Jacob M. Dickinson, Dec. 20, 1899, and Jerome Hill to Mayes & Harris, Feb. 9, 1900, Fish Letters; Kirwan, *Revolt of the Rednecks*, 119, 140, 142.

[56] Fish to Fentress, May 1, 1899, Fish Letters.

of this appeal led him to believe that he could use it as a club over the heads of the legislators. "Should our proposition be carried out in good faith," he wrote, "we will welcome the day, but if attempts are made to trifle with us or to squeeze more money or other concessions out of us, we will simply let the cases at Washington take their course. In this we are fully determined."[57]

Having finally made the decision to compromise, Fish's offer left his negotiators with very little to negotiate. He proposed to settle at $750,000, or about half the contested sum. Attached were offensive conditions. If the legislature would accept Fish's figure, he would be willing to forfeit seven years of future exemptions, which he reckoned at $1,000,000. In addition, the legislative enactment incorporating the settlement was to state explicitly that Adams was to receive not a penny more than 20 per cent of the back taxes and nothing of the future exemption money. The rest was to go directly to the state treasury and not to hungry local governments. "They," he declared, "would fritter it away." Moreover, any enactment would have to preclude the state, Adams, or any other governmental body from bringing new tax suits against the entire Illinois Central system in Mississippi.[58]

Given the atmosphere of the 1900 session of the Mississippi legislature, it is doubtful if even a more generous proposal would have been accepted. The campaign of the previous year had been an especially polemical one, and as usual in the heat of political rhetoric, many candidates for office had made irretrievable promises. Typical was the case of E. N. Thomas of Washington County in the Yazoo Delta. He was the chairman of the House Ways and Means Committee through which the railroad's compromise bill would have to go. Neither he

---

[57] Fish to Jerome Hill, Feb. 15, 1900, *ibid.*
[58] Fish to Dickinson, Dec. 20, 1899, *ibid.*

nor the Washington County Executive Committee, which was the ruling political organization in his district, savored Mc-Laurin's demagoguery or the nepotism and corruption with which the outgoing governor was charged. But though Thomas had campaigned on a strict anti-McLaurinism platform, he pledged himself not to vote for any measure affecting the railroad's back tax suit. A public word of approval for the railroad's measure from either the outgoing governor[59] or the incoming Longino would have been enough to free Thomas from his anti-railroad pledge.[60] But with public sentiment strongly against the Illinois Central as a result of the campaign, neither McLaurin nor Longino dared show any signs of supporting the railroad's campaign. On the contrary, Mc-Laurin's last message to the legislature at the opening of the session contained a ringing blast against the Illinois Central accusing it of bad faith, of stalling for time to avoid paying the taxes the state's highest court had declared were due. And as a parting shot, he brought up again the old specter of the railroad leviathan: "Large sums of money," he said, "concentrated in the hands of gigantic railroad companies enable them, if they are so disposed, to protract resistance to the just process of law."[61]

Unable to get anyone to champion the measure in the House, railroad lobbyists turned to the Senate Judiciary Committee where a majority slowly ground out the bill for final floor consideration.[62] In the meantime, Adams' forces were

[59] Curiously, the railroad's lawyers never took McLaurin's fulminations against them seriously. In January 1900 they vainly tried to persuade Mc-Laurin to oppose Adams' forces in the legislature. Jacob Dickinson to Stuyvesant Fish, Jan. 11, 1900, *ibid.*

[60] Mayes & Harris to J. M. Dickinson, Feb. 9, 1900, and Leroy Percy to J. M. Dickinson, Feb. 15, 1900, *ibid.*

[61] Mississippi, *Governor's Messages, 1900* (Anselm J. McLaurin), Department of Archives and History, Jackson.

[62] Mississippi, *Senate Journal, 1900* (S.B. 197), 263, 295, 318, 431.

not idle. They canvassed the legislators urging them to stand firm before the intimidating influences of Stuyvesant Fish and assuring them that in time the railroad would be forced to lose everything. Besides, they argued, it was a moral question, a matter of simple justice. If the railroad did not owe the money, then the state had no right to take it, but if the railroad did owe the money, then the state had the right to take it all, not half or any other fraction. Moreover, they insisted, this was a question solely for the courts and not the legislature, and the courts had already ruled against the railroad.[63] The angry minority report accompanying the Judiciary Committee's recommendation for passage repeated these arguments with telling rhetoric:

> Nothing but the full realization of its affording the only avenue of escape could have induced these corporations to transfer their fight from the courts to the Legislature, and to thus obtain by means of more than questionable constitutionality, special relief, which the law now denies to them and to all other tax delinquents. If the railroads are legally liable for taxes . . . they should discharge that liability by a full payment to the public treasury. If they are not liable legally, they should pay nothing; and that property which is legally liable to taxation should alone defray the expenses of government.

Alluding to the heavy-handed political meddling of the railroad lobbyists, and Fish's threats of economic and legal reprisals, the minority report concluded with an emotional appeal to preserve the state's self-respect: "There can be no compromise of such litigation without compromising the dignity of the state and violating a duty it owes to every citizen."[64] The minority and not the majority of the Judiciary Committee represented the feelings of the rest of the Senate.

[63] Mayes & Harris to J. M. Dickinson, Feb. 10, 15, 1900, Fish Letters.
[64] Mississippi, *Senate Journal, 1900*, pp. 452-459.

Near the end of the session the railroad's compromise bill was defeated by a decisive two-thirds majority.[65] Fish seemed almost relieved that the Mississippi legislature had refused his compromise proposal, for now, he confidently believed, the United States Supreme Court would tellingly repudiate the "repudiators" of Mississippi. Moreover, since the return of prosperity to the Yazoo Delta, surplus earnings from merely two years of Yazoo and Mississippi Valley Railroad's operations would be more than sufficient to cover all back taxes. "Bearing in mind," he wrote to Vice President J. C. Welling, "that I feel very confident that we will save some part of these taxes, if not the whole,—this leaves the Yazoo and Mississippi Valley Railroad Company in a very strong position."[66] Fish's optimism was very short-lived, for the decision of the United States Supreme Court in November 1900 upheld every point made by the Mississippi high court. Not even the high-priced legal talent of William D. Guthrie, whose arguments helped defeat the income tax in the celebrated case of Pollack vs. Farmer's Loan and Trust Company, had much effect. In addition to ruling that the Yazoo and Mississippi Valley Railroad after 1892 was a new corporation and ineligible under Mississippi law for tax exemptions claimed by the Louisville, New Orleans and Texas Railroad, the high court went on to overturn the central thesis of the Illinois Central—that tax exemptions granted by state governments to attract capital investments were sacred irrepealable contracts. On the contrary, it held that these kinds of tax exemptions were decisions of state policy that could be retracted as freely as they were given. The Court was always ready to defend contractual obligations, and its sympathies for the

---

[65] *Ibid.*, 521-523; Stuyvesant Fish to E. L. Russell, March 3, 1900, and Mayes & Harris to Dickinson, March 6, 1900, Fish Letters.

[66] Fish to J. C. Welling, July 10, 1900, *ibid.*

railroad's cause were evident, but, it continued, "whatever policy the state may choose to adopt with respect to encouraging or discouraging the investment of capital from abroad, the duty of the courts is to declare the law as they find it, and avoid the discussion of questions of policy, which are clearly beyond their province. Certainly this court is not the keeper of the state's conscience."[67] It is ironic that this part of the high court's decision not only legalized the demands of Mississippi extremists who called for outright repeal of the railroad's tax exemptions but made academic the legislative fight over the railroad's compromise bill.

Wholesale repeal of the exemptions by the legislature was now possible. But this was not done. A pronouncement from the highest court in the land could not overnight change the long-held popular belief that tax exemptions were contracts. The Mississippi state government, as well as the railroad, clung to that view and continued to operate on that assumption. Although outright repeal of the exemptions would not now, because of the Supreme Court's ruling, legally be repudiation, future investors of capital, the state feared, would continue to think so. Thus, the slower course of court litigation was continued with every certainty that the railroad would lose the suits that were remanded to local jurisdiction.[68] While Governor Longino, in 1902, congratulated the legislature for having taken "the high ground" by refusing to acquiesce in the railroad's compromise proposition, local courts awarded Adams a total of $1,443,683 in Illinois Central taxes "illegally withheld." In adition, the same local courts declared forfeit tax exemptions due to expire by 1907 on the grounds

[67] Yazoo and Mississippi Valley Railroad Co. *vs.* Adams, 180 U.S. 25; William D. Guthrie to Fish, May 23, 1901, Fish Letters.

[68] Mississippi, *Biennial Report of the Revenue Agent, 1901*, pp. 5-6, 8; Mayes & Harris, Summary of Mississippi Back Tax Cases (Feb. 1901), Fish Letters.

that those railroads in the Illinois Central system that did have tax privileges had violated the conditions under which they held them.[69]

Large as it was, the loss of these back taxes was hardly felt by the Illinois Central Railroad, especially the Yazoo and Mississippi Valley Railroad, whose gross receipts in any single year after 1900 amounted to more than double its total taxes for twenty years. The back tax episode caused the railroad little financial pain. It did, however, reveal its utter political weakness and was an invitation to further attacks by a rising element of "bottom rail" politicians. Political impotence was new to the history of the Illinois Central Railroad, whose officials attributed their helplessness in Mississippi to demagogic persecution peculiar to the naturally violent southern temperament. But this was a description of symptoms, not an explanation of causes. Whatever the sectional and economic differences among them, the people of Mississippi were united in the harassment of their greatest potential benefactor for the reason that it had remained only a potential. Despite long years of economic adversity and rhetoric, southerners never lost their old faith in the efficacy of northern capital to put the South's economy upon a sound prosperous basis. For example, in the midst of the back tax trial with the railroad, Mississippi's legislature passed a law to encourage outside manufacturers to establish themselves in the state by granting a ten-year tax exemption.[70] What caused the resentment against capitalism was the southerner's frustration at its seeming unwillingness to utilize its power for southern benefit. In his view, the objective of the Illinois Central in Mississippi

---

[69] Mississippi, *Governor's Messages, 1902* (Andrew H. Longino), Department of Archives and History, Jackson; J. C. Welling to Stuyvesant Fish, Jan. 7, 1903, Fish Letters; Mayes & Harris, Memorandum for Mr. Fish, June [?], 1903, *ibid.*

[70] Mississippi, *Laws, 1896*, Ch. LIV.

had been to exploit rather than to contribute. It refused to become a part of Mississippi, holding itself aloof and alienated from every interest group, such as the Yazoo Delta planters, with whom it could have allied. Basic to this problem was, of course, the loose definition by southerners and northerners alike of what part investment capital from abroad was supposed to play. Since Mississippi's greatest problem at the turn of the century was the need for revenue, it was decided that capital's role in the economic life of the state should be as a source of tax money. For this reason the revenue agent received unanimous support in his attempts to force the Illinois Central to "carry its share of the public burden." To be sure, in the light of the Illinois Central's tremendous earnings from Mississippi, credit must be given to the state's restraint in taking relatively little. But this restraint stemmed from the persistent belief that northern capital had other roles to play besides that of making profits for itself.

# Bibliography and Index

# Bibliography

## MANUSCRIPT SOURCES

Most of the material in this book has been derived from the Illinois Central Railroad Archives deposited in the Newberry Library, Chicago, Illinois. This splendid source of material, given by the Railroad Company to the Newberry Library in 1943, contains over "400,000 letters, 126 bundles or boxes of miscellaneous material, and 2,000 bound volumes of account books." A detailed and descriptive guide to these archives is given in Carolyn Curtis Mohr, *Guide to the Illinois Central Archives in the Newberry Library, 1851-1906*, Chicago, 1951. The collection's material terminates at the end of the presidency of Stuyvesant Fish. I have used his letters extensively. In general, they are broken up into eighty volumes of Out-letters, each volume containing about 1,000 pages of letter press copies, and 426 volumes of In-letters. There is an index to the In-letters, but it is neither reliable nor complete. Consequently, I have searched through each volume of the In-letters. More reliable, and of great help, is the volume-by-volume index of the Out-letters. In addition to the separate index at the beginning of each volume, many of these letters are individually cross-indexed.

Extensive use was also made of the W. K. Ackerman letters (Out-letters and In-letters) and the letters of Vice-President J. C. Welling. Unfortunately, the letters of Edward P. Skene, Land Commissioner, are not included in this collection. Neither are they to be found among the records in the Illinois Central's depot at Dearborn Street in Chicago. Many of his letters, however, are interspersed among the letters of Welling and Fish.

Some of the materials listed in Mohr's *Guide*, such as the records of committees and minute books, have been removed from the

Newberry Library, put on microfilm, and deposited in the Illinois Central's depot in Champaign, Illinois. Papers supporting the minutes of the board of directors and stockholders are on microfilm at the depot in Dearborn Street in Chicago. Minutes of the board are also housed in the Chicago depot.

In additon, I have made use of the forty volumes of printed *Laws and Documents* relating to Illinois Central matters (see Mohr, *Guide*, 14), and the *Annual Reports*.

The second large manuscript source used consisted of federal case files for the following:

Byron H. Evers *vs.* Thomas Watson, No. 314 District Court of the United States, Western Division of Southern District, Mississippi. (Included in this file are fragments of the case file of Jordan and Jordan *vs.* Phillips, Marshall and Co., No. 71262 Court of Common Pleas, Hamilton County, Cincinnati, Ohio.) Jordan and Jordan were suing Phillips, Marshall and Co. for their fees and thus a great deal of information was derived from the exhibits in that case.

Byron H. Evers *vs.* Thomas Watson, No. 363 U.S. Circuit Court, Western Division, Northern District of Mississippi, November Term, 1890.

Byron H. Evers *vs.* S. Gwin, Auditor, No. 392 U.S. Circuit Court, District of Mississippi, 1884.

Dysart *vs.* Phillips et al., No. 397 U.S. District Court, Mississippi.

The material in these cases included copies of contracts among the different land speculators, briefs, petitions, exhibits, memorandums, inventories, and reports. All these records for the Fifth U.S. Circuit are housed in the Federal Records Center, East Point (Atlanta), Georgia. Though full of vital information, there is absolutely no order to these records. Some of the material is missing and much is duplication. Nevertheless, these types of records are invaluable for a study of southern economic development during this period.

The third manuscript source used was numerous letters of Delta planters found in the Agricultural Division of the National Archives in Washington. I was particularly interested in these manuscripts from the point of view of drainage activities (see National Archives, Record Group 8, 114). But I found them to be a very valuable source for other things as well. Also in the Justice and Treasury Division of the National Archives (Record Group 267) some per-

tinent material about the Delta was found in the case of Ford and
Levy *vs.* L.N.O. & T. and the Delta & Pine Land Company (File No.
15168).

The state of Mississippi's manuscript sources are a frustrating
experience. The scores of boxes of Governor's Papers of Robert
Lowry (1882-1890), John M. Stone (1876-1882; 1890-1896), and
Andrew H. Longino (1900-1904) housed in the Department of
Archives and History, Jackson, Mississippi, are filled with petitions
for pardons and little else. There are, however, noteworthy docu-
ments scattered through the thirty-six boxes of Governor Anselm J.
McLaurin's papers (1896-1900). For the flamboyant James K.
Vardaman administration (1904-1908) there is only one box, and
this contains little but more petitions for pardons.

The carefully edited papers of John C. Burrus, a Delta planter-
politician and member of the Mississippi legislature, at the Department of Archives and History, Jackson, were of some help in describ-
ing the local agricultural scene in the Delta. In addition, there are
a few relevant letters in the archives of the state auditor, also at the
Department of Archives and History. Of newspapers, the Department of Archives and History has the best collection, but even these
are incomplete. Moreover, the reporting is not of the first quality.

Another Mississippi source is case files and records in the Hinds
County (1st District) Chancery Court in Jackson. Again, many of
these are misfiled, and materials that should be in the files are missing. The following case files were used:

State *vs.* Delta & Pine Land Company, No. 762.
Delta & Pine Land Company *vs.* Edgar S. Wilson, No. 915.
L.N.O. & T. R.R. *vs.* Edgar S. Wilson, No. 916.
State *vs.* Delta & Pine Land Company, No. 922.
Andrew Gilchrist *vs.* Edgar S. Wilson, No. 924.
Augustus Hawks *vs.* Edgar S. Wilson, No. 931.
Delta & Pine Land Company *vs.* Callie Mizell, No. 2302.
Delta & Pine Land Company *vs.* E. N. Nall, No. 2705.
Delta & Pine Land Company and Charles Scott *vs.* E. N. Nall, No.
   2706.

Also used were the *Minute Books*, vols. 1-4, of the Hinds County
Chancery Court.

Of particular importance to drainage matters in the northern
Delta are the case files of The State of Mississippi *vs.* H. W. Cren-

shaw et al., No. 15703, Supreme Court, State of Mississippi; and T. G. James et al. *vs.* The Tallahatchie Drainage Commission, No. 14386.

Also examined were records in Coahoma and Washington counties. In Coahoma County (Courthouse, Clarksdale) use was made of the Land Rolls (2d District) 1915-16, 1925-26, Fishing Bayou Drainage District, Chancery Docket No. 1009, and Hopson Bayou Drainage District, Chancery Docket No. 993.

Found in the office of Harding Corley, Clarksdale, Mississippi, were the *Minute Books* of the Drainage Commissioners of Coahoma County, 4 vols.: Minute Book "A"—Minutes of Hopson's Bayou Drainage District from 22 March, 1907, to 6 December, 1921; Minute Book "A"—Sever Lake Drainage District from 30 December, 1912, to 12 October, 1921; Annis Lake Drainage District, 4 September, 1921, to 7 August, 1923; Annis Lake Drainage District, 3 July, 1923, to 2 August, 1932.

In Washington County (Courthouse, Greenville), much use was made of the Washington County *Deed Books,* and *Deeds of Trust.* The earliest extant *Land Roll* in Washington County dates from 1900. Also used were *Minutes,* Washington County Chancery Court; Mississippi Levee Board *vs.* Y. & M.V. R.R. (1897), File No. 2211; T. W. Valliant et al. *vs.* Washington Bayou Drainage District (1913), File No. 5082.

In the law office of Farish, Keady and Campbell, Greenville, Mississippi, is the correspondence of the Bogue Phalia Drainage District, Nos. 1-7, July 1912-1915. These are the files of the law firm of Percy and Percy and include papers dealing with the difficulties in getting a drainage district in operation in Washington County. Also, some use was made of the *Minutes* of the Board of Mississippi Levee Commissioners, Greenville.

## PRINTED SOURCES

Adams, Samuel H. "Yellow Fever: The Problem Solved," *McClure's Magazine,* XXVII (June 1906), 179-192.

American Agricultural Association. *Journal.* New York, 1881-1882.

*American Lumbermen.* 1st Series, Chicago, 1905. 2d and 3d Series, Chicago, 1906.

Atkinson, Edward. *Address Given in Atlanta, Georgia in October, 1880.* Boston, 1881. Available at Widener Library, Harvard University.

—— "The Cotton Resources of the South, Present and Future," *DeBow's Review,* New Series, II (August 1866), 132-144.

Baker, Ray S. *Following the Color Line.* New York: Doubleday, Page, 1908.

Bazley, Thomas. "Cotton as an Element of Industry," *Lectures on the Results of the Great Exhibition of 1851.* London, 1853.

Bearss, Edwin C. *Decision in Mississippi.* Jackson, Miss.: Mississippi Commission on the War Between the States, 1962.

Berthoff, Rowland T. "Southern Attitudes Toward Immigration, 1865-1914," *Journal of Southern History,* XVII (August 1951), 328-360.

Blackburn, Glen A. et al. *The John Tipton Papers With an Introduction by Wallace Gates.* 3 vols. Indianapolis: Indiana History Bureau, 1942.

Blegen, T. C. "The Competition of the Northwestern States for Immigrants," *Wisconsin Magazine of History,* III (September 1939), 3-29.

Blicksilver, Jack. *Cotton Manufacturing in the Southeast: An Historical Analysis.* Georgia State College of Business Administration, Studies in Business and Economics, Bulletin No. 5. Atlanta, 1959.

Bogue, Margaret B. "The Swamp Land Act and Wet Land Utilization in Illinois, 1850-1890," *Agricultural History,* XXV (October 1951), 169-180.

Bond, Horace Mann. "Social and Economic Forces in Alabama Reconstruction," *Journal of Negro History,* XXIII (July 1938), 290-348.

*The Book of the World Cotton Conference, New Orleans, Louisiana, October 13-16, 1919.* Boston, 1919.

Brough, Charles H. "The History of Banking in Mississippi," *Publications of the Mississippi Historical Society,* III (Oxford, Miss., 1900), 317-340.

—— "History of Taxation in Mississippi," *Publications of the Mississippi Historical Society,* II (Oxford, Miss., 1899), 113-132.

Brown, Arthur J., "The Promotion of Emigration to Washington, 1854-1909," *Pacific Northwest Quarterly,* XXXVI (January 1945), 3-17.

Buck, Paul H. *The Road to Reunion.* Boston: Little, Brown, 1937.

Busbey, T. A., ed. *The Biographical Directory of the Railway Officials of America.* Chicago: The Railway Age and Northwestern Railroads, 1893.

Campbell, Edward G. *The Reorganization of the American Railroad System, 1893-1900.* New York: Columbia University Press, 1938.

Campbell, John L. and W. H. Ruffner. *A Physical Survey in Georgia, Alabama, and Mississippi Along the Line of the Georgia Pacific Railway.* New York, 1883. Available at Baker Library, Harvard University.

Carlisle, George W. *Are You Coming South? Handbook of the State of Mississippi.* Jackson, Miss., 1888.

Carlson, Theodore L. *The Illinois Military Tract: A Study of Land Occupation Utilization and Tenure.* Illinois Studies in the Social Sciences, XXXII, No. 2. Urbana, Ill.: University of Illinois Press, 1951.

Cash, Wilbur J. *The Mind of the South.* New York: Knopf, 1946.

Clapham, J. H. *An Economic History of Modern Britain,* vol. III: *Machinery and National Rivalries.* Cambridge, Eng.: University Press, 1938.

Clark, Thomas D. *A Pioneer Southern Railroad from New Orleans to Cairo.* Chapel Hill, N.C.: University of North Carolina Press, 1936.

Cohn, David L. *God Shakes Creation.* New York: Harper, 1935.

────── *The Life and Times of King Cotton.* New York: Oxford University Press, 1956.

Cole, Arthur H. *Business Enterprise in Its Social Setting.* Cambridge, Mass.: Harvard University Press, 1959.

*Commercial and Financial Chronicle.* New York, 1871-1906.

Conkling, Frederick A. *On the Production and Consumption of Cotton.* New York, 1865.

Conover, Milton. *The General Land Office: Its History, Activities and Organization.* Institute for Government Research Service Monographs of the United States Government, No. 13. Baltimore: Johns Hopkins Press, 1923.

Corliss, Carleton J. *Main Line of Mid-America: The Story of the Illinois Central.* New York: Creative Age Press, 1950.

Corthell, E. L. *A History of the Jetties at the Mouth of the Mississippi River.* New York: J. Wiley and Sons, 1880.

*Cotton Facts.* New York, 1876-1931.

Cotton Planter's Convention of Georgia. *Organization of the Cotton Power: Communication of the President.* Macon, Ga., 1858.

*Cotton Trade Journal.* New Orleans, 1921-1925.

*DeBow's Commercial Review of the South and West.* New Orleans, 1846-1880.

Decker, Leslie E. *Railroads, Lands and Politics: The Taxation of the Railroad Land Grants, 1864-1897.* Providence: Brown University Press, 1964.

DiPalma-Castiglione, G. E. "Italian Immigration into the United States, 1901-1904," *American Journal of Sociology,* XI, No. 2 (1905), 202-206.

Donald, David H. "The Scalawag in Mississippi Reconstruction," *Journal of Southern History,* X (November 1944), 447-460.

Dorsey, Florence L. *Road to the Sea and the Mississippi River.* New York: Rinehart, 1947.

Douglass, Frederick. *Life and Times of Frederick Douglass.* Hartford, Conn.: Park Publishing, 1881.

Dowd, Douglas F. "A Comparative Analysis of Economic Development in the American West and South," *Journal of Economic History,* XVI (December 1956), 558-574.

Elliott, D. O. *The Improvement of the Lower Mississippi River for Flood Control and Navigation.* 3 vols. Vicksburg, Miss.: U.S. Waterways Experiment Station, 1932.

Erickson, Charlotte. *American Industry and the European Immigrant, 1860-1885.* Cambridge, Mass.: Harvard University Press, 1957.

Etcheverry, Bernard A. *Land Drainage and Flood Protection.* Stanford, Calif.: Stanford University Press, 1940.

Evans, Cerinda W. *Collis Potter Huntington.* 2 vols. Newport News, Va.: Mariners' Museum, 1954.

Fairchild, Walter. "Tax Titles in New York State," *Brooklyn Law Review,* VIII (1938-39), 61-80.

Fish, Stuyvesant. *The Development of the Natural Resources of the State of Mississippi.* New York, 1901.

Fleming, Walter L. "Immigration to the Southern States," *Political Science Quarterly,* XX (June 1905), 276-297.

Foerster, Robert F. *The Italian Emigration of Our Times.* Cambridge, Mass.: Harvard University Press, 1919.

Frank, Arthur DeWitt. *The Development of the Federal Program of Flood Control on the Mississippi River.* New York: Columbia University Press, 1930.

Fries, Robert F. *Empire in Pine: The Story of Lumbering in Wisconsin, 1830-1900.* Madison, Wis.: State Historical Society, 1951.

Garner, James W. *Reconstruction in Mississippi.* New York: Macmillan, 1901.

Gates, Paul W. "Frontier Landlords and Pioneer Tenants," *Journal of the Illinois State Historical Society,* XXXVIII (June 1945), 143-206.

────── "Federal Land Policy in the South 1866-1888," *Journal of Southern History* VI (July 1940), 303-330.

────── *The Illinois Central and Its Colonization Work.* Cambridge, Mass.: Harvard University Press, 1934.

*The Georgia Pacific Railway: Prospects and Reports.* New York, 1882. Available at Baker Library, Harvard University.

Goodspeed Publishing Company. *Biographical and Historical Memoirs of Mississippi.* 2 vols. Chicago: Goodspeed Publishing, 1891.

Grady, Henry W. "Cotton and Its Kingdom," *Harper's New Monthly Magazine,* LXIII (October 1881), 719-734.

Great Britain. *Parliamentary Papers.* London, 1877-1884.

*The Great Railroad Route to the Pacific . . . Showing the Relation of the Alabama and Chattanooga Railroad to the Proposed Southern Line to the Pacific.* Boston, 1870.

Green, Fletcher M. "Origins of the Credit Mobilier of America," *Mississippi Valley Historical Review,* XLVI (September 1959), 243.

Gregg, William. *Essays on Domestic Industry.* Charleston, 1845.

Griggs, Richard. *Guide to Mississippi.* Jackson, 1874.

Hammond, James H. "Southern Industry," *The Industrial Resources of the Southern and Western States,* ed. James D. B. DeBow. New Orleans, 1953.

Harman, Jacob A. "Flood Protection and Drainage of the Yazoo Delta, State of Mississippi," *Journal of the Engineers' Club of St. Louis,* V (October-November-December 1920), 13-17 (with map).

Harper, L. *Preliminary Report on the Geology and Agriculture of the State of Mississippi.* Jackson, Miss., 1857.

Harrison, Fairfax. *A History of the Legal Development of the Railroad System of Southern Railway Company.* Washington, D.C., 1901.

Harrison, Robert W. "The Formative Years of the Yazoo-Mississippi Delta Levee District," *Journal of Mississippi History,* XIII (October 1951), 236-248.

—————— "Levee Building in Mississippi Before the Civil War," *Journal of Mississippi History*, XII (April 1950), 63-97.

—————— *Levee Districts and Levee Building in Mississippi*. Stoneville, Miss.: Delta Council, 1951.

Haven, J. E. and A. T. Hurd. "Share System in Italian Agriculture," *Monthly Labor Review*, XXVII (July 1928), 31-32.

Haywood, Atticus G. *The New South: Gratitude, Amendment, Hope.* Oxford, Ga., 1880. Available at Widener Library, Harvard University.

Henry, R. H. *Editors I Have Known Since the Civil War.* Jackson, Miss., 1922.

Hibbard, Benjamin H. *A History of the Public Land Policies.* New York: Macmillan, 1924.

Hickman, Nollie. *Mississippi Harvest: Lumbering in the Longleaf Pine Belt, 1840-1915.* University, Miss.: University of Mississippi, 1962.

Higham, John. *Strangers in the Land: Patterns of American Nativism, 1860-1925.* New Brunswick, N.J.: Rutgers University Press, 1955.

Horn, Stanley F. *This Fascinating Lumber Business.* Indianapolis, Ind.: Bobbs-Merrill, 1951.

Hughes, H. Stuart. *The United States and Italy.* Cambridge, Mass.: Harvard University Press, 1953.

Hutton, J. Arthur. *The Cotton Crisis.* Manchester, Eng., 1904.

*I'll Take My Stand: The South and the Agrarian Tradition, by Twelve Southerners.* New York: Harper, 1930.

Illinois Central Railroad. *600,000 Acres of Railroad Lands for Sale Owned by the Yazoo & Mississippi Valley Railroad Company in the Famous Yazoo Valley of Mississippi. Chicago,* 1896.

James, Charles T. *Practical Hints on the Comparative Cost and Productiveness of the Culture of Cotton and the Cost and Productiveness of Its Manufacture.* Providence, 1849. Available at Widener Library, Harvard University.

Jenkins, William Dunbar. "The Mississippi River and the Efforts to Confine It in Its Channel," *Publications of the Mississippi Historical Society*, VI (Oxford, Miss., 1902), 283-306.

Jones, Robert H. "Long Live the King?" *Agricultural History*, XXXVII (July 1963), 166-169.

Keith, Jean. "The Role of the Louisville and Nashville Railroad in the Early Development of Alabama Coal and Iron," *Business Historical Society Bulletin*, XXVI (September 1962), 165-174.

Kelley, Arthell. Some Aspects of the Geography of the Yazoo Basin, Mississippi. Unpublished Ph.D. dissertation, University of Nebraska, 1954.

Key, V. O. *Southern Politics in State and Nation.* New York: Knopf, 1950.

King, Edward. *The Great South.* Hartford, Conn.: American Publishing Company, 1875.

Kirkland, Edward C. *Men, Cities, and Transportation: A Study in New England History, 1820-1900.* Cambridge, Mass.: Harvard University Press, 1948.

Kirwan, Albert Dennis. *Revolt of the Rednecks.* Lexington, Ky.: University of Kentucky Press, 1951.

Langley, Lee J. "Italians in the Cotton Fields," *Manufacturer's Record,* XLIV (August 6, 1903), 250-251.

Larson, Agnes M. *History of the White Pine Industry in Minnesota.* Minneapolis: University of Minnesota Press, 1949.

Lea, James J. *Lea's Cotton Book and Statistical History of the American Cotton Crop.* New Orleans: Press of Houser Printing, 1914.

Leake, Hunter C., comp. *Illinois Central and Yazoo & Mississippi Valley Railroad Co. v. Wirt Adams, Mississippi State Revenue Agent, Briefs.* Jackson, Miss., 1908. Department of Archives and History, Jackson.

Leowenberg, Bert J. "Efforts of the South to Encourage Immigration, 1865-1900," *South Atlantic Quarterly,* XXXIII (1943), 363-385.

Lowe, E. N. *Our Waste Lands: A Preliminary Study of Erosion in Mississippi.* Jackson, 1910.

McCain, William D. The Populist Party in Mississippi. Unpublished M.A. thesis, University of Mississippi, 1931.

———— and Charlotte Capers, eds. *Memoirs of Henry Tillinghast Ireys. Papers of the Washington County Historical Society, 1910-1915.* Jackson: Mississippi Department of Archives and History, 1954.

McMain, Eleanor. "Behind the Yellow Fever in Little Palermo," *Charities,* XV (November 4, 1905), 152-159.

McNeily, J. S. "Climax and Collapse of Reconstruction in Mississippi," *Publications of the Mississippi Historical Society,* XII (Oxford, Miss., 1912), 283-474.

*Manufacturers' Record.* Baltimore, 1894-1906.

Martin, Rex B. "Taxation—Tax Delinquent Lands—The Michigan
Land Board Act as a Solution to the Delinquency Problem,"
*Michigan Law Review*, XXXIX (1940-41), 800-811.

Massachusetts Bureau of [Labor] Statistics. *Cotton Manufacturing
in Massachusetts and the Southern States: Part II of the Annual
Report for 1905*. Boston, 1905.

Mathews, John Lathrop. *Remaking the Mississippi*. New York:
Houghton Mifflin, 1909.

Mayor des Planches, Edmondo. "A Model Italian Colony in Arkansas," *American Monthly Review of Reviews*, XXXIV (September 1906), 361-362.

——— *Attraverso Gli Stati Uniti*. Turin, Italy: Unione Tipografico-
editrice Torinese, 1913.

Mississippi, State of.

Board of Immigration and Agriculture. *Mississippi Homes*.
July 1878. Department of Archives and History, Jackson,
Miss.

——— *State of Mississippi*. Jackson, 1879.

*Constitution and Ordinances of the State of Mississippi, Adopted
in Convention Assembled in Pursuance of the Reconstruction
Acts of Congress . . . in 1868*. Jackson, 1868.

*Constitution of the State of Mississippi, Adopted November 1,
1890*. Jackson, 1891.

*Departmental Reports*. Jackson, Miss., 1868-1920. These include
the *Messages of the Governor*, and *Annual* and *Biennial
Reports* of the Secretary of State, the Attorney-General, the
Treasurer, the Auditor of Public Accounts, the Superintendent
of Public Education, the Board of Education, the Commissioner of Immigration and Agriculture, the Board of Immigration and Agriculture, the Revenue Agent, Railroad
Commissioners, and others.

Geological Survey. Bulletin No. 7. C. E. Dunston. *Preliminary
Examination of the Forest Conditions of Mississippi*. Brandon,
Miss., 1910.

——— Bulletin No. 8. E. N. Lowe. *A Preliminary Study of
Soils of Mississippi*. Brandon, Miss., 1911.

*Handbook of the State of Mississippi*. Jackson, 1882, 1885.

*Journal of the House of Representatives, 1865-1912*. Jackson,
1865-1912.

*Journal of the Senate, 1865-1912*. Jackson, 1865-1912.

*Journal of the Proceedings of the Constitutional Convention of the State of Mississippi, Begun at the City of Jackson on August 12, 1890, and Concluded November 1, 1890.* Jackson, 1890.

*Laws of the State of Mississippi (Session Laws), 1865-1912.* Jackson, 1865-1912.

*Official and Statistical Register of the State of Mississippi.* Nashville, 1904, 1908, 1912.

*Records of Incorporation.* Office of the Secretary of State, Jackson.

*Revised Code of the Statute Laws of the State of Mississippi.* Jackson, 1848, 1857, 1871, 1880, 1892, 1906.

Supreme Court, *Reports.* Various cases concerning Mississippi in relation to railroads and land speculation, 1866-1903.

*The Testimony in the Impeachment of Adelbert Ames, Governor of Mississippi.* Jackson, 1877.

*The Mobile and Northwestern Railroad: Address to the People of Mobile.* Mobile, 1870. Available at Baker Library, Harvard University.

Montgomery, Frank A. *Reminiscences of a Mississippian in Peace and War.* Cincinnati: Robert Clark, 1901.

Moore, John T. and Austin P. Foster, eds. *Tennessee: The Volunteer State.* 4 vols. Chicago: S. J. Clarke, 1923.

National Cotton Planter's Association of America. *Charter of Incorporation.* Vicksburg, Miss., 1881. Available at Widener Library, Harvard University.

*National Cyclopedia of American Biography.* New York: J. T. White and Co., 1937.

New England Cotton Manufacturing Association. *Proceedings.* Boston, 1866-1884.

*New Outlook.* New York, 1879-1910.

Newton, J. C. C. *The New South and the Methodist Episcopal Church, South.* Baltimore, 1887. Available at Widener Library, Harvard University.

New York Cotton Exchange. *Market Reports.* New York, 1879-1927.

*New York Geneological and Biographical Record.* New York, 1870-1907.

Nixon, Raymond B. *Henry W. Grady: Spokesman of the New South.* New York: Knopf, 1943.

*Official Report, Second International Conference of Cotton Growers, Spinners and Manufacturers.* Atlanta, October 7-9, 1907.

*Official Report, World Cotton Conference.* New Orleans, October 13-16, 1919.

Overton, R. C. *Burlington West.* Cambridge, Mass.: Harvard University Press, 1941.

Owsley, Frank L. *King Cotton Diplomacy.* 2d ed. Chicago: University of Chicago Press, 1959.

————— *Plain People of the Old South.* Baton Rouge: Louisiana State University Press, 1949.

Percy, William Alexander. *Lanterns on the Levee.* New York: Knopf, 1941.

Pierantoni, Augusto. "Italian Feeling on American Lynching," *The Independent,* LV (August 27, 1903), 2040-2042.

*Planters Journal.* Vicksburg, Miss., 1880, 1883.

Poor, Henry V. *Manual of the Railroads of the United States.* New York, 1868-1924.

"The Proceedings of a Mississippi Convention in 1879," *Journal of Negro History,* IV (January 1919), 51-54.

*Proceedings of the 1st Annual Session of the Southern Immigration Association of America.* Nashville, 1884.

*Proceedings of the International Congress of Delegated Representatives of Master Cotton Spinners and Manufacturer's Associations.* 9 vols. Manchester, 1904-1912.

*Proceedings of the Southern Interstate Immigration Convention, December 12-13, 1888, Convened in Montgomery, Alabama.* Dallas, 1888.

*Railway Review.* Chicago, 1880-1900.

Reed, John C. *The Brother's War.* Boston: Little, Brown, 1905.

————— *The Old and New South.* New York, 1876. Available at Widener Library, Harvard University.

*Report of the Trustee for the First Mortgage Bondholders of the Alabama and Chattanooga Railroad, December 1, 1874.* New York, 1874.

Rhodes, M. C. "History of Taxation in Mississippi," *Contribution to Education, George Peabody College for Teachers.* No. 79. Nashville, Tenn., 1930.

Ripley, William Z. *Railroads: Finance and Organization.* New York: Longmans, 1915.

Robinson, Mary Risher. "A Sketch of James Lusk Alcorn," *Journal of Mississippi History,* XII (January 1950), 28-45.

Robson, Robert. *The Cotton Industry in Britain.* London: Macmillan, 1957.

Rogers, William E. *Report on the Louisville, New Orleans and Texas Railroad to the President of the Illinois Central Railroad Company, May 16, 1892.* Chicago, 1892. Available at Baker Library, Harvard University.

Ross, W. H. et al. *The Mobile and Northwestern Railroad: Address to the People of Mobile.* Mobile, 1870.

Rowland, Dunbar. *History of Mississippi, Heart of the South.* 2 vols. Chicago: S. J. Clarke, 1925.

—— *Courts, Judges and Lawyers of Mississippi 1798-1935.* Jackson, Miss.: Hederman Brothers, 1935.

Rubin, Morton. *Plantation County.* Chapel Hill: University of North Carolina Press, 1951.

Russel, Robert R. *Economic Aspects of Southern Sectionalism 1840-1861.* Urbana: University of Illinois Press, 1924.

Saloutos, Theodore. *Farmer Movements in the South, 1865-1933.* Berkeley, Calif.: University of California Press, 1960.

Schmidt, Carl T. *The Plough and the Sword.* New York: Columbia University Press, 1938.

Scruggs, Otey. "Evolution of the Mexican Farm Labor Agreement of 1942," *Agricultural History,* XXXIV (July 1960), 140-149.

Sheehan, Donald H. and Syrett, H. C., eds. *Essays in American Historiography: Papers Presented in Honor of Allan Nevins.* New York: Columbia University Press, 1960.

Silver, James W. "Land Speculation in the Chickasaw Cession," *Journal of Southern History,* X (February 1944), 83-92.

—— "Paul Bunyan Comes to Mississippi," *Journal of Mississippi History,* XIX (April 1957), 93-119.

Simkins, Francis B. *Pitchfork Ben Tillman.* Baton Rouge: Louisiana State University Press, 1944.

—— *The South, Old and New: A History, 1820-1947.* New York: Knopf, 1947.

Smith, Frank E. *The Yazoo River.* New York: Rinehart, 1954.

Smyer, Sidney W. "Tax Titles," *The Alabama Lawyer,* III (January 1942), 31-39.

Somers, Robert. *The Southern States since the War, 1870-71.* New York: Macmillan, 1871.

South Carolina. Department of Agriculture. *The Cotton Mills of South Carolina, Their Names, Location, Capacity and History.* Charleston, 1880.

Southern Alluvial Lands Association. *The Call of the Alluvial Empire.* Memphis, 1919.

Steadman, E. *A Brief Treatise on Manufacturing in the South.* Clarksdale, Tenn., 1851.

Sterne, Simon. *Railway Reorganization.* New York, 1890.

—— *Railways in the United States.* New York: G. P. Putnam's Sons, 1912.

—— *Recent Railroad Failures and Their Lessons.* New York, 1894.

Stevenson, Frederick B. "Italian Colonies in the U.S.: A New Solution for the Immigration Problem," *Public Opinion,* XXXIX (1906), 453-456.

Stone, Alfred H. "Italian Cotton-Growers in Arkansas," *American Monthly Review of Reviews,* XXXV (February 1907), 209-213.

—— *Studies in the American Race Problem.* New York: Doubleday, Page, 1908.

—— and Julien H. Fort. *The Truth About the Boll Weevil.* Greenville, Miss., 1911.

Stover, John F. *The Railroads of the South, 1865-1900.* Chapel Hill: University of North Carolina Press, 1955.

Sunderland, Edwin S. S. *Illinois Central Railroad, Main Line of Mid-America: The Simplification of Its Debt Structure, 1938-1952.* New York: Privately printed, 1952.

Tankersley, Allen P. *John B. Gordon: A Study in Gallantry.* Atlanta: Whitehall Press, 1955.

Taylor, George R. and Irene D. Neu. *The American Railroad Network, 1861-1890.* Cambridge, Mass.: Harvard University Press, 1956.

Taylor, Paul S. *Mexican Labor in the United States,* vol. V: *Demmit County, Winter Garden District, South Texas.* Berkeley: University of California Press, 1930.

Tiffany, Herbert T. *The Law of Real Property.* 3d ed. rev. Vol. IV. Chicago: Callaghan, 1939.

Tilford, John E. *L & N: Its First Hundred Years.* New York: Newcomen Society in North America, 1951.

United States.
  Army, Chief of Engineers. *Annual Reports, 1873-1919.* Washington, 1873-1919.

Bureau of Labor, Commissioner of Labor. "Wages and Hours of Labor," *Nineteenth Annual Report, 1904.* Washington, 1905.

Bureau of Statistics (Treasury Department). *Report on the Internal Commerce of the United States.* Washington, 1879, 1881.

Congress, House. *Biographical Dictionary of the American Congress, 1774-1961.* 85th Cong., 2d Sess. (1961), House Doc. 442.

—— Various House Reports and Documents on the Mississippi River and flood control, 1875-1934, as cited in footnotes.

Congress, Senate. Various Senate Reports and Documents on the Mississippi River and on immigration, 1870-1916, as cited in footnotes.

Department of Agriculture. Bulletin No. 1119. Robert V. Reynolds and Albert H. Pierson. *Lumber Cut of the United States, 1870-1920.* Washington, 1923.

—— Bureau of Statistics. Bulletin No. 28. James L. Watkins. *The Commercial Cotton Crops of 1900-1901, 1901-1902, and 1902-1903.* Washington, 1904.

—— Bureau of Statistics. Bulletin No. 34. James L. Watkins. *The Commercial Cotton Crop of 1903-1904.* Washington, 1905.

—— Bureau of Statistics. Miscellaneous Series Bulletin No. 26. James H. Blodgett. *Wages of Farm Labor in the United States: Results of Twelve Statistical Investigations, 1866-1902.* Washington, 1903.

—— Department Bulletin No. 1207. George R. Boyd and R. A. Hart. *Drainage District Assessments: A Study of Present Practices in Assessing Benefits under the State Drainage Laws.* Washington, 1924.

—— Department Bulletin No. 1224. Clyde R. Chambers. *Relation of Land Income to Land Value.* Washington, 1924.

—— Division of Statistics. Miscellaneous Series Bulletin No. 9. James L. Watkins. *Production and Price of Cotton for 100 Years.* Washington, 1895.

—— Division of Statistics. Miscellaneous Series Bulletin No. 17. James L. Watkins. *The Cotton Crop of 1898-1899.* Washington, 1900.

—— Farmer's Bulletin No. 344. W. D. Hunter. *The Boll Weevil Problem.* Washington, 1909.

—— Farmer's Bulletin No. 512. W. D. Hunter. *The Boll Weevil Problem.* Washington, 1912.

—— Miscellaneous Special Report No. 3. A. B. Hunt. *Mississippi: Its Climate, Soil, Productions and Agricultural Capabilities.* Washington, 1883.

—— Office of Experiment Stations. Bulletin No. 244. H. A. Kipp. *Report on the Belzoni Drainage District in Washington County, Mississippi.* Washington, 1912.

—— Office of Experiment Stations. Circular No. 88. *Organization Work and Publications of Drainage Investigations.* Washington, 1909.

—— Technical Bulletin No. 682. E. L. Langsford and B. H. Thibodeaux. *Plantation Organization and Operation in the Yazoo-Mississippi Delta Area.* Washington, 1939.

—— Weather Bureau Bulletin E. Park Morril. *Floods of the Mississippi River.* Washington, 1897.

—— *Yearbook of Agriculture, 1903-1911, 1938.* Washington, 1904-1912, 1939.

Department of Agriculture and Mississippi Department of Agriculture and Commerce. *Base Book of Mississippi Agriculture, 1866-1953.* Jackson, Miss., 1955.

Department of Commerce. Bureau of the Census. Bulletin No. 129. *Negroes in the United States.* Washington, 1915.

—— Bureau of the Census. Decennial Censuses for 1850, 1870, 1880, 1890, 1900, 1910, 1920, 1930. Census of Agriculture, 1925.

—— Bureau of the Census. *Ravages of the Boll Weevil.* Washington, 1941.

Department of Commerce and Labor. Bureau of the Census. Bulletin No. 8. *Negroes in the United States.* Washington, 1904.

—— Bureau of the Census. Bulletin No. 95. *Cotton Production, 1907.* Washington, 1908. Bulletin No. 107. *Cotton Production, 1909.* Washington, 1910. Bulletin No. 110. *Supply and Distribution of Cotton.* Washington, 1911. Bulletin No. 114. *Cotton Production, 1911.* Washington, 1912. Bulletin No. 125. *Cotton Production, 1913.* Washington, 1914. Bulletin No. 134. *Cotton Production and Distribution, 1915-1916.* Washington, 1916.

Federal Court Decisions.
Evers *vs.* Watson, 13 Fed. 194; 156 U.S. 527.
Stansell *vs.* Levee Board of Mississippi District No. 1, 13 Fed. 846.
Ford & Levy *vs.* The Delta & Pine Land Company, 43 Fed. 181; 164 U.S. 662.
Yazoo and Mississippi Valley Railroad *vs.* Adams, 180 U.S. 1.
Illinois Central Railroad *vs.* Adams, 180 U.S. 28.
Federal Trade Commission. *Report on War-Time Costs and Profits of Southern Pine Lumber Companies.* Washington, 1922.
Immigration and Naturalization Bureau. *Annual Reports, 1904-1909.* Washington, 1905-1910.
Immigration Service. *Report of the Immigration Investigation Committee to the Secretary of the Treasury.* Washington, 1895.
Interstate Commerce Commission. *Annual Report, 1888.* Washington, 1889.
Treasury Department. Immigration Bureau. Commissioner-General of Immigration. *Annual Reports, 1895-1907.* Washington, 1896-1908.
Vance, Rupert B. *Human Factors in Cotton Culture.* Chapel Hill: University of North Carolina Press, 1929.
Wade, Emmie Ellen. The Office of Commissioner of Immigration and Agriculture in Mississippi from 1873 to 1890. Unpublished M.A. thesis, University of Mississippi, 1940.
Wade, John W. "Lands of the Liquidating Levee Board Through Litigation and Legislation," *Publications of the Mississippi Historical Society,* IX (Oxford, Miss., 1906), 273-313.
Weaver, Herbert. *Mississippi Farmers, 1850-1860.* Nashville, Tenn.: Vanderbilt University Press, 1945.
Wellington, Arthur M. *The Economic Theory of the Location of Railways.* New York: J. Wiley and Sons, 1887.
Wharton, Vernon L. *The Negro in Mississippi, 1865-1890.* James Sprunt Studies in History and Political Science, vol. XXVIII. Chapel Hill: University of North Carolina Press, 1947.
Williams, Wirt A., ed. *History of Bolivar County, Mississippi.* Jackson, Miss.: Hederman Brothers, 1948.
Woodward, C. Vann. *Origins of the New South, 1877-1913.* Baton Rouge: Louisiana State University Press, 1951.

—— *Reunion and Reaction.* Boston: Little, Brown, 1951.
—— *The Strange Career of Jim Crow.* New York: Oxford University Press, 1955.
—— *Tom Watson: Agrarian Rebel.* New York: Macmillan, 1938.

## NEWSPAPERS

*Atlanta Constitution*
*Clarksdale Daily Register* (Clarksdale, Miss.)
*Daily Clarion-Ledger* (Jackson, Miss.)
*Daily Democrat [Times]* (Greenville, Miss.)
*Friars Point Coahomian* (Friar's Point, Miss.)
*Hinds County Gazette* (Raymond, Miss.)
*Jackson Daily [Evening] News* (Jackson, Miss.)
*London Times*
*Memphis Commercial Appeal*
*Natchez Democrat* (Natchez, Miss.)
*New York Times*
*New York Tribune*
*Manchester Guardian* (Manchester, Eng.)
*Southern Livestock Journal* (Meridian, Miss.)
*Tallahatchie Herald* (Charleston, Miss.)
*Weekly Clarion-Ledger* (Jackson, Miss.)
*Weekly Democrat* (Greenville, Miss.)

# Index